D0722094

NELSON'S
ROYAL
CLASSICS

THE PRACTICE OF THE PRESENCE OF GOD

THE WAY OF PERFECTION

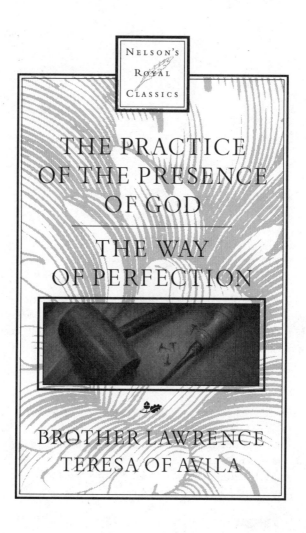

BROTHER LAWRENCE
TERESA OF AVILA

Publishers since 1798

THOMAS NELSON PUBLISHERS
Nashville

Copyright © 1999 by Thomas Nelson, Inc.

Published in Nashville, Tennessee, by Thomas Nelson, Inc.

All rights reserved. Written permission must be secured from the publisher to use or reproduce any part of this book except for brief quotations in critical reviews or articles.

Library of Congress Cataloging-in-Publication Data

Lawrence, of the Resurrection, Brother, 1611–1691.
    [Pratique de la présence de Dieu. English]
    The practice of the presence of God / Brother Lawrence ; and, The way of perfection / Teresa of Ávila.
    p. cm.
    ISBN 0-7852-4227-9
    1. Spiritual life—Catholic Church Early works to 1800.
I. Teresa, of Ávila, Saint, 1515–1582. Way of perfection.
II. Title.   III. Title: Way of perfection.
BX2349.L   1999
248.4′82—dc21   99-32606
                                           CIP

Printed in the United States of America
2 3 4 5 6 7 — 04 03 02 01 00

PUBLISHER'S PREFACE

Since the birth of the Christian church, thousands of writers have examined the teachings of the church and chronicled the experience of faith. Yet only a few of these works stand out as true classics—books that had and continue to have a significant impact on the church and the everyday lives of believers. They describe the core of our beliefs and capture the essence of our Christian experience. They remain an essential part of every Christian's library, and they continue to challenge the way we conceive our faith and our world.

Welcome to Nelson's Royal Classics—our commitment to preserving these treasures and presenting them to a new generation of believers. Every book contains an introduction that will detail the life and faith of the author and define why these works have such an important place in the history of our faith. As you read, you'll find that the timeless wisdom of the writers in this series is not only encouraging and enlightening but also very stimulating. These rich resources will strengthen your spiritual growth and show you ways to grow ever closer to God.

Each volume, such as Sheldon's *In His Steps*, Bunyan's *Pilgrim's Progress*, or St. Augustine's *Confessions*, is a treasure to be read and cherished. As a series, they become an heirloom library of invaluable worth. Read them now, and share them with others as a way to pass on the heart of Christianity.

THE PRACTICE
OF THE PRESENCE
OF GOD

BROTHER LAWRENCE

BROTHER LAWRENCE, 1605–1691

HIS LIFE	1605–1691	WORLD EVENTS
Born in the province of Lorraine, France	**1605**	Gunpowder Plot conspiracy to kill King and Parliament; *Don Quixote* published by Miguel Cervantes
Spends childhood and is educated in Lorraine	**1606–1617**	Jamestown, Virginia, settled (1607); Hudson discovers the river and bay that bear his name (1609); Louis XII gains throne of France (1610); King James Version of the Bible and Shakespeare's *The Tempest* are published (1611); Dutch build on Manhattan for fur trade with Indians (1614); Pocahontas dies (1617).
Fights in the Thirty Years' War, is wounded, and goes to work for Mr. Fieubert.	**1618–1622**	First African slaves arrive in Virginia (1619); *Mayflower* lands in Plymouth, Massachusetts (1620); first Thanksgiving—Governor Bradford invites Indians to join the Pilgrims (1621).
Converts to Christianity.	**1623**	Shakespeare's *First Folio* of plays is published.
Continues working for Mr. Fieubert while increasing his study of Scripture; grows increasingly dissatisfied with his life in the world.	**1624–1650**	Charles becomes engaged to Henrietta Maria of France and shows toleration toward English Catholics (1624); Francis Bacon dies from a cold he caught while stuffing snow into a chicken as part of an experiment (1626); William Harvey discovers the circulation of blood (1628); Mt. Vesuvius erupts (1631); Galileo is forced to renounce his beliefs (1632); Oberammergau performs a passion play (9 hours long) every tenth year to ward off the plague—thousands attend (1633); L'Academie Francaise resolves to purify the French language (1635); first printing press in North America (1639); Descartes' *Meditations* attempts to logically prove the existence of God (1641); Oliver Cromwell's army wins at Naseby (1642); Cromwell defeats King Charles I, who is beheaded (1648); Milton publishes *The Tenure of Kings and Magistrates* (1649).
Joins the Discalced Carmelite monastery in Paris.	**1651**	Hobbs publishes his masterpiece, *Leviathan*.
Grudgingly takes charge of the monastery kitchen; increases his study of Scripture and hours of devotion but without enthusiasm for any task.	**1652–1654**	First coffeehouses open in London (1652); Pascal and Fermat formulate the probability theory; Dutch in New Amsterdam build a wall for protection from outsiders, which later becomes Wall Street (1653); Ferdinand II of Tuscany improves Galileo's thermometer (1654).

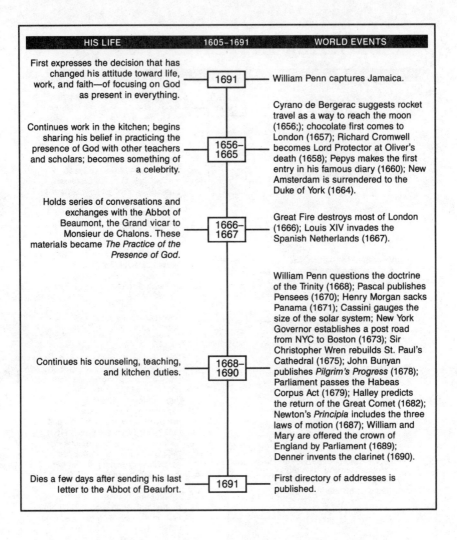

HIS LIFE	1605–1691	WORLD EVENTS
First expresses the decision that has changed his attitude toward life, work, and faith—of focusing on God as present in everything.	1691	William Penn captures Jamaica.
Continues work in the kitchen; begins sharing his belief in practicing the presence of God with other teachers and scholars; becomes something of a celebrity.	1656–1665	Cyrano de Bergerac suggests rocket travel as a way to reach the moon (1656;); chocolate first comes to London (1657); Richard Cromwell becomes Lord Protector at Oliver's death (1658); Pepys makes the first entry in his famous diary (1660); New Amsterdam is surrendered to the Duke of York (1664).
Holds series of conversations and exchanges with the Abbot of Beaumont, the Grand vicar to Monsieur de Chalons. These materials became *The Practice of the Presence of God*.	1666–1667	Great Fire destroys most of London (1666); Louis XIV invades the Spanish Netherlands (1667).
Continues his counseling, teaching, and kitchen duties.	1668–1690	William Penn questions the doctrine of the Trinity (1668); Pascal publishes Pensees (1670); Henry Morgan sacks Panama (1671); Cassini gauges the size of the solar system; New York Governor establishes a post road from NYC to Boston (1673); Sir Christopher Wren rebuilds St. Paul's Cathedral (1675); John Bunyan publishes *Pilgrim's Progress* (1678); Parliament passes the Habeas Corpus Act (1679); Halley predicts the return of the Great Comet (1682); Newton's *Principia* includes the three laws of motion (1687); William and Mary are offered the crown of England by Parliament (1689); Denner invents the clarinet (1690).
Dies a few days after sending his last letter to the Abbot of Beaufort.	1691	First directory of addresses is published.

INTRODUCTION

A t first, there was nothing special about the man who worked in the monastery's kitchen. Nicholas was just one of the many lay brothers who cared for the day-to-day functions of the monastery so that the monks could concentrate on their prayer and study. He cooked the meals and cleaned the pots thoroughly, but without any real enthusiasm. No one could have foretold the radical impact this ordinary man would make on Christianity.

Unlike the monks who came to the order at a young age, Nicholas Herman had come to monastic life much later than most men had. Born in 1605, Nicholas had been raised at a time of tremendous religious unrest. Protestantism was growing in his native France, but the welfare of the reformers was completely dependent upon the monarch who sat on the Parisian throne. Some of kings granted the Protestants a limited freedom; others persecuted them mercilessly. This made for some odd alliances, as when the French crown joined with the German Protestants to attack the Catholic government of the Holy Roman Empire. Nicholas, who had been raised a devout Catholic, was a member of the French army when this conflict came to a head in the much-disputed territory of Lorraine.

Nicholas was severely wounded in the battle. After spending time as a prisoner of war, he faced a slow and painful recovery, which left him partially disabled. Afterwards, he went to work for a local treasury official, Mr. Fieubert. During this time, his relationship with God grew, leading to his conversion at eighteen. His moment of complete surrender was later described in *The Practice of the Presence of God* with reverent and poetic images: "In the winter, seeing a tree stripped of its leaves, and considering that within a little time, the leaves would be renewed, and after that the flowers and fruit appear, he received a high view of the providence and power of God, which has never since been effaced from his soul."

The impact of this conversion profoundly changed the way Nicholas saw the world. He continued to work, but he became more and more dissatisfied with his life. Finally, at the age of fifty, he decided to enter the Discalced Carmelite monastery in Paris. As a lay brother, Nicholas had regular hours of devotion, and he was given a new name, Brother Lawrence. But lay brothers were responsible for the mundane tasks of keeping the monastery functioning, and Brother Lawrence was put in charge of the kitchen.

The former soldier was not thrilled by this assignment, and for the next four years, he did his job grudgingly, considering it a penance for his prior sins. He was miserable and tormented by the idea that his soul was so wrecked that God should lead him to this. As he dwelled on this idea, he slowly realized that he was focusing too much time and energy on himself. He had joined the monastery out of a love for God, and he decided that he needed to concentrate on that simple idea: loving God in whatever he did.

This decision changed his life. His conscious desire to approach even the most menial task out of his love for God and as a part of his service to God altered his attitude, filling him with an unexpected joy. Others in the monastic community noticed the surprising change in Brother

Lawrence, and they started asking him about his philosophy. His reputation spread beyond the monastery, and religious leaders from all walks of life came to him for advice, while others wrote endless letters asking for spiritual counsel and direction.

One of these correspondents was the Abbot of Beaufort. The Abbot and Brother Lawrence exchanged fifteen letters and met four times to discuss what Brother Lawrence had learned by focusing his mind on the constant presence of God in everyday life. The Abbot recorded the conversations, and later edited them, with the letters, to create the book known today as *The Practice of the Presence of God*. The book was first published in the mid-1690s, just after Brother Lawrence died.

The demand for the book was immediate, and it has remained constant for the past 300 years. Perhaps the reason for this is that Brother Lawrence was intensely personal about religion and the presence of God in our lives, which is intimately appealing to those who are seeking to expand and deepen their relationship with God.

What Brother Lawrence had discovered was that experiencing God's presence was not a one-time feeling or a program to follow step-by-step. Experiencing God's presence was a way of life—a practice. It means concentrating on God constantly, making whatever the individual feels or experiences secondary in the light of loving God.

This all sounds very simple, but Brother Lawrence was well aware of how difficult it was to maintain this focus. In his first conversation with the Abbot, he describes how hard he had to work at this, forcing himself to make it a disciplined habit. Only after a long time did the habit become second nature—an unconscious way of seeing everyday life that brought Brother Lawrence, an ordinary man, the feelings of joy and deep satisfaction that characterized the last years of his extraordinary life.

PREFACE

A friend of mine likes to say that the biggest problem with the Christian life is that it is so daily.[1] Most believers have times when God seems very close. Some people experience God's presence during life's high points: the birth of a child, a wedding day, walking alongside a beautiful mountain stream, or any moment when it looks like all their dreams may come true. But other people feel closest to God during life's low points: the death of a friend, a serious illness, the loss of a job, or those moments when they feel trapped in their worst nightmares. Even then—some might say, especially then—one can have a "peace that passes all understanding" (Phil. 4:7).

Life at the extremes—in the best and worst of times—is where most people experience God's presence most easily. For many believers, however, finding God is much more difficult during the in-between times. For most of us, it is the daily grind that wears us out and does us in. Many Christians cannot locate God in the sameness of every day responsibilities and in the unending cycles of what we do most of the time.

The big question, then, for us is this: Where is God when one day seems pretty much like another, when nothing much seems to be happening in our lives? Where is God in the dullness of daily living? At least part of the answer to that question can be found in the thoughtful life-experience of Brother Lawrence, a seventeenth-century Frenchman, who learned how to "practice the presence of God" in a kitchen.

BROTHER LAWRENCE (C. 1605–1691)

Not much is known about the early life of Brother Lawrence. We believe that he was born Nicholas Herman in about 1605 in the French province of Lorraine. His parents were poor but respectable; and they raised Nicholas as a devout Catholic.

Like much of Europe, France had been deeply divided by the Protestant Reformation of the sixteenth century. French Protestants, who were called Huguenots, had grown rapidly after the 1530s, prompting the Catholic monarchy to take strong measures against them. After decades of religious strife and even armed conflict between French Catholics and Huguenots, in 1598 the Edict of Nantes created an uneasy peace between the warring parties.

By the time Nicholas was born, then, the Catholic majority had guaranteed the Huguenots certain rights, including possession of a number of fortified cities to call their own. Huguenot security actually depended on who was in control of the French government. Fearing their growing strength, in 1629 Cardinal Richelieu, King Louis XIII's most powerful adviser, drove the Huguenots from their fortified cities, then rather surprisingly granted them extensive religious and civil toleration. The next king, Louis XIV, was much less accommodating. He demanded that Huguenots re-convert to Catholicism or be driven from France. To that end, in 1685 the king issued the Edict of Fontainebleau, which abolished the religious guarantees of the Edict of Nantes and outlawed Protestantism throughout the realm.

In short, because Nicholas Herman was a Roman Catholic, he did not experience religious persecution himself; but his religious loyalties did not keep him completely out of harm's way. According to our sketchy sources, Nicholas may have been a soldier in the French army during the Thirty Years' War (1618–1648), in which Catholic France sided with German Protestants against the Hapsburgs, the Catholic dynasty that ruled both Spain and the Holy Roman Empire. In a fierce battle fought near Lorraine, Nicholas was severely wounded.

After a slow and painful recovery which left him partially disabled, he became a footman for a local official, Mr. Fieubert. Nicholas later described himself as "a great awkward fellow who broke everything." Nevertheless, during his years of service for Mr. Fieubert, his relationship with God began to grow. In 1623, when Nicholas was eighteen, he experienced a religious conversion. "In the winter, seeing a tree stripped of its leaves, and considering that within a little time the leaves would be renewed, and after that the flowers and fruit appear, he received a high view of the providence and power of God, which has never since been effaced from his soul." This personal experience of God's sovereignty and power "set him loose from the world, and kindled in him such a love for God" that its impact never left him.[2]

Over the years, Nicholas became dissatisfied with his life in the world. Some historians believe that he may have tried his hand at living as a hermit. One thing is certain: when he was about fifty years of age, he decided to enter the Discalced Carmelite monastery in Paris. Looking back years later, Nicholas was quite honest about his motives. Because of his love for God, he wanted to sacrifice his life and all its pleasures in order to serve Him. He also hoped that in the rigors of monastic life he would "be made to smart for his awkwardness and the faults he should commit."[3]

The Carmelites were a religious order that had been founded in the thirteenth century and named after Mount Carmel in Israel. For a while, the Carmelites had been known for their strict discipline; but over the years standards declined. In the early sixteenth century, the order was reformed by St. Theresa of Ávila. New Carmelite convents and monasteries were founded, and much of the old discipline returned. The strictest of the Carmelites broke off from the main body and established their own separate order in 1593. They called themselves barefoot (discalced) Carmelites because they preferred sandals to shoes and socks.

Nicholas joined the Carmelites as a lay brother, which meant that he was part of the work force that allowed the rest of the community to study, teach, preach, and copy manuscripts. As part of the monastery, the lay brothers prayed and kept regular hours of devotion, to be sure; but they were there mainly to work hard for everyone else. When Nicholas Herman entered the community, he received a new name and got a new job: he was now Brother Lawrence and was put in charge of the kitchen.

Because Brother Lawrence had no natural inclination for such work, he figured that it was God's way of making him "smart for his awkwardness" and his faults. He had come to the monastery to learn discipline, so spending the rest of his life up to his elbows in dirty pots and pans seemed like a fitting venue for self-sacrifice. But, he said years later, in this God disappointed him. Instead of being a life-long penance for his sins, over time the kitchen work brought him "nothing but satisfaction." Much to his surprise, slaving over a hot stove taught him how to practice the presence of God.

It took him a while to figure it out, however. For the first four years, Brother Lawrence did not like his work; in fact, he had a great aversion to it. He also anguished over the condition of his soul, convinced that if there were any justice in the world, God should damn him. Despite his best efforts, he was miserable. Finally he had a breakthrough. To put it simply, he evaluated his condition to find out where he had gone wrong. Eventually he understood that he was spending too much time and energy worrying about himself. He decided to get back to basics and focus his life on loving God. Years later, he put it this way: "I engaged in a religious life only for the love of God, and I have endeavored to act only for Him; whatever becomes of me, whether I be lost or saved, I will always continue to act purely for the love of God. I shall have this good at least, that till death I shall have done all that is in me to love Him."[4]

That is what made all the difference in his life. From that time on, he found joy in his work. He was "pleased when he could take up a straw from the ground for the love of God." Even the most menial and unwelcome tasks took on new meaning. When he consciously decided to do everything out of his love for God, his life changed. In fact, he became famous, at least after a fashion.

Other people in the community noticed that something had happened to the lay brother in charge of the kitchen. When they asked him about it, he told them about practicing the presence of God in life's little duties. There was no real trick to it, he said, nothing all that mysterious. All one had to do was remember God as one went around one's work. Of course, it was a bit more complicated than that, but for Brother Lawrence experiencing God's presence in daily life consisted of thinking about God all the time.

Over the years, then, Brother Lawrence's life proved that he had discovered something of enormous importance. He never promoted himself, but he was eager to share what he had learned. Fellow Carmelites consulted with him about practicing God's presence, as did people from outside the monastery. Religious leaders came to him for advice; and other people wrote him letters seeking spiritual counsel. What he learned in the kitchen he practiced until he died in Paris, in his mid-eighties.

THE PRACTICE OF THE PRESENCE OF GOD

The book that has become a Christian spiritual classic consists of a summary of four conversations between Brother Lawrence and the Abbot of Beaufort, the Grand Vicar to Monsieur de Chalons, which occurred in 1666–67, and fifteen letters whose dates are uncertain, but may extend to just before his death in 1691. These materials were edited by the Abbot of Beaufort and published in Paris during the mid-1690s.

Despite the fact that the conversations and letters were intensely personal in nature, they contain very little autobiographical information. Brother Lawrence was much more interested in telling what he had learned than the story of his own life. As a result, the book includes few details about monastic life and virtually nothing about what was going on in the outside world. Brother Lawrence's focus was on his personal experience with God and little else. "I renounced, for the love of Him, everything that was not He, and I began to live as if there was none but He and I in the world."[5]

Possibly that is the reason why *The Practice of the Presence of God* still speaks to people three hundred years after it was first published: much of modern religious life remains centered on the self and the quest for an intensely personal experience of God. Pollsters keep finding evidence of deep religious longings in modern life. Americans are the most church-going people in the western, industrialized world; and even among those who have sworn off religious institutions, there is widespread interest in "spirituality." Similarly, modern people demand that religion be practical, that it speak to personal needs. In short, in most circles today, the emphasis is on relevance, not religious dogma or denominational loyalty.

Naturally, not everyone is happy about this individualistic and even consumeristic approach to things spiritual. Religious experience cut off from religious communities can easily become eccentric and self-absorbed. But Brother Lawrence was intensely personal about religion without being self-centered. After all, to practice the presence of God, one needed to concentrate on God, not on one's self. How one felt and what one experienced were always secondary to loving and remembering God during one's daily routine.

In a world awash with twelve-step programs for breaking old addictions and how-to manuals on everything from losing weight to getting everything we want in life, one is struck by Brother Lawrence's almost total lack of concern with *methodology*. Modern readers will not find any clearly-spelled-out, step-by-step process for experiencing the presence of God. According to this kitchen saint, experiencing God's presence is not a program; it is a practice, a way of life. There is nothing all that complex about it. One has to set priorities, eliminate distractions, and decide to think about God—a lot. In one of his letters, Brother Lawrence put it this way: "Pray remember what I have recommended to you, which is, to think often on God, by day, by night, in your business, and even in your diversions. He is always near you and with you; leave Him not alone. You would think it rude to leave a friend alone who came to visit you; why, then, must God be neglected?"[6]

What about distractions? Some people are surprised to learn that there were any in monasteries: Did not people join religious communities in order to serve God without any diversions? True enough, but it is much easier to take the monk out of the world than it is to take the world out of the monk. The history of Christianity is filled with stories of exasperated monastic men and women who lived behind cloistered walls or even in hermit caves, only to be consumed with thoughts of the life they left behind.

Brother Lawrence struggled here too. He did not find structured times of prayer and devotion all that helpful at first. Like many others, he discovered that the more he tried to rid his mind of wandering thoughts, the more he had them. So he took another approach: He worked, he stayed busy, he kept his hands occupied, and he thought about God while he went about his business in the kitchen. In this way, much to his surprise, he could concentrate more easily on God. The harder he worked, the better he prayed.

Dr. Wayne Oates, one of the pioneers of pastoral counseling, finds real wisdom in Brother Lawrence's approach. He notes that sometimes manual labor is the best way to reconnect with the life of the spirit. "As a minister-teacher, I have times of unproductive doldrums of spirit as I search for some new revealing of the Spirit. I have found that to clean a basement room, to paint a door, to fix a bothersome piece of tile in the kitchen releases many unaccustomed sources of thought and revelation."[7] Most monastic leaders who drew up the rules that monks and nuns lived by understood that to keep spiritual lives healthy, there must be a balance between prayer and work.

But by itself, Brother Lawrence discovered, hard work was never enough. One also had to keep one's mind fixed on God while working. He said that it was easier to keep his mind from wandering during prayer if he had not let it wander too far at other times: "You should keep it strictly in the presence of God; and being accustomed to think of Him often, you will find it easy to keep your mind calm in the time of prayer, or at least to recall it from its wanderings."[8] Would Brother Lawrence find life's distractions more numerous today than in his time? Probably. No seventeenth century lay brother could have imagined the flood of distractions competing for our attention. Nevertheless, one suspects that his advice to us would be the same: Eliminate distractions whenever possible and remember that the still, small voice of God's presence is hard to hear over blaring televisions and CD players.

What about sin? How does practicing the presence of God relate to the problem of sin in one's life? Brother Lawrence was no sinless saint. He sinned and he knew it. But he did not dwell on his sins. By faith he got over his fear of damnation. He confessed his sins and moved on, confident of the love and grace of God.[9] In the Second Conversation Brother Lawrence said "that all possible kinds of mortification, if they were void of the love of God, could not efface a single sin. That we ought, without anxiety, to expect the pardon of our sins from the blood of Jesus Christ, only endeavoring to love Him with all our hearts. That God seemed to have granted the greatest favors to the greatest sinners, as more signal monuments of His mercy."

Does practicing the presence of God come easily? Not according to Brother Lawrence. One has to work at it. In the First Letter, he described how he developed "that habitual sense of God's presence." Practicing God's presence must become a habit (*habitus* in Latin), a regular and disciplined way of life that in time becomes a natural and almost involuntary response. But even Brother Lawrence had to start slowly; over time he learned to see God in everything he did and everything that happened to him. But it took practice.

In the long run, maybe that is what separates Brother Lawrence from most people. Over 90 percent of Americans polled say they believe in God. But how many of them think about God, look for those signs of God's presence in their work, in the daily grind, in the middle of exhausting family or business obligations? How many people go through their daily lives without giving God a second thought? They say they believe in God, but they never pay God any mind. Anyone interested in living daily with a keen sense of God's presence cannot go through life that way. According to the author of Hebrews, "Without faith it is impossible to please God, because anyone who comes to him must believe that he exists and that he rewards those who earnestly seek him" (11:6).

CONVERSATIONS

FIRST CONVERSATION

T he first time I saw Brother Lawrence was upon the 3rd of August, 1666. He told me that God had done him a singular favor in his conversion at the age of eighteen.

BROTHER LAWRENCE'S CONVERSION AND EARLY LIFE

That in the winter, seeing a tree stripped of its leaves, and considering that within a little time the leaves would be renewed, and after that the flowers and fruit appear, he received a high view of the providence and power of God, which has never since been effaced from his soul. That this view had perfectly set him loose from the world, and kindled in him such a love for God that he could not tell whether it had increased during the more than forty years he had lived since.

That he had been footman to M. Fieubert, the treasurer, and that he was a great awkward fellow who broke everything.

That he had desired to be received into a monastery, thinking that he would there be made to smart for his awkwardness and the faults he should commit, and so he should sacrifice to God his life, with its pleasures; but that God had disappointed him, he having met with nothing but satisfaction in that state.

That we should establish ourselves in a sense of God's presence by continually conversing with Him. That it was a shameful thing to quit His conversation to think of trifles and fooleries.

THE NEED OF DEDICATION TO GOD

That we should feed and nourish our souls with high notions of God; which would yield us great joy in being devoted to Him.

That we ought to *quicken*—i.e., to *enliven*—*our faith*. That it was lamentable we had so little; and that instead of taking *faith* for the rule of their conduct, men amused themselves with trivial devotions, which changed daily. That the way of faith was the spirit of the church, and that it was sufficient to bring us to a high degree of perfection.

That we ought to give ourselves up to God, with regard both to things temporal and spiritual, and seek our satisfaction only in the fulfilling of His will, whether He lead us by suffering or by consolation, for all would be equal to a soul truly resigned. That there needed fidelity in those drynesses or insensibilities and irksomenesses in prayer by which God tries our love to Him; that *then* was the time for us to make good and effectual acts of resignation, whereof one alone would oftentime very much promote our spiritual advancement.

LAWRENCE'S VIEW OF SIN

That as for the miseries and sins he heard of daily in the world, he was so far from wondering at them that, on the contrary, he was surprised that there were not more, considering the malice sinners were capable of; that, for his part, he prayed for them; but knowing that God could remedy the mischiefs they did when He pleased, he gave himself no further trouble.

That to arrive at such resignation as God requires, we should watch attentively over all the passions which mingle as well in spiritual things as in those of a grosser nature; that God would give light concerning those passions to those who truly desire to serve Him. That if this was my design, viz., sincerely to serve God, I might come to him (Brother Lawrence) as often as I pleased, without any fear of being troublesome; but if not, that I ought no more to visit him.

SECOND CONVERSATION

That he had always been governed by love, without selfish views; and that having resolved to make the love of God the *end* of all his actions, he had found reasons to be well satisfied with his method. That he was pleased when he could take up a straw from the ground for the love of God, seeking Him only, and nothing else, not even His gifts.

LAWRENCE'S FEARS OF DAMNATION

That he had been long troubled in mind from a certain belief that he should be damned; that all the men in the world could not have persuaded him to the contrary; but that he had thus reasoned with himself about it: *I engaged in a religious life only for the love of God, and I have endeavored to act only for Him; whatever becomes of me, whether I be lost or saved, I will always continue to act purely for the love of God. I shall have this good at least, that till death I shall have done all that is in me to love Him.*

That this trouble of mind had lasted four years, during which time he had suffered much; but that at last he had seen that this trouble arose from want of faith, and that since he had passed his life in perfect liberty and continual joy. That he had placed his sins betwixt him and God, as it were, to tell Him that he did not deserve His favors but that God still continued to bestow them in abundance.

LAWRENCE'S APPROACH
TO THE SPIRITUAL LIFE

That in order to form a habit of conversing with God continually, and referring all we do to Him, we must at first apply to Him with some diligence; but that after a little care we should find His love inwardly excite us to it without any difficulty.

That he expected, after the pleasant days God had given him, he should have his turn of pain and suffering; but that he was not uneasy about it, knowing very well that as he could do nothing of himself, God would not fail to give him the strength to bear it.

That when an occasion of practising some virtue offered, he addressed himself to God, saying, *Lord, I cannot do this unless Thou enablest me;* and that then he received strength more than sufficient.

That when he had failed in his duty, he only confessed his fault, saying to God, *I shall never do otherwise if You leave me to myself; it is You who must hinder my falling, and mend what is amiss.* That after this he gave himself no further uneasiness about it.

That we ought to act with God in the greatest simplicity, speaking to Him frankly and plainly, and imploring His assistance in our affairs, just as they happen. That God never failed to grant it, as he had often experienced.

DO ALL FOR THE LOVE OF GOD

That he had been lately sent into Burgundy, to buy the provision of wine for the society, which was a very unwelcome task for him, because he had no turn for business, and because he was lame and could not go about the boat but by rolling himself over the casks. That, however, he gave himself no uneasiness about it, nor about the purchase of the wine. That he said to God, *It was His business he was about,* and that he afterward found it very well performed. That he had been sent into Auvergne, the year before, upon the same account; that he could not tell how the matter passed, but that it proved very well.

So, likewise, in his business in the kitchen (to which he had naturally a great aversion), having accustomed himself to do everything there for the love of God, and with prayer, upon all occasions, for His grace to do his work well, he had found everything easy, during fifteen years that he had been employed there.

That he was very well pleased with the post he was now in; but that he was as ready to quit that as the former, since he was always pleasing himself in every condition by doing little things for the love of God.

OBSTACLES TO PRAYER

That with him the set times of prayer were not different from other times; that he retired to pray, according to the directions of his superior, but that he did not want such retirement, nor ask for it, because his greatest business did not divert him from God.

That as he knew his obligation to love God in all things, and as he endeavored so to do, he had no need of a director to advise him, but that he needed much a confessor to absolve him. That he was very sensible of his faults, but not discouraged by them; that he confessed them to God, but did not plead against Him to excuse them. When he had so done, he peaceably resumed his usual practice of love and adoration.

That in his trouble of mind he had consulted nobody, but knowing only by the light of faith that God was present, he contented himself with directing all his actions to Him, i.e., doing them with a desire to please Him, let what would come of it.

That useless thoughts spoil all; that the mischief began there; but that we ought to reject them as soon as we perceived their impertinence to the matter in hand, or our salvation, and return to our communion with God.

That at the beginning he had often passed his time appointed for prayer in rejecting wandering thoughts and falling back into them. That he could never regulate his devotion by certain methods as some do.

That, nevertheless, at first he had *meditated* for some time, but afterward that went off, in a manner he could give no account of.

THE PLACE OF
BODILY MORTIFICATION

That all bodily mortification and other exercises are useless, except as they serve to arrive at the union with God by love; that he had well considered this, and found it the shortest way to go straight to Him by a continual exercise of love and doing all things for His sake.

That we ought to make a great difference between the acts of the *understanding* and those of the *will;* that the first were comparatively of little value, and the others all. That our only business was to love and delight ourselves in God.

That all possible kinds of mortification, if they were void of the love of God, could not efface a single sin. That we ought, without anxiety, to expect the pardon of our sins from the blood of Jesus Christ, only endeavoring to love Him with all our hearts. That God seemed to have granted the greatest favors to the greatest sinners, as more signal monuments of His mercy.

That the greatest pains or pleasures of this world were not to be compared with what he had experienced of both kinds in a spiritual state; so that he was careful for nothing and feared nothing, desiring only one thing of God, viz., that he might not offend Him.

That he had no scruples; for, said he, when I *fail* in my duty, I readily acknowledge it, saying, *I am used to do so; I shall never do otherwise if I am left to myself.* If I fail not, then I give God thanks, acknowledging that the strength comes from Him.

THIRD CONVERSATION

He told me that the *foundation of the spiritual life* in him had been a high notion and esteem of God in faith; which when he had once well conceived, he had no other care at first but faithfully to reject every other thought, *that he might perform all his actions for the love of God*. That when sometimes he had not thought of God for a good while, he did not disquiet himself for it; but, after having acknowledged his wretchedness to God, he returned to Him with so much the greater trust in Him as he had found himself wretched through forgetting Him.

GOD'S GRACE

That the trust we put in God honors Him much and draws down great graces.

That it was impossible not only that God should deceive, but also that He should long let a soul suffer which is perfectly resigned to Him, and resolved to endure everything for His sake.

That he had so often experienced the ready succors of divine grace upon all occasions, that from the same experience, when he had business to do, he did not think of it beforehand; but when it was time to do it, he found in God, as in a clear mirror, all that was fit for him to do. That of late he had acted thus, without anticipating care; but before the experience above mentioned, he had used it in his affairs.

LAWRENCE'S DESIRE FOR GOD

When outward business diverted him a little from the thought of God, a fresh remembrance coming from God invested his soul, and so inflamed and transported him that it was difficult for him to contain himself.

That he was more united to God in his outward employments than when he left them for devotion and retirement.

That he expected hereafter some great pain of body or mind; that the worst that could happen to him was to lose that sense of God which he had enjoyed so long; but that the goodness of God assured him He would not forsake him utterly, and that He would give him strength to bear whatever evil He permitted to happen to him; and therefore that he feared nothing, and had no occasion to consult with anybody about his state. That when he had attempted to do it, he had always come away more perplexed; and that as he was conscious of his readiness to lay down his life for the love of God, he had no apprehension of danger. That perfect resignation to God was a sure way to heaven, a way in which we had always sufficient light for our conduct.

HINDRANCES TO SPIRITUAL GROWTH

That in the beginning of the spiritual life we ought to be faithful in doing our duty and denying ourselves; but after that, unspeakable pleasures followed. That in difficulties we need only have recourse to Jesus Christ, and beg His grace; with that everything became easy.

That many do not advance in the Christian progress because they stick in penances and particular exercises, while they neglect the love of God, which is the *end*. That this appeared plainly by their works, and was the reason why we see so little solid virtue.

That there needed neither art nor science for going to God, but only a heart resolutely determined to apply itself to nothing but Him, or for *His* sake, and to love Him only.

FOURTH CONVERSATION

He discoursed with me frequently, and with great openness of heart, concerning his manner of *going* to God, whereof some part is related already.

ENGAGE IN A CONTINUAL CONVERSATION WITH GOD

He told me that all consists *in one hearty renunciation* of everything which we are sensible does not lead to God. That we might accustom ourselves to a continual conversation with Him, with freedom and in simplicity. That we need only to recognize God intimately present with us, to address ourselves to Him every moment, that we may beg His assistance for knowing His will in things doubtful, and for rightly performing those which we plainly see He requires of us, offering them to Him before we do them, and giving Him thanks when we have done.

That in this conversation with God we are also employed in praising, adoring, and loving Him incessantly, for His infinite goodness and perfection.

WHY GOD'S GRACE "FAILS"

That, without being discouraged on account of our sins, we should pray for His grace with a perfect confidence, as relying upon the infinite merits of our Lord Jesus Christ. That God never failed offering us His grace at each action; that he distinctly perceived it, and never failed of it, unless when his thoughts had wandered from a sense of God's presence, or he had forgotten to ask His assistance.

That God always gave us light in our doubts when we had no other design but to please Him.

That our sanctification did not depend upon *changing* our works, but in doing that for God's sake, which we commonly do for our own. That it was lamentable to see how many people mistook the means for the end, addicting themselves to certain works, which they performed very imperfectly, by reason of their human or selfish regards.

LAWRENCE'S APPROACH TO PRAYER

That the most excellent method he had found of going to God was that of doing our common business without any view of pleasing men, and (as far as we are capable) purely for the love of God.

That it was a great delusion to think that the times of prayer ought to differ from other times; that we are as strictly obliged to adhere to God by action in the time of action as by prayer in the season of prayer.

That his prayer was nothing else but a sense of the presence of God, his soul being at that time insensible to everything but divine love; and that when the appointed times of prayer were past, he found no difference, because he still continued with God, praising and blessing Him with all his might, so that he passed his life in continual joy; yet hoped that God would give him somewhat to suffer when he should grow stronger.

FAITH, HOPE, AND CHARITY

That we ought, once for all, heartily to put our whole trust in God, and make a total surrender of ourselves to Him, secure that He would not deceive us.

That we ought not to be weary of doing little things for the love of God, who regards not the greatness of the work, but the love with which it is performed. That we should not wonder if, in the beginning, we often failed in our endeavors, but that at last we should gain a habit, which will naturally produce its acts in us, without our care, and to our exceeding great delight.

That the whole substance of religion was faith, hope, and charity, by the practice of which we become united to the will of God; that all besides is indifferent, and to be used as a means that we may arrive at our end, and be swallowed up therein, by faith and charity.

That all things are possible to him who *believes;* that they are less difficult to him who *hopes;* that they are more easy to him who *loves,* and still more easy to him who perseveres in the practice of these three virtues.

THE PLACE OF SELF-EXAMINATION

That the end we ought to propose to ourselves is to become, in this life, the most perfect worshipers of God we can possibly be, as we hope to be through all eternity.

That when we enter upon the spiritual life, we should consider and examine to the bottom, what we are. And then we should find ourselves worthy of all contempt, and not deserving indeed the name of Christians; subject to all kinds of misery and numberless accidents, which trouble us and cause perpetual vicissitudes in our health, in our humors, in our internal and external dispositions; in fine, persons whom God would humble by many pains and labors, as well within as without. After this we should not wonder that troubles, temptations, oppositions, and contradictions happen to us from men. We ought, on the contrary, to submit ourselves to them, and bear them as long as God pleases, as things highly advantageous to us.

That the greater perfection a soul aspires after, the more dependent it is upon divine grace.

BROTHER LAWRENCE'S PERSONAL EXPERIENCE

*Being questioned by one of his own society (to whom he was obliged to open himself) by what means he had attained such an habitual sense of God, he told him that, since his first coming to the monastery, he had considered God as the end of all his thoughts and desires, as the mark to which they should tend, and in which they should terminate.

That in the beginning of his novitiate he spent the hours appointed for private prayer in thinking of God, so as to convince his mind of, and to impress deeply upon his heart, the divine existence, rather by devout sentiments, and submission to the lights of faith, than by studied reasonings and elaborate meditations. That by this short and sure method he exercised himself in the knowledge and love of God, resolving to use his utmost endeavor to live in a continual sense of His presence, and, if possible, never to forget Him more.

That when he had thus in prayer filled his mind with great sentiments of that infinite Being, he went to his work appointed in the kitchen (for he was cook to the society). There having first considered severally the things his office required, and when and how each thing was to be done, he spent all the intervals of his time, as well before as after his work, in prayer.

---

*The particulars which follow are collected from other accounts of Brother Lawrence.

11

That when he began his business, he said to God, with a filial trust in Him: *O my God, since Thou art with me, and I must now, in obedience to Thy commands, apply my mind to these outward things, I beseech Thee to grant me the grace to continue in Thy presence; and to this end do Thou prosper me with Thy assistance, receive all my works, and possess all my affections.*

As he proceeded in his work he continued his familiar conversation with his Maker, imploring His grace, and offering to Him all his actions.

When he had finished he examined himself how he had discharged his duty; if he found *well,* he returned thanks to God; if otherwise, he asked pardon, and, without being discouraged, he set his mind right again, and continued his exercise of the *presence* of God, as if he had never deviated from it. "Thus," said he, "by rising after my falls, and by frequently renewed acts of faith and love, I am come to a state wherein it would be as difficult for me not to think of God as it was at first to accustom myself to it."

BROTHER LAWRENCE'S EXAMPLE

As Brother Lawrence had found such an advantage in walking in the presence of God, it was natural for him to recommend it earnestly to others; but his example was a stronger inducement than any arguments he could propose. His very countenance was edifying, such a sweet and calm devotion appearing in it as could not but affect the beholders. And it was observed that in the greatest hurry of business in the kitchen he still preserved his recollection and heavenly-mindedness. He was never hasty nor loitering, but did each thing in its season, with an even, uninterrupted composure and tranquillity of spirit. "The time of business," said he, "does not with me differ from the time of prayer, and in the noise and clatter of my kitchen, while several persons are at the same time calling for different things, I possess God in as great tranquillity as if I were upon my knees at the blessed sacrament."

LETTERS

FIRST LETTER

Since you desire so earnestly that I should communicate to you the method by which I arrived at that *habitual sense of God's presence,* which our Lord, of His mercy, has been pleased to vouchsafe to me, I must tell you that it is with great difficulty that I am prevailed on by your importunities; and now I do it only upon the terms that you show my letter to nobody. If I knew that you would let it be seen, all the desire that I have for your advancement would not be able to determine me to it. The account I can give you is [this.]

BECOMING HIS ALONE

Having found in many books different methods of going to God, and divers practices of the spiritual life, I thought this would serve rather to puzzle me than facilitate what I sought after, which was nothing but how to become wholly God's. This made me resolve to give the all for the all; so after having given myself wholly to God, that He might take away my sins, *I renounced, for the love of Him, everything that was not He, and I began to live as if there was none but He and I in the world.*

UNINTERRUPTED THOUGHTS OF GOD

Sometimes I considered myself before Him as a poor criminal at the feet of his judge; at other times I beheld Him in my heart as my Father, as my God. I worshipped Him the oftenest that I could, keeping my mind in His holy presence, and recalling it as often as I found it wandered from Him. I found no small pain in this exercise, and yet I continued it, notwithstanding all the difficulties that occurred, without troubling or disquieting myself when my mind had wandered involuntarily. I made this my business as much all the day long as at the appointed times of prayer; for at all times, every hour, every minute, even in the height of my business, I drove away from my mind everything that was capable of interrupting my thoughts of God.

A NATURAL, HABITUAL PRACTICE

Such has been my common practice ever since I entered in religion; and though I have done it very imperfectly, yet I have found great advantages by it. These, I well know, are to be imputed to the mere mercy and goodness of God, because we can do nothing without Him, and *I* still less than any. But when we are faithful to keep ourselves in His holy presence, and set Him always before us, this not only hinders our offending Him and doing anything that may displease Him, at least wilfully, but it also begets in us a holy freedom, and, if I may so speak, a familiarity with God, wherewith we ask and, that successfully, the graces we stand in need of.

In fine, by often repeating these acts, they become *habitual,* and the presence of God rendered as it were *natural* to us. Give Him thanks, if you please, with me, for His great goodness toward me, which I can

14

never sufficiently admire, for the many favors He has done to so miserable a sinner as I am. May all things praise Him. Amen.

I am, in our Lord,

Yours, etc.

SECOND LETTER

To the Reverend ——

Not finding my manner of life in books, although I have no difficulty about it, yet, for greater security, I shall be glad to know your thoughts concerning it.

In a conversation some days since with a person of piety, he told me the spiritual life was a life of grace, which begins with servile fear, which is increased by hope of eternal life, and which is consummated by pure love; that each of these states had its different stages, by which one arrives at last at that blessed consummation.

HOW THE "PRACTICE" DEVELOPED

I have not followed all these methods. On the contrary, from I know not what instincts, I found they discouraged me. This was the reason why, at my entrance into religion, I took a resolution to give myself up to God, as the best return I could make for His love, and, for the love of Him, to renounce all besides.

For the first year I commonly employed myself during the time set apart for devotion with the thought of death, judgment, heaven, hell, and my sins. Thus I continued some years, applying my mind carefully the rest of the day, and even in the midst of my business, *to the presence of God*, whom I considered always as *with* me, often as *in* me.

At length I came insensibly to do the same thing during my set time of prayer, which caused in me great delight and consolation. This practice

15

produced in me so high an esteem for God that *faith* alone was capable to satisfy me in that point.*

BROTHER LAWRENCE'S
EARLY STRUGGLES

Such was my beginning, and yet I must tell you that for the first ten years I suffered much. The apprehension that I was not devoted to God as I wished to be, my past sins always present to my mind, and the great unmerited favors which God did me, were the matter and source of my sufferings. During this time I fell often, and rose again presently. It seemed to me that all creatures, reason, and God Himself were against me, and *faith* alone for me. I was troubled sometimes with thoughts that to believe I had received such favors was an effect of my presumption, which pretended to be *at once* where others arrive with difficulty; at other times, that it was a wilful delusion, and that there was no salvation for me.

When I thought of nothing but to end my days in these troubles (which did not at all diminish the trust I had in God, and which served only to increase my faith), I found myself changed all at once; and my soul, which till that time was in trouble, felt a profound inward peace, as if she were in her center and place of rest.

HIS PRESENT STATE

Ever since that time I walk before God simply, in faith, with humility and with love, and I apply myself diligently to do nothing and think nothing which may displease Him. I hope that when I have done what I can, He will do with me what He pleases.

---

*I suppose *he means* that all distinct notions he could form of God were unsatisfactory, because he perceived them to be unworthy of God; and therefore his mind was not to be satisfied but by the views of *faith,* which apprehended God as infinite and incomprehensible, as He is in Himself, and not as He can be conceived by human ideas.

As for what passes in me at present, I cannot express it. I have no pain or difficulty about my state, because I have no will but that of God, which I endeavor to accomplish in all things, and to which I am so resigned that I would not take up a straw from the ground against His order, or from any other motive than purely that of love to Him.

I have quitted all forms of devotion and set prayers but those to which my state obliges me. And I make it my business only to persevere in His holy presence, wherein I keep myself by a simple attention, and a general fond regard to God, which I may call an *actual presence* of God; or, to speak better, an habitual, silent, and secret conversation of the soul with God, which often causes me joys and raptures inwardly, and sometimes also outwardly, so great that I am forced to use means to moderate them and prevent their appearance to others.

BROTHER LAWRENCE'S VIEW OF HIMSELF

In short, I am assured beyond all doubt that my soul has been with God above these thirty years. I pass over many things that I may not be tedious to you, yet I think it proper to inform you after what manner I consider myself before God, whom I behold as my King.

I consider myself as the most wretched of men, full of sores and corruption, and who has committed all sorts of crimes against his King. Touched with a sensible regret, I confess to Him all my wickedness, I ask His forgiveness, I abandon myself in His hands that He may do what He pleases with me. The King, full of mercy and goodness, very far from chastising me, embraces me with love, makes me eat at His table, serves me with His own hands, gives me the key of His treasures; He converses and delights Himself with me incessantly, in a thousand and a thousand ways, and treats me in all respects as His favorite. It is thus I consider myself from time to time in His holy presence.

My most useful method is this simple attention, and such a general passionate regard to God, to whom I find myself often attached with greater sweetness and delight than that of an infant at the mother's breast; so that, if I dare use the expression, I should choose to call this state the bosom of God, for the inexpressible sweetness which I taste and experience there.

If sometimes my thoughts wander from it by necessity or infirmity, I am presently recalled by inward motions so charming and delicious that I am ashamed to mention them. I desire your Reverence to reflect rather upon my great wretchedness, of which you are fully informed, than upon the great favors which God does me, all unworthy and ungrateful as I am.

HIS APPROACH TO PRAYER

As for my set hours of prayer, they are only a continuation of the same exercise. Sometimes I consider myself there as a stone before a carver, whereof he is to make a statue; presenting myself thus before God, I desire Him to form His perfect image in my soul, and make me entirely like Himself.

At other times, when I apply myself to prayer, I feel all my spirit and all my soul lift itself up without any care or effort of mine, and it continues as it were suspended and firmly fixed in God, as in its center and place of rest.

I know that some charge this state with inactivity, delusion, and self-love. I confess that it is a holy inactivity, and would be a happy self-love if the soul in that state were capable of it, because, in effect, while she is in this repose, she cannot be disturbed by such acts as she was formerly accustomed to, and which were then her support, but which would now rather hinder than assist her.

Yet I cannot bear that this should be called delusion, because the soul which thus enjoys God desires herein nothing but Him. If this be delusion in me, it belongs to God to remedy it. Let Him do what He pleases with me: I desire only Him, and to be wholly devoted to Him. You will, however, oblige me in sending me your opinion, to which I always pay a great deference, for I have a singular esteem for your Reverence, and am, in our Lord,

Yours, etc.

THIRD LETTER

We have a God who is infinitely gracious and knows all about our wants. I always thought that He would reduce you to extremity. He will come in His own time, and when you least expect it. Hope in Him more than ever; thank Him with me for the favors He does you, particularly for the fortitude and patience which He gives you in your afflictions. It is a plain mark of the care He takes of you. Comfort yourself, then, with Him, and give thanks for all.

ADVICE FOR A FELLOW BELIEVER

I admire also the fortitude and bravery of Mr. ——. God has given him a good disposition and a good will; but there is in him still a little of the world and a great deal of youth. I hope the affliction which God has sent him will prove a wholesome remedy to him, and make him enter into himself. It is an accident which should engage him to put all his trust in *Him* who accompanies him everywhere. Let him think of Him as often as he can, especially in the greatest dangers. A little lifting up of the heart suffices. A little remembrance of God, one act of inward worship, though upon a march, and a sword in hand, are prayers, which, however short, are nevertheless very acceptable to God; and far from lessening a soldier's courage in occasions of danger, they best serve to fortify it.

ENGAGE IN LITTLE INTERNAL ADORATIONS

Let him then think of God the most he can. Let him accustom himself, by degrees, to this small but holy exercise. No one will notice it, and nothing is easier than to repeat often in the day these little internal adorations. Recommend to him, if you please, that he think of God the most he can, in the manner here directed. It is very fit and most necessary for a soldier who is daily exposed to the dangers of life. I hope that God will assist him and all the family, to whom I present my service, being theirs and

Yours, etc.

FOURTH LETTER

I have taken this opportunity to communicate to you the sentiments of one of our society, concerning the admirable effects and continual assistances which he receives from *the presence of God*. Let you and me both profit by them.

ADMIRABLE EFFECTS OF PRACTICING THE PRESENCE OF GOD

You must know his continual care has been, for about forty years past that he has spent in religion, to be *always with God,* and to do nothing, say nothing, and think nothing which may displease Him, and this without any other view than purely for the love of Him, and because He deserves infinitely more.

He is now so accustomed to that *divine presence* that he receives from it continual succors upon all occasions. For about thirty years his soul has been filled with joy so continual, and sometimes so great, that he is forced to use means to moderate them, and to hinder their appearing outwardly.

WHEN THE SOUL DRIFTS

If sometimes he is a little too much absent from that *divine presence,* God presently makes Himself to be felt in his soul to recall Him, which often happens when he is most engaged in his outward business. He answers with exact fidelity to these inward drawings, either by an elevation of his heart toward God, or by a meek and fond regard to Him; or by such words as love forms upon these occasions, as, for instance, *My God, here I am all devoted to Thee. Lord, make me according to Thy heart.*

And then it seems to him (as in effect he feels it) that this God of love, satisfied with such few words, reposes again, and rests in the fund and center of his soul. The experience of these things gives him such an assurance that God is always in the fund or bottom of his soul that it renders him incapable of doubting it upon any account whatever.

Judge by this what content and satisfaction he enjoys while he continually finds in himself so great a treasure. He is no longer in an anxious search after it, but has it open before him, and may take what he pleases of it.

ON THE FAILURE TO ENJOY THE INFINITE TREASURE OF GOD'S PRESENCE

He complains much of our blindness, and cries often that we are to be pitied who content ourselves with so little. *God,* saith he, *has infinite treasure to bestow, and we take up with a little sensible devotion, which passes in a moment. Blind as we are, we hinder God and stop the current of His graces. But when He finds a soul penetrated with a lively faith, He pours into it His graces and favors plentifully; there they flow like a torrent which, after being forcibly stopped against its ordinary course, when it has found a passage, spreads itself with impetuosity and abundance.*

Yes, we often stop this torrent by the little value we set upon it. But let us stop it no more; let us enter into ourselves and break down the bank which hinders it. Let us make way for grace; let us redeem the lost time, for perhaps we have but little left. Death follows us close; let us be well prepared for it; for we die but once, and a miscarriage *there* is irretrievable.

A CHALLENGE TO ADVANCE SPIRITUALLY

I say again, let us enter into ourselves. The time presses, there is no room for delay; our souls are at stake. I believe you have taken such effectual measures that you will not be surprised. I commend you for it; it is the one thing necessary. We must, nevertheless, always work at it, because not to advance in the spiritual life is to go back. But those who have the gale of the Holy Spirit go forward even in sleep. If the vessel of our soul is still tossed with winds and storms, let us awake the Lord, who reposes in it, and He will quickly calm the sea.

I have taken the liberty to impart to you these good sentiments, that you may compare them with your own. It will serve again to kindle and inflame them, if by misfortune (which God forbid, for it would be indeed a great misfortune) they should be, though never so little, cooled. Let us then *both* recall our first fervors. Let us profit by the example and the sentiments of this brother, who is little known of the world, but known to God, and extremely caressed by Him. I will pray for you; do you pray instantly for me, who am, in our Lord,

Yours, etc.

FIFTH LETTER

I received this day two books and a letter from Sister ——, who is preparing to make her profession, and upon that account desires the prayers of your holy society, and yours in particular. I perceive that she reckons much upon them; pray do not disappoint her. Beg of God that she may make her sacrifice in the view of His love alone, and with a firm resolution to be wholly devoted to Him. I will send you one of these books, which treat of *the presence of God,* a subject which, in my opinion, contains the whole spiritual life; and it seems to me that whoever duly practises it will soon become spiritual.

THE PLEASURE OF A CONTINUAL CONVERSATION WITH GOD

I know that for the right practice of it the heart must be empty of all other things, because God will possess the heart *alone;* and as He cannot possess it *alone* without emptying it of all besides, so neither can

He act *there,* and do in it what He pleases, unless it be left vacant to Him.

There is not in the world a kind of life more sweet and delightful than that of a continual conversation with God. Those only can comprehend it who practise and experience it; yet I do not advise you to do it from that motive. It is not pleasure which we ought to seek in this exercise; but let us do it from a principle of love, and because God would have us.

Were I a preacher, I should, above all other things, preach the practice of *the presence of God;* and were I a director, I should advise all the world to do it, so necessary do I think it, and so easy, too.

A PLEA TO PRACTICE GOD'S PRESENCE

Ah! knew we but the want we have of the grace and assistance of God, we should never lose sight of Him—no, not for a moment. Believe me, make immediately a holy and firm resolution nevermore wilfully to forget Him, and to spend the rest of your days in His sacred presence, deprived, for the love of Him, if He thinks fit, of all consolations.

Set heartily about this work, and if you do it as you ought, be assured that you will soon find the effects of it. I will assist you with my prayers, poor as they are. I recommend myself earnestly to yours and those of your holy society, being theirs, and more particularly,

Yours, etc.

SIXTH LETTER

To the Same

I have received from Mrs. —— the things which you gave her for me. I wonder that you have not given me your thoughts of the little book I sent to you, and which you must have received. Pray set heartily about the practice of it in your old age; it is better late than never.

LAWRENCE'S EXPERIENCE
OF GOD'S PRESENCE

I cannot imagine how religious persons can live satisfied without the practice of *the presence of God*. For my part, I keep myself retired with Him in the fund or center of my soul as much as I can; and while I am so with Him I fear nothing, but the least turning from Him is insupportable.

This exercise does not much fatigue the body; it is, however, proper to deprive it sometimes, nay, often, of many little pleasures which are innocent and lawful, for God will not permit that a soul which desires to be devoted entirely to Him should take other pleasures than with Him: that is more than reasonable.

LAY ASIDE ALL OTHER CARES

I do not say that therefore we must put any violent constraint upon ourselves. No, we must serve God in a holy freedom; we must do our business faithfully, without trouble or disquiet, recalling our mind to God mildly, and with tranquillity, as often as we find it wandering from Him.

It is, however, necessary to put our whole trust in God, laying aside all other cares, and even some particular forms of devotion, though very good in themselves, yet such as one often engages in unreasonably, because these devotions are only means to attain to the end. So when by this exercise of *the presence of God* we are *with Him* who is our end, it is then useless to return to the means; but we may continue with Him our commerce of love, persevering in His holy presence, one while by an act of praise, of adoration, or of desire; one while by an act of resignation or thanksgiving; and in all the ways which our spirit can invent.

Be not discouraged by the repugnance which you may find in it from nature; you must do yourself violence. At the first one often thinks it lost time, but you must go on, and resolve to persevere in it to death, notwithstanding all the difficulties that may occur. I recommend myself to the prayers of your holy society, and yours in particular. I am, in our Lord,

Yours, etc.

SEVENTH LETTER

I pity you much. It will be of great importance if you can leave the care of your affairs to ——, and spend the remainder of your life only in worshiping God. He requires no great matters of us: a little remembrance of Him from time to time; a little adoration; sometimes to pray for His grace, sometimes to offer Him your sufferings, and sometimes to return Him thanks for the favors He has given you, and still gives you, in the midst of your troubles, and to console yourself with Him the oftenest you can. Lift up your heart to Him, sometimes even at your meals, and when you are in company; the least little remembrance will always be acceptable to Him. You need not cry very loud; He is nearer to us than we are aware of.

ENJOY GOD'S PRESENCE
EVERYWHERE

It is not necessary for being with God to be always at church. We may make an oratory of our heart wherein to retire from time to time to converse with Him in meekness, humility, and love. Everyone is capable of such familiar conversation with God, some more, some less. He knows what we can do. Let us begin, then.

Perhaps He expects but one generous resolution on our part. Have courage. We have but little time to live; you are near sixty-four, and I am almost eighty. Let us live and die with God. Sufferings will be sweet and pleasant to us while we are with Him; and the greatest pleasures will be, without Him, a cruel punishment to us. May He be blessed for all. Amen.

ACT WITH CONFIDENCE IN GOD

Accustom yourself, then, by degrees thus to worship Him, to beg His grace, to offer Him your heart from time to time in the midst of your business, even every moment, if you can. Do not always scrupulously confine yourself to certain rules, or particular forms of devotion, but act with a general confidence in God, with love and humility. You may assure —— of my poor prayers, and that I am their servant, and particularly

Yours in our Lord, etc.

EIGHTH LETTER

Concerning Wandering Thoughts in Prayer

You tell me nothing new; you are not the only one that is troubled with wandering thoughts. Our mind is extremely roving; but, as the will is mistress of all our faculties, she must recall them, and carry them to God as their last end.

When the mind, for want of being sufficiently reduced by recollection at our first engaging in devotion, has contracted certain bad habits of wandering and dissipation, they are difficult to overcome, and commonly draw us, even against our wills, to the things of the earth.

A REMEDY FOR WANDERING THOUGHTS

I believe one remedy for this is to confess our faults and to humble ourselves before God. I do not advise you to use multiplicity of words in prayer, many words and long discourses being often the occasions of wandering. Hold yourself in prayer before God like a dumb or paralytic beggar at a rich man's gate. Let it be *your* business to keep your mind in the presence of the Lord. If it sometimes wander and withdraw itself from Him, do not much disquiet yourself for that: trouble and disquiet serve rather to distract the mind than to recollect it; the will must bring it back in tranquillity. If you persevere in this manner, God will have pity on you.

KEEP STRICTLY IN THE PRESENCE OF GOD

One way to recollect the mind easily in the time of prayer, and preserve it more in tranquillity, *is not to let it wander too far at other times.* You should keep it strictly in the presence of God; and being accustomed to think of Him often, you will find it easy to keep your mind calm in the time of prayer, or at least to recall it from its wanderings.

I have told you already at large, in my former letters, of the advantages we may draw from this practice of the presence of God. Let us set about it seriously, and pray for one another.

Yours, etc.

NINTH LETTER

The enclosed is an answer to that which I received from ——; pray deliver it to her. She seems to me full of good will, but she would go faster than grace. One does not become holy all at once. I recommend her to you; we ought to help one another by our advice, and yet more by our good examples. You will oblige me to let me hear of her from time to time, and whether she be very fervent and very obedient.

OUR ONLY BUSINESS IN LIFE

Let us thus think often that our only business in this life is to please God, and that all besides is but folly and vanity. You and I have lived about forty years in religion (i.e., a monastic life). Have we employed them in loving and serving God, who by His mercy has called us to this state, and for that very end? I am filled with shame and confusion when I reflect, on one hand, upon the great favors which God has done, and incessantly continues to do me; and on the other, upon the ill use I have made of them, and my small advancement in the way of perfection.

Since by His mercy He gives us still a little time, let us begin in earnest; let us repair the lost time; let us return with a full assurance to that Father of mercies, who is always ready to receive us affectionately. Let us renounce, let us generously renounce, for the love of Him, all that is not Himself; He deserves infinitely more.

Let us think of Him perpetually. Let us put all our trust in Him. I doubt not but we shall soon find the effects of it in receiving the abundance of His grace, with which we can do all things, and without which we can do nothing but sin.

THINK OF HIM OFTEN

We cannot escape the dangers which abound in life without the actual and *continual* help of God. Let us, then, pray to Him for it *continually*. How can we pray to Him without being with Him? How can we be with Him but in thinking of Him often? And how can we often think of Him but by a holy habit which we should form of it?

You will tell me that I am always saying the same thing. It is true, for this is the best and easiest method I know; and as I use no other, I advise all the world to do it. We must *know* before we can *love*. In order to *know* God, we must often *think* of Him; and when we come to *love* Him, we shall then also think of Him often, for our heart will be with our treasure. This is an argument which well deserves your consideration.

I am,
Yours, etc.

TENTH LETTER

I have had a good deal of difficulty to bring myself to write to Mr. ——, and I do it now purely because you and Madam —— desire me. Pray write the directions and send it to him. I am very well pleased with the trust which you have in God; I wish that He may increase it in you more and more. We cannot have too much in so good and faithful a Friend, who will never fail us in this world nor in the next.

LOVE FOR GOD MUST EXCEED LOVE FOR FRIENDS

If Mr. —— makes his advantage of the loss he has had, and puts all his confidence in God, He will soon give him another friend, more powerful and more inclined to serve him. He disposes of hearts as He pleases. Perhaps Mr. —— was too much attached to him he has lost. We ought to love our friends, but without encroaching upon the love due to God, which must be the principal.

Pray remember what I have recommended to you, which is, to think often on God, by day, by night, in your business, and even in your diversions. He is always near you and with you; leave Him not alone. You would think it rude to leave a friend alone who came to visit you; why, then, must God be neglected?

Do not, then, forget Him, but think on Him often, adore Him continually, live and die with Him; this is the glorious employment of a Christian. In a word, this is our profession; if we do not know it, we must learn it. I will endeavor to help you with my prayers, and am, in our Lord,

Yours, etc.

ELEVENTH LETTER

I do not pray that you may be delivered from your pains, but I pray God earnestly that He would give you strength and patience to bear them as long as He pleases. Comfort yourself with Him who holds you fastened to the cross. He will loose you when He thinks fit. Happy those who suffer with Him. Accustom yourself to suffer in that manner, and seek from Him the strength to endure as much, and as long, as He shall judge to be necessary for you.

A PROPER VIEW
OF SICKNESS

The men of the world do not comprehend these truths, nor is it to be wondered at, since they suffer like what they are, and not like Christians. They consider sickness as a pain to nature, and not as a favor from God; and seeing it only in that light, they find nothing in it but grief and distress. But those who consider sickness as coming from the hand of God, as the effect of His mercy, and the means which He employs for their salvation—such commonly find in it great sweetness and sensible consolation.

THE SOVEREIGN PHYSICIAN

I wish you could convince yourself that God is often (in some sense) nearer to us, and more effectually present with us, in sickness than in health. Rely upon no other physician; for, according to my apprehension, He reserves your cure to Himself. Put, then, all your trust in Him, and you will soon find we often retard by putting greater confidence in physic than in God.

Whatever remedies you make use of, they will succeed only so far as He permits. When pains come from God, He only can cure them. He often sends diseases of the body to cure those of the soul. Comfort yourself with the sovereign Physician both of the soul and body.

BE SATISFIED WITH YOUR CONDITION

Be satisfied with the condition in which God places you; however happy you may think me, I envy you. Pains and sufferings would be a paradise to me while I should suffer with my God, and the greatest pleasures would be hell to me if I could relish them without Him. All my consolation would be to suffer something for His sake.

I must, in a little time, go to God. What comforts me in this life is that I now see Him by *faith;* and I see Him in such a manner as might make me say sometimes, *I believe no more, but I see.* I feel what faith teaches us, and in that assurance and that practice of faith I will live and die with Him.

Continue, then, always with God; it is the only support and comfort for your affliction. I shall beseech Him to be with you. I present my service.

Yours, etc.

TWELFTH LETTER

If we were well accustomed to the exercise of *the presence of God,* all bodily diseases would be much alleviated thereby. God often permits that we should suffer a little to purify our souls and oblige us to continue *with* Him.

HOW TO DEAL WITH PAIN

Take courage; offer Him your pains incessantly; pray to Him for strength to endure them. Above all, get a habit of entertaining yourself often with God, and forget Him the least you can. Adore Him in your infirmities, offer yourself to Him from time to time, and in the height of your sufferings beseech Him humbly and affectionately (as a child his father) to make you conformable to His holy will. I shall endeavor to assist you with my poor prayers.

God has many ways of drawing us to Himself. He sometimes hides Himself from us; but *faith* alone, which will not fail us in time of need, ought to be our support, and the foundation of our confidence, which must be all in God.

OUR NEED FOR GOD'S PRESENCE

I know not how God will dispose of me. I am always happy. All the world suffers; and I, who deserve the severest discipline, feel joys so continual and so great that I can scarce contain them.

I would willingly ask of God a part of your sufferings, but that I know my weakness, which is so great that if He left me one moment to myself I should be the most wretched man alive. And yet I know not how He can leave me alone, because faith gives me as strong a conviction as sense can do, that He never forsakes us until we have first forsaken Him. Let us fear to leave Him. Let us be always with Him. Let us live and die in His presence. Do you pray for me as I for you. I am,

Yours, etc.

THIRTEENTH LETTER

To the Same

I am in pain to see you suffer so long. What gives me some ease and sweetens the feelings I have for your griefs is that they are proofs of God's love toward you. See them in that view and you will bear them more easily. As your case is, it is my opinion that you should leave off human remedies, and resign yourself entirely to the providence of God. Perhaps He stays only for that resignation and a perfect trust in Him to cure you. Since, notwithstanding all your cares, physic has hitherto proved unsuccessful, and your malady still increases, it will not be tempting God to abandon yourself in His hands and expect all from Him.

HOW TO PRAY IN TIME OF PAIN

I told you in my last that He sometimes permits bodily diseases to cure the distempers of the soul. Have courage, then; make a virtue of necessity. Ask of God, not deliverance from your pains, but strength to bear resolutely, for the love of Him, all that He should please, and as long as He shall please.

Such prayers, indeed, are a little hard to nature, but most acceptable to God and sweet to those that love Him. Love sweetens pains; and when one loves God, one suffers for His sake with joy and courage. Do you so, I beseech you; comfort yourself with Him, who is the only Physician of all our maladies. He is the Father of the afflicted, always ready to help us. He loves us infinitely, more than we imagine. Love Him, then, and seek no consolation elsewhere. I hope you will soon receive it. Adieu. I will help you with my prayers, poor as they are, and shall always be, in our Lord,

Yours, etc.

FOURTEENTH LETTER

To the Same

I render thanks to our Lord for having relieved you a little, according to your desire. I have been often near expiring, but I never was so much satisfied as then. Accordingly, I did not pray for any relief, but I prayed for strength to suffer with courage, humility, and love. Ah, how sweet it is to suffer with God! However great the sufferings may be, receive them with love.

ADORE HIM INCESSANTLY

It is paradise to suffer and be with Him; so that if in this life we would enjoy the peace of paradise we must accustom ourselves to a familiar, humble, affectionate conversation with Him. We must hinder our spirits' wandering from Him upon any occasion. We must make our heart a spiritual temple, wherein to adore Him incessantly. We must watch continually over ourselves, that we may not do nor say nor think anything that may displease Him. When our minds are thus employed about God, suffering will become full of unction and consolation.

I know that to arrive at this state the beginning is very difficult, for we must act purely in faith. But though it is difficult, we know also that we can do all things with the grace of God, which He never refuses to them who ask it earnestly. Knock, persevere in knocking, and I answer for it that He will open to you in His due time, and grant you all at once what He has deferred during many years. Adieu. Pray to Him for me as I pray to Him for you. I hope to see Him quickly. I am,

Yours, etc.

FIFTEENTH LETTER

To the Same

God knoweth best what is needful for us, and all that He does is for our good. If we knew how much He loves us, we should always be ready to receive equally and with indifference from His hand the sweet and the bitter. All would please that came from Him.

The sorest afflictions never appear intolerable, except when we see them in the wrong light. When we see them as dispensed by the hand of God, when we know that it is our loving Father who abases and distresses us, our sufferings will lose their bitterness and become even matter of consolation.

TO KNOW GOD BETTER IS TO LOVE HIM MORE

Let all our employment be to *know* God; the more one *knows* Him, the more one *desires* to know Him. And as *knowledge* is commonly the measure of *love,* the deeper and more extensive our *knowledge* shall be, the greater will be our *love;* and if our love of God were great, we should love Him equally in pains and pleasures.

SEEK GOD BY FAITH

Let us not content ourselves with loving God for the mere sensible favors, how elevated soever, which He has done or may do us. Such favors, though never so great, cannot bring us so near to Him as faith does in one simple act. Let us seek Him often by faith. He is within us; seek Him not elsewhere. If we do love Him alone, are we not rude, and do we not deserve blame, if we busy ourselves about trifles which do not please and perhaps offend Him? It is to be feared these *trifles* will one day cost us dear.

LAWRENCE'S DESIRE TO SEE GOD

Let us begin to be devoted to Him in good earnest. Let us cast everything besides out of our hearts. He would possess them alone. Beg this favor of Him. If we do what we can on our parts, we shall soon see that change wrought in us which we aspire after. I cannot thank Him sufficiently for the relaxation He has vouchsafed you. I hope from His mercy the favor to see Him within a few days.* Let us pray for one another. I am, in our Lord,

Yours, etc.

---

*He took to his bed two days after, and died within the week.

NOTES

1. The friend is Bruce Shelley, now senior professor of church history at Denver Seminary.
2. First Conversation in the text following.
3. Ibid.
4. Second Conversation.
5. First Letter.
6. Tenth Letter.
7. Wayne E. Oates's psychological commentary on *The Practice of the Presence of God* is found in E. Glenn Hinson, *Seekers After Mature Faith: A Historical Introduction to the Classics of Christian Devotion* (Nashville: Broadman Press, 1968), 158.
8. Eighth Letter.
9. Second and Fourth Conversations.

THE
WAY OF
PERFECTION

TERESA OF ÁVILA

TERESA OF ÁVILA, 1515–1582

HER LIFE	1515–1582	WORLD EVENTS

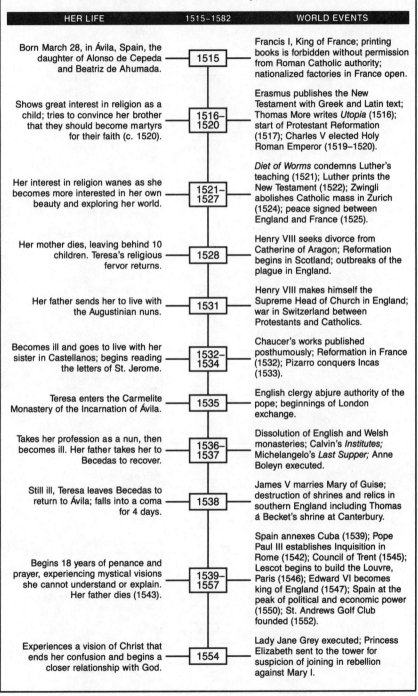

HER LIFE — Born March 28, in Ávila, Spain, the daughter of Alonso de Cepeda and Beatriz de Ahumada. **1515** — **WORLD EVENTS** Francis I, King of France; printing books is forbidden without permission from Roman Catholic authority; nationalized factories in France open.

Shows great interest in religion as a child; tries to convince her brother that they should become martyrs for their faith (c. 1520). — **1516–1520** — Erasmus publishes the New Testament with Greek and Latin text; Thomas More writes *Utopia* (1516); start of Protestant Reformation (1517); Charles V elected Holy Roman Emperor (1519–1520).

Her interest in religion wanes as she becomes more interested in her own beauty and exploring her world. — **1521–1527** — *Diet of Worms* condemns Luther's teaching (1521); Luther prints the New Testament (1522); Zwingli abolishes Catholic mass in Zurich (1524); peace signed between England and France (1525).

Her mother dies, leaving behind 10 children. Teresa's religious fervor returns. — **1528** — Henry VIII seeks divorce from Catherine of Aragon; Reformation begins in Scotland; outbreaks of the plague in England.

Her father sends her to live with the Augustinian nuns. — **1531** — Henry VIII makes himself the Supreme Head of Church in England; war in Switzerland between Protestants and Catholics.

Becomes ill and goes to live with her sister in Castellanos; begins reading the letters of St. Jerome. — **1532–1534** — Chaucer's works published posthumously; Reformation in France (1532); Pizarro conquers Incas (1533).

Teresa enters the Carmelite Monastery of the Incarnation of Ávila. — **1535** — English clergy abjure authority of the pope; beginnings of London exchange.

Takes her profession as a nun, then becomes ill. Her father takes her to Becedas to recover. — **1536–1537** — Dissolution of English and Welsh monasteries; Calvin's *Institutes;* Michelangelo's *Last Supper;* Anne Boleyn executed.

Still ill, Teresa leaves Becedas to return to Ávila; falls into a coma for 4 days. — **1538** — James V marries Mary of Guise; destruction of shrines and relics in southern England including Thomas á Becket's shrine at Canterbury.

Begins 18 years of penance and prayer, experiencing mystical visions she cannot understand or explain. Her father dies (1543). — **1539–1557** — Spain annexes Cuba (1539); Pope Paul III establishes Inquisition in Rome (1542); Council of Trent (1545); Lescot begins to build the Louvre, Paris (1546); Edward VI becomes king of England (1547); Spain at the peak of political and economic power (1550); St. Andrews Golf Club founded (1552).

Experiences a vision of Christ that ends her confusion and begins a closer relationship with God. — **1554** — Lady Jane Grey executed; Princess Elizabeth sent to the tower for suspicion of joining in rebellion against Mary I.

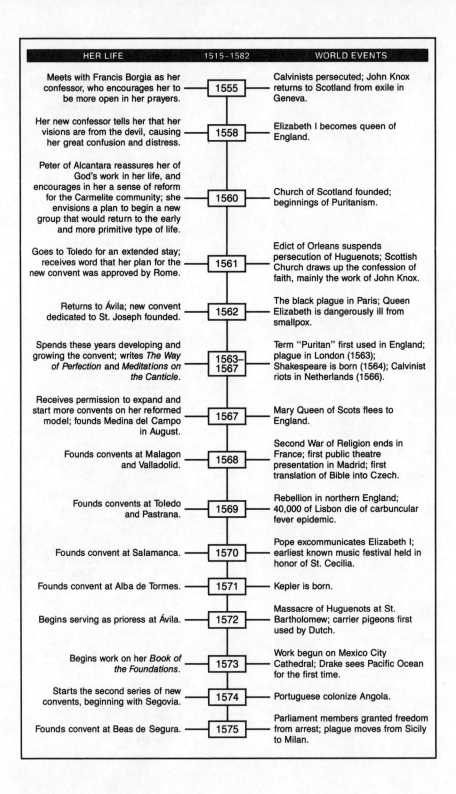

HER LIFE	1515–1582	WORLD EVENTS
Meets with Francis Borgia as her confessor, who encourages her to be more open in her prayers.	1555	Calvinists persecuted; John Knox returns to Scotland from exile in Geneva.
Her new confessor tells her that her visions are from the devil, causing her great confusion and distress.	1558	Elizabeth I becomes queen of England.
Peter of Alcantara reassures her of God's work in her life, and encourages in her a sense of reform for the Carmelite community; she envisions a plan to begin a new group that would return to the early and more primitive type of life.	1560	Church of Scotland founded; beginnings of Puritanism.
Goes to Toledo for an extended stay; receives word that her plan for the new convent was approved by Rome.	1561	Edict of Orleans suspends persecution of Huguenots; Scottish Church draws up the confession of faith, mainly the work of John Knox.
Returns to Ávila; new convent dedicated to St. Joseph founded.	1562	The black plague in Paris; Queen Elizabeth is dangerously ill from smallpox.
Spends these years developing and growing the convent; writes *The Way of Perfection* and *Meditations on the Canticle*.	1563–1567	Term "Puritan" first used in England; plague in London (1563); Shakespeare is born (1564); Calvinist riots in Netherlands (1566).
Receives permission to expand and start more convents on her reformed model; founds Medina del Campo in August.	1567	Mary Queen of Scots flees to England.
Founds convents at Malagon and Valladolid.	1568	Second War of Religion ends in France; first public theatre presentation in Madrid; first translation of Bible into Czech.
Founds convents at Toledo and Pastrana.	1569	Rebellion in northern England; 40,000 of Lisbon die of carbuncular fever epidemic.
Founds convent at Salamanca.	1570	Pope excommunicates Elizabeth I; earliest known music festival held in honor of St. Cecilia.
Founds convent at Alba de Tormes.	1571	Kepler is born.
Begins serving as prioress at Ávila.	1572	Massacre of Huguenots at St. Bartholomew; carrier pigeons first used by Dutch.
Begins work on her *Book of the Foundations*.	1573	Work begun on Mexico City Cathedral; Drake sees Pacific Ocean for the first time.
Starts the second series of new convents, beginning with Segovia.	1574	Portuguese colonize Angola.
Founds convent at Beas de Segura.	1575	Parliament members granted freedom from arrest; plague moves from Sicily to Milan.

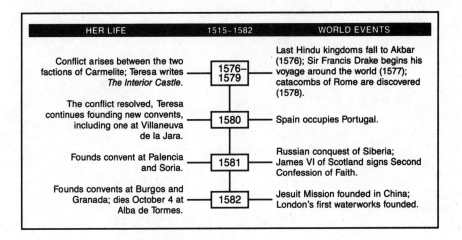

HER LIFE	1515–1582	WORLD EVENTS
Conflict arises between the two factions of Carmelite; Teresa writes *The Interior Castle*.	1576–1579	Last Hindu kingdoms fall to Akbar (1576); Sir Francis Drake begins his voyage around the world (1577); catacombs of Rome are discovered (1578).
The conflict resolved, Teresa continues founding new convents, including one at Villaneuva de la Jara.	1580	Spain occupies Portugal.
Founds convent at Palencia and Soria.	1581	Russian conquest of Siberia; James VI of Scotland signs Second Confession of Faith.
Founds convents at Burgos and Granada; dies October 4 at Alba de Tormes.	1582	Jesuit Mission founded in China; London's first waterworks founded.

INTRODUCTION

A lthough she was only five years old, Teresa Sanchez Cepeda Davila y Ahumada was already charismatic and persuasive. Caught up in a sense of religious piety she had acquired from her father, she convinced her older brother that they should become martyrs for Christ. She thought they should "go off to the land of the Moors and beg them, out of love of God, to cut off our heads." The two adventurous children set out on their ambitious journey, only to have an uncle interrupt the plans by taking them home.

Although this early seriousness about religion did not last, her ability to persuade remained one of Teresa's best assets, helping her influence priests, politicians, and popes as she became one of medieval Europe's best known figures and a writer whose works changed the way Christians viewed prayer and a personal relationship with God.

Teresa's early childhood piety gave way to the concerns of a typical teenaged girl. She was enthusiastic, outgoing, and beautiful, and she loved finding ways to enhance her beauty. She adored the romance stories her mother kept carefully hidden from Teresa's strict father, and she dreamed of boys and marriage. Her father became concerned about the wildness of his daughter's ways, but her mother, Beatriz, protected her beloved child.

Then, when Teresa was fifteen, her mother died, leaving behind not only Teresa but nine other children. Overwhelmed by the loss, Teresa's father no longer had patience or time to give his daughter the proper guidance. Feeling she was out of control, he sent her to an Augustinian convent in Ávila. Under the nuns' tutoring, Teresa began to wonder if she had a true vocation. As she was working out her feelings about the church and marriage, however, she became ill, and left the convent after eighteen months. Returning home to recover, Teresa began to read the letters of St. Jerome, which had been given to her by an uncle.

Through reading and prayer, Teresa decided that she needed to enter a convent. Her father refused to grant his permission, so in November 1535, Teresa ran away from home, entering the Carmelite Monastery of the Incarnation at Ávila. Her father finally acquiesced to this development, and Teresa took the habit the next year. However, Teresa became ill shortly thereafter, and her father took her to Becedas for medical help. Her health continued to deteriorate, and her father finally carried her home to Ávila, where she fell into a coma and was believed to be dead. Although she revived after four days, she was unable to walk for another three years, and never regained her full health again.

For the next eighteen years, Teresa languished spiritually and mentally. She struggled with her faith, her beliefs about prayer, and her desire to be liked and approved of by other people. Although she had begun to have mystical visions, she and those counseling her discounted them. Then she had a vision of Christ that completely converted her from her doubts and allowed her to release her own ego in her search for a deeper faith and conviction. Shortly afterward, her confession about the vision was heard by Francis Borgia, who encouraged her to focus on Christ and her prayer life.

Concentrating on her prayer time, Teresa began to formulate a vision of reform of her world as well as herself. Vowing to follow a life of poverty that was devoted to prayer, she then turned her mind toward starting a new Carmelite convent—one that was centered on the basics of prayer and poverty. She was met with much opposition from within her order as well as from other clergy, church administrators and from the laity. Teresa's personal charisma and persuasive powers went into play, however, and six months later, she was granted permission to start the new convent. On August 24, 1562, the convent of Discalced Carmelite Nuns of the Primitive Rule of St. Joseph was dedicated, with four young women entering as novices.

The next five years were the most uneventful of Teresa's life. She expanded her time in prayer and meditation, and wrote two books, including *The Way of Perfection*. The book, which was originally addressed to her nuns, is the heart of her spiritual doctrine, detailing her beliefs in the merit of virtue, prayer, and an ascetic life. Teresa was content.

Then, in 1567, the head of the Carmelite order visited her convent. Impressed, he commanded her to start other convents—as well as monasteries—on the model of St. Joseph's. Thus began the most frenetic, and sometimes frustrating, stage of Teresa's life. Over the next four years, she founded seven new communities. Her work was then interrupted as she served for a short period as prioress at her old order. Then, on March 19, 1574, she opened a new convent at Segovia, which started the second stage of her foundations. Over the next eight years, Teresa of Ávila struggled with conflict within the order, visited her existing convents, established eight more, and wrote one of her finest books, *The Interior Castle*. She died on October 4, 1582, while visiting one of those convents.

Teresa of Ávila holds a decidedly unique place in the history of Christian literature and theology. Because her doctrine was developed out of her own experience as well as her study of Scripture and church history, she was one of the first to place an emphasis on the vital need for prayer and an intimate and personal relationship with God. Undoubtedly one of the finest books written on the subject of living devotedly in the presence of God, *The Way of Perfection* remains relevant to today's believer because of its common sense approach and practical advice from a woman who knew all too well how *imperfect* life could be.

PREFACE

Although St. Teresa of Ávila lived and wrote almost four centuries ago, her superbly inspiring classic on the practice of prayer is as fresh and meaningful today as it was when she first wrote it. *The Way of Perfection* is a practical guide to prayer setting forth the Saint's counsels and directives for the attainment of spiritual perfection.

Through the entire work there runs the author's desire to teach a deep and lasting love of prayer beginning with a treatment of the three essentials of the prayer-filled life—fraternal love, detachment from created things, and true humility. St. Teresa's counsels on these are not only the fruit of lofty mental speculation, but of mature practical experience. The next section develops these ideas and brings the reader directly to the subjects of prayer and contemplation. St. Teresa then gives various maxims for the practice of prayer and leads up to the topic which occupies the balance of the book—a detailed and inspiring commentary on the Lord's Prayer.

Of all St. Teresa's writings, *The Way of Perfection* is the most easily understood. Although it is a work of sublime mystical beauty, its outstanding hallmark is its simplicity which instructs, exhorts, and inspires all those who are seeking a more perfect way of life.

"I shall speak of nothing of which I have no experience, either in my own life or in observation of others, or which the Lord has not taught me in prayer."—Prologue

Almost four centuries have passed since St. Teresa of Ávila, the great Spanish mystic and reformer, committed to writing the experiences which brought her to the highest degree of sanctity. Her search for, and eventual union with, God have been recorded in her own world-renowned writings—the autobiographical *Life,* the celebrated masterpiece *Interior Castle* and *The Way of Perfection*—as well as in the other numerous works which flowed from her pen while she lived.

The Way of Perfection was written during the height of controversy which raged over the reforms St. Teresa enacted within the Carmelite Order. Its specific purpose was to serve as a guide in the practice of prayer and it sets forth her counsels and directives for the attainment of spiritual perfection through prayer. It was composed by St. Teresa at the express command of her superiors, and was written during the late hours in order not to interfere with the day's already crowded schedule.

Without doubt it fulfills the tribute given all St. Teresa's works by E. Allison Peers, the outstanding authority on her writings: "Work of a sublime beauty bearing the ineffaceable hallmark of genius."

To the gracious memory of

P. EDMUND GURDON

sometime prior of the Carthusian
monastery of Miraflores
a man of God

Translator's Notes

In the text of each of the chapters, of the Valladolid autograph there
are omissions—some merely verbal, often illustrating the author's
aim in making the new redaction, others more fundamental. If the
Valladolid manuscript represents *The Way of Perfection* as St. Teresa wrote
it in the period of her fullest powers, the greater freshness and individual-
ity of the Escorial manuscript are engaging qualities, and there are many
passages in it, omitted from the later version, which one would be sorry
to sacrifice.

In what form, then, should the book be presented to English readers?
It is not surprising if this question is difficult to answer, since varying
procedures have been adopted for the presentation of it in Spain. Most
of them amount briefly to a re-editing of the Valladolid manuscript. The
first edition of the book, published at Évora in the year 1583, follows
this manuscript, apparently using a copy (the so-called "Toledo" copy)
made by Ana de San Pedro and corrected by St. Teresa; it contains a
considerable number of errors, however, and omits one entire chapter—

the thirty-first, which deals with the Prayer of Quiet, a subject that was arousing some controversy at the time when the edition was being prepared. In 1585, a second edition, edited by Fray Jerónimo Gracián, was published at Salamanca: the text of this follows that of the Évora edition very closely, as apparently does the text of a rare edition published at Valencia in 1586. When Fray Luis de Leon used the Valladolid manuscript as the foundation of his text (1588) he inserted for the first time paragraphs and phrases from that of El Escorial, as well as admitting variants from the copies corrected by the author: he is not careful however, to indicate how and where his edition differs from the manuscript.

Since 1588, most of the Spanish editions have followed Fray Luis de León with greater or less exactness. The principal exception is the well-known "Biblioteca de Autores Españoles" edition, in which La Fuente followed a copy of the then almost forgotten Escorial manuscript, indicating in footnotes some of the variant readings in the codex of Valladolid. In the edition of 1883, the work of a Canon of Valladolid Cathedral, Francisco Herrero Bayona, the texts of the two manuscripts are reproduced in parallel columns. P. Silverio de Santa Teresa gives the place of honour to the Valladolid codex, on which he bases his text, showing only the principal variants of the Escorial manuscript but printing the Escorial text in full in an appendix as well as the text of the Toledo copy referred to above.

The first translations of this book into English, by Woodhead (1675: reprinted 1901) and Dalton (1852), were based, very naturally, on the text of Luis de León, which in less critical ages than our own enjoyed great prestige and was considered quite authoritative. The edition published in 1911 by the Benedictines of Stanbrook, described on its title-page as "including all the variants" from both the Escorial and the Valladolid manuscript, uses Herrero Bayona and gives an eclectic text based on the two originals but with no indications as to which is which. The editors' original idea of using one text only, and showing variants in footnotes, was rejected in the belief that "such an arrangement would prove bewildering for the generality of readers" and that anyone who could claim the title of "student" would be able to read the original

Spanish and would have access to the Herrero Bayona edition. Father Zimmerman, in his introduction, claimed that while the divergences between the manuscripts are sometimes "so great that the [Stanbrook] translation resembles a mosaic composed of a large number of small bits, skilfully combined," "the work has been done most conscientiously, and while nothing has been added to the text of the Saint, nothing has been omitted, except, of course, what would have been mere repetition."

This first edition of the Benedictines' translation furnished the general reader with an attractive version of what many consider St. Teresa's most attractive book, but soon after it was published a much more intelligent and scholarly interest began to be taken in the Spanish mystics and that not only by students with ready access to the Spanish original and ability to read it. So, when a new edition of the Stanbrook translation was called for, the editors decided to indicate the passages from the Escorial edition which had been embodied in the text by enclosing these in square brackets. In 1911, Father Zimmerman, suspecting that the procedure then adopted by the translators would not "meet with the approval of scholars," had justified it by their desire "to benefit the souls of the faithful rather than the intellect of the student"; but now, apparently, he thought it practicable to achieve both these aims at once. This resolution would certainly have had the support of St. Teresa, who in this very book describes intelligence as a useful staff to carry on the way of perfection. The careful comparison of two separate versions of such a work of genius may benefit the soul of an intelligent reader even more than the careful reading of a version compounded of both by someone else.

When I began to consider the preparation of the present translation it seemed to me that an attempt might be made to do a little more for the reader who combined intelligence with devoutness than had been done already. I had no hesitation about basing my version on the Valladolid MS., which is far the better of the two, whether we consider the aptness of its illustrations, the clarity of its expression, the logical development of its argument or its greater suitability for general reading. At the same time, no Teresan who has studied the Escorial text can fail to have an affection for it: its greater intimacy and spontaneity and its appeal to personal experience make it one of the most characteristic of all the Saint's writings—indeed, excepting the *Letters* and a few chapters of the *Foundations,* it reveals her better than any. Passages from the Escorial MS. must therefore be given: thus far I followed the reasoning of the Stanbrook nuns.

Where this translation diverges from theirs is in the method of presentation. On the one hand I desired, as St. Teresa must have desired, that it should be essentially her mature revision of the book that should be read. For this reason I have been extremely conservative as to the interpolations admitted into the text itself: I have rejected, for example, the innumerable phrases which St. Teresa seems to have cut out in making her new redaction because they were trivial or repetitive, because they weaken rather than reinforce her argument, because they say what is better said elsewhere, because they summarize needlessly[1] or because they are mere personal observations which interrupt the author's flow of thought, and sometimes, indeed, are irrelevant to it. I hope it is not impertinent to add that, in the close study which the adoption of this procedure has involved, I have acquired a respect and admiration for St. Teresa as a reviser, to whom, as far as I know, no one who has written upon her has done full justice. Her shrewdness, realism and complete lack of vanity make her an admirable editor of her own work, and, in debating whether or no to incorporate some phrase or passage in my text I have often asked myself: "Would St. Teresa have included or omitted this if she had been making a fresh revision for a world-wide public over a period of centuries?"

At the same time, though admitting only a minimum of interpolations into my text, I have given the reader all the other important variants in footnotes. I cannot think, as Father Zimmerman apparently thought, that anyone can find the presence of a few notes at the foot of each page "bewildering." Those for whom they have no interest may ignore them; others, in studying them, may rest assured that the only variants not included (and this applies to the variants from the Toledo copy as well as from the Escorial MS.) are such as have no significance in a translation.

I have been rather less meticulous here than in my edition of St. John of the Cross, where textual problems assumed greater importance. Thus, except where there has been some special reason for doing so, I have not recorded alterations in the order of clauses or words; the almost regular use by E. of the second person of the plural where V. has the first; the frequent and often apparently purposeless changes of tense; such substitutions, in the Valladolid redaction, as those of "Dios" or "Ṣeñior mío" for "Señior"; or merely verbal paraphrases as (to take an example at random) "Todo esto que he dicho es para . . ." for "En todo esto que he dicho no trato . . ." Where I have given variants which may seem trivial (such as "hermanas" for "hijas," or the insertion of an explanatory word, like "digo") the reason is generally that there seems to me a possibility that some difference in tone is intended, or that the alternative phrase gives some slight turn to the thought which the phrase in the text does not.

The passages from the Escorial version which I have allowed into my text are printed in italics. Thus, without their being given undue prominence (and readers of the Authorized Version of the Bible will know how seldom they can recall what words are italicized even in the passages they know best) it is clear at a glance how much of the book was intended by its author to be read by a wider public than the nuns of St. Joseph's. The interpolations may be as brief as a single expressive word, or as long as a paragraph, or even a chapter: the original Chapter 17 of the Valladolid MS., for example, which contains the famous similitude of the Game of Chess, was torn out of the codex by its author (presumably with the idea that so secular an illustration was out of place) and has been restored from the Escorial MS. as part of Chapter 16 of this translation. No doubt the striking bullfight metaphor at the end of Chapter 39 was suppressed in the Valladolid codex for the same reason. With these omissions may be classed a number of minor ones—of words or phrases which to the author may have seemed too intimate or colloquial but do not seem so to us. Other words and phrases have apparently been suppressed because St. Teresa thought them redundant, whereas a later reader finds that they make a definite contribution to the sense or give explicitness and detail to what would otherwise be vague, or even obscure.[4] A few suppressions seem to have been due to pure oversight. For the omission of other passages it is difficult to find any reason, so good are they: the conclusion of Chapter 38 and the opening of Chapter 41 are cases in point.

The numbering of the chapters, it should be noted, follows neither of the two texts, but is that traditionally employed in the printed editions. The chapter headings are also drawn up on an eclectic basis, though here the Valladolid text is generally followed.

The system I have adopted not only assures the reader that he will be reading everything that St. Teresa wrote and nothing that she did not write, but that he can discern almost at a glance, what she meant to be read by her little group of nuns at St. Joseph's and also how she intended her work to appear in its more definitive form. Thus we can see her both as the companion and Mother and as the writer and Foundress. In both roles she is equally the Saint.

But it should be made clear that, while incorporating in my text all important passages from the Escorial draft omitted in that of Valladolid, I have thought it no part of my task to provide a complete translation of the Escorial draft alone, and that, therefore, in order to avoid the multiplication of footnotes, I have indicated only the principal places where some expression in the later draft is not to be found in the earlier. In other words, although, by omitting the italicized portions of my text, one will be able to have as exact a translation of the Valladolid version as it is possible to get, the translation of the Escorial draft will be only approximate. This is the sole concession I have made to the ordinary reader as opposed to the student, and it is hardly conceivable, I think, that any student to whom this could matter would be unable to read the original Spanish.

One final note is necessary on the important Toledo copy, the text of which P. Silverio also prints in full. This text I have collated with that of the Valladolid autograph, from which it derives. In it both St. Teresa herself and others have made corrections and additions—more, in fact, than in any of the other copies extant. No attempt has been made here either to show what the Toledo copy omits or to include those of its corrections and additions—by far the largest number of them—which are merely verbal and unimportant, and many of which, indeed, could not be embodied in a translation at all. But the few additions which are really worth noting have been incorporated in the text (in square brackets so as to distinguish them from the Escorial additions) and all corrections which have seemed to me of any significance will be found in footnotes.

BOOK CALLED WAY OF PERFECTION[3]

Composed by TERESA OF JESUS, Nun of the Order of Our Lady of Carmel, addressed to the Discalced Nuns of Our Lady of Carmel of the First Rule.[4]

General Argument of this Book
J. H. S.

T his book treats of maxims and counsels which Teresa of Jesus gives to her daughters and sisters in religion, belonging to the Convents which, with the favour of Our Lord and of the glorious Virgin, Mother of God, Our Lady, she has founded according to the First Rule of Our Lady of Carmel. In particular she addresses it to the sisters of the Convent of Saint Joseph of Ávila, which was the first Convent, and of which she was Prioress when she wrote it.[5]

PROTESTATIONS[8]

In all that I shall say in this Book, I submit to what is taught by Our Mother, the Holy Roman Church; if there is anything in it contrary to this, it will be without my knowledge. Therefore, for the love of Our Lord, I beg the learned men who are to revise it to look at it very carefully and to amend any faults of this nature which there may be in it and the many others which it will have of other kinds. If there is anything good in it, let this be to the glory and honour of God and in the service of His most sacred Mother, our Patroness and Lady, whose habit, though all unworthily, I wear.

PROLOGUE

J. H. S.

The sisters of this Convent of Saint Joseph, knowing that I had had leave from Father Presentado Fray Domingo Bañes,[9] of the Order of the glorious Saint Dominic, who at present is my confessor, to write certain things about prayer, which it seems I may be able to succeed in doing since I have had to do with many holy and spiritual persons, have, *out of their great love for me,* so earnestly begged me to say something to them about this that I have resolved to obey them. I realize that the great love which they have for me may render the imperfection and the poverty of my style in what I shall say to them more acceptable than other books which are very ably written by those who[10] have known what they are writing about. I rely upon their prayers, by means of which the Lord may be pleased to enable me to say something concerning the way and method of life which it is fitting should be practised in this house. If I do not succeed in doing this, Father Presentado, who will first read what I have written, will either put it right or burn it, so that I shall have lost nothing by obeying these servants of God, and they will see how useless I am when His Majesty does not help me.

My intent is to suggest a few remedies for a number of small temptations which come from the devil, and which, because they are so slight, are apt to pass unnoticed. I shall also write of other things, according as the Lord reveals them to me and as they come to my mind; since I do not know what I am going to say I cannot set it down in suitable order; and I think it is better for me not to do so, for it is quite unsuitable that I should be writing in this way at all. May the Lord lay His hand on all that I do so that it may be in accordance with His holy will; this is always my desire, although my actions may be as imperfect as I myself am.

I know that I am lacking neither in love nor in desire to do all I can to help the souls of my sisters to make great progress in the service of the Lord. It may be that this love, together with my years and the experience which I have of a number of convents, will make me more successful in writing about small matters than learned men can be. For these, being themselves strong and handing other and more important occupations, do not always pay such heed to things which in themselves seem of no importance but which may do great harm to persons as weak as we women are. For the snares laid by the devil for strictly cloistered nuns are numerous and he finds that he needs new weapons if he is to do them harm. I, being a wicked woman, have defended myself but ill, and so I should like my sisters to take warning by me. I shall speak of nothing of which I have no experience, either in my own life or in the observation of others, *or which the Lord has not taught me in prayer.*

A few days ago I was commanded to write an account of my life in which I also dealt with certain matters concerning prayer. It may be that my confessor will not wish you to see this, for which reason I shall set down here some of the things which I said in that book and others which may also seem to me necessary. May the Lord direct this, as I have begged Him to do, and order it for His greater glory. Amen.

PRINCIPAL ABBREVIATIONS

A.V.—Authorized Version of the Bible (1611).

D.V.—Douai Version of the Bible (1609).

Letters—*Letters of St. Teresa.* Unless otherwise stated, the numbering of the Letters follows Vols. VII–IX of P. Silverio. *Letters* (St.) indicates the translation of the *Benedictines of Stanbrook* (London, 1919–24, 4 vols.).

Lewis—*The Life of St. Teresa of Jesus,* etc., translated by David Lewis, 5th ed., with notes and introductions by the Very Rev. Benedict Zimmerman, O.C.D., London, 1916.

P. Silverio—*Obras de Santa Teresa de Jesús,* editadas y anotadas por el P. Silverio de Santa Teresa, C.D., Durgos, 1915–24, 9 vols.

Ribera—Francisco de Ribera, *Vida de Santa Teresa de Jesús,* Nueva ed. aumentada, con introduction, etc., por el P. Jaime Pons, Barcelona, 1908.

S.S.M.—E. Allison Peers, *Studies of the Spanish Mystics,* London, 1927–30, 2 vols.

St. John of the Cross—*The Complete Works of Saint John of the Cross, Doctor of the Church,* translated from the critical edition of P. Silverio de Santa Teresa, C.D., and edited by E. Allison Peers, London, 1934–35, 3 vols.

Yepes—Diego de Yepes, *Vida de Santa Teresa,* Madrid, 1615.

CHAPTER ONE

*Of the reason which moved me to found this convent
in such strict observance.*

When this convent was originally founded, for the reasons set down in the book which, as I say, I have already written, and also because of certain wonderful revelations by which the Lord showed me how well He would be served in this house, it was not my intention that there should be so much austerity in external matters, nor that it should have no regular income: on the contrary, I should have liked there to be no possibility of want. I acted, in short, like the weak and wretched woman that I am, although I did so with good intentions and not out of consideration for my own comfort.

At about this time there came to my notice the harm and havoc that were being wrought in France by these Lutherans and the way in which their unhappy sect was increasing.[11] This troubled me very much, and, as though I could do anything, or be of any help in the matter, I wept before the Lord and entreated Him to remedy this great evil. I felt that I would have laid down a thousand lives to save a single one of all the souls that were being lost there. And, seeing that I was a woman, and a sinner,[12] and incapable of doing all I should like in the Lord's service, and as my whole yearning was, and still is, that, as He has so many enemies and so few friends, these last should be trusty ones, I determined to do the little that was in me—namely, to follow the evangelical counsels as perfectly as I could, and to see that these few nuns who are here should do the same, confiding in the great goodness of God, Who never fails to help those who resolve to forsake everything for His sake. As they are all that I have ever painted them as being in my desires, I hoped that their virtues would more than counteract my defects, and I should thus be able to give the Lord some pleasure, and all of us, by busying ourselves in prayer for those who are defenders of the Church, and for the preachers and learned men who defend her, should do every-thing we could to aid this Lord of mine Who is so much oppressed by those to whom He has shown so much good that it seems as though these traitors would send Him to the Cross again and that He would have nowhere to lay His head.

Oh, my Redeemer, my heart cannot conceive this without being sorely distressed! What has become of Christians now? Must those who owe Thee most always be those who distress Thee? Those to whom Thou doest the greatest kindnesses, whom Thou dost choose for Thy friends, among whom Thou dost move, communicating Thyself to them through the Sacraments? Do they not think, *Lord of my soul,* that they have made Thee endure more than sufficient torments?

It is certain, my Lord, that in these days withdrawal from the world means no sacrifice at all. Since worldly people have so little respect for Thee, what can we expect them to have for us? Can it be that we deserve that they should treat us any better than they have treated Thee? Have we done more for them than Thou hast done that they should be friendly to us? What then? What can we expect—we who, through the goodness of the Lord, are free from that pestilential infection, and do not, like those others, belong to the devil? They have won severe punishment at his hands and their pleasures have richly earned them eternal fire. So to eternal fire they will have to go,[13] though none the less it breaks my heart to see so many souls travelling to perdition. I would the evil were not so great and I did not see more being lost every day.

Oh, my sisters in Christ! Help me to entreat this of the Lord, Who has brought you together here for that very purpose. This is your vocation; this must be your business; these must be your desires; these your tears; these your petitions. Let us not pray for worldly things, my sisters. It makes me laugh, and yet it makes me sad, when I hear of the things which people come here to beg us to pray to God for; we are to ask His Majesty to give them money and to provide them with incomes—I wish that some of these people would entreat God to enable them to trample all such things beneath their feet. Their intentions are quite good, and I do as they ask because I see that they are really devout people, though I do not myself believe that God ever hears me when I pray for such things. The world is on fire. Men try to condemn Christ once again, as it were, for they bring a thousand false witnesses against Him. They would raze His Church to the ground—and are we to waste our time upon things which, if God were to grant them, would perhaps bring one soul less to Heaven? No, my sisters, this is no time to treat with God for things of little importance.

Were it not necessary to consider human frailty, which finds satisfaction in every kind of help—and it is always a good thing if we can be of any help to people—I should like it to be understood that it is not for things like these that God should be importuned with such anxiety.

CHAPTER TWO

Treats of how the necessities of the body should be disregarded and of the good that comes from poverty.

Do not think, my sisters, that because you do not go about trying to please people in the world you will lack food. You will not, I assure you: never try to sustain yourselves by human artifices, or you will die of hunger, and rightly so. Keep your eyes fixed upon your Spouse: it is for Him to sustain you; and, if He is pleased with you, even those who like you least will give you food, if unwillingly, as you have found by experience. If you should do as I say and yet die of hunger, then happy are the nuns of Saint Joseph's! For the love of the Lord, let us not forget this: you have forgone a regular income; forgo worry about food as well, or thou will lose everything. Let those whom the Lord wishes to live on an income do so: if that is their vocation, they are perfectly justified; but for us to do so, sisters, would be inconsistent.

Worrying about getting money from other people seems to me like thinking about what other people enjoy. However much you worry, you will not make them change their minds nor will they become desirous of giving you alms. Leave these anxieties to Him Who can move every-one, Who is the Lord of all money and of all who possess money. It is by His command that we have come here and His words are true—they cannot fail: Heaven and earth will fail first.[14] Let us not fail Him, and let us have no fear that He will fail us; if He should ever do so it will be for our greater good, just as the saints failed to keep their lives when they were slain for the Lord's sake, and their bliss was increased through their martyrdom. We should be making a good exchange if we could have done with this life quickly and enjoy everlasting satiety.

Remember, sisters, that this will be important when I am dead; and that is why I am leaving it to you in writing. For, *with God's help,* as long as I live, I will remind you of it myself, as I know by experience what a great help it will be to you. It is when I possess least that I have the fewest worries and the Lord knows that, as far as I can tell, I am more afflicted when there is excess of anything than when there is lack of it; I am not sure if that is the Lord's doing, but I have noticed that He provides for us immediately. To act otherwise would be to deceive the world by pretending to be poor when we are not poor in spirit but only outwardly. My conscience would give me a bad time. It seems to me it would be like stealing what was being given us, as one might say; for I should feel as if we were rich people asking alms: please God this may never be so. Those who worry too much about the alms that they are likely to be given will find that sooner or later this bad habit will lead them to go and ask for something which they do not need, and perhaps from someone who needs it more than they do. Such a person would gain rather than lose by giving it us but we should certainly be the worse off for having it. God forbid this should ever happen, my daughters; if it were likely to do so, I should prefer you to have a regular income.

I beg you, for the love of God, just as if I were begging alms for you, never to allow this to occupy your thoughts. If the very least of you ever hears of such a thing happening in this house, cry out about it to His Majesty and speak to your Superior. Tell her humbly that she is doing wrong; this is so serious a matter that it may cause true poverty gradually to disappear. I hope in the Lord that this will not be so and that He will not forsake His servants; and for that reason, if for no other, what you have told me to write may be useful to you as a reminder.

My daughters must believe that it is for their own good that the Lord has enabled me to realize in some small degree what blessings are to be found in holy poverty. Those of them who practise it will also realize this, though perhaps not as clearly as I do; for, although I had professed poverty, I was not only without poverty of spirit, but my spirit was devoid of all restraint. Poverty is good and contains within itself all the good things in the world. It is a great domain—I mean that he who cares nothing for the good things of the world has dominion over them all. What do kings and lords matter to me if I have no desire to possess their money, or to please them, if by so doing I should cause the least displeasure to God? And what do their honours mean to me if I have realized that the chief honour of a poor man consists in his being truly poor?

For my own part, I believe that honour and money nearly always go together, and that he who desires honour never hates money, while he who hates money cares little for honour. Understand this clearly, for I think this concern about honour always implies some *slight* regard for endowments or money: seldom or *never* is a poor man honoured by the world; however worthy of honour he may be, he is apt rather to be despised by it. With true poverty there goes a different kind of honour to which nobody can take objection. I mean that, if poverty is embraced for God's sake alone, no one has to be pleased save God. It is certain that a man who has no need of anyone has many friends: in my own experience I have found this to be very true.

A great deal has been written about this virtue which I cannot understand, still less express, and I should only be making things worse if I were to eulogize it, so I will say no more about it now. I have only spoken of what I have myself experienced and I confess that I have been so much absorbed that until now I have hardly realized what I have been writing. However, it has been said now. Our arms are holy poverty, which was so greatly esteemed and so strictly observed by our holy Fathers at the beginning of the foundation of our Order. (Someone who knows about this tells me that they never kept anything from one day to the next.) For the love of the Lord, then, [I beg you] now that the rule of poverty is less perfectly observed as regards outward things, let us strive to observe it inwardly. Our life lasts only for a couple of hours; our reward is boundless; and, if there were no reward but to follow the counsels given us by the Lord, to imitate His Majesty in any degree would bring us a great recompense.

These arms must appear on our banners and at all costs we must keep this rule—as regards our house, our clothes, our speech, and (which is much more important) our thoughts. So long as this is done, there need be no fear, with the help of God, that religious observances in this house will decline, for, as Saint Clare said, the walls of poverty are very strong. It was with these walls, she said, and with those of humility, that she wished to surround her convents; and assuredly, if the rule of poverty is truly kept, both chastity and all the other virtues are fortified much better than by the most sumptuous edifices. Have a care to this, for the love of God; and this I beg of you by His blood. If I may say what my conscience bids me, I should wish that, on the day when you build such edifices, they[15] may fall down *and kill you all.*

It seems very wrong, my daughters, that great houses should be built with the money of the poor; may God forbid that this should be done; let our houses be small and poor in every way. Let us to some extent resemble our King, Who had no house save the porch in Bethlehem where He was born and the Cross on which He died. These were houses where little comfort could be found. Those who erect large houses will no doubt have good reasons for doing so. *I do not utterly condemn them:* they are moved by various holy intentions. But any corner is sufficient for thirteen poor women. If grounds should be thought necessary on account of the strictness of the enclosure, and also as an aid to prayer and devotion, *and because our miserable nature needs such things,* well and good; and let there be a few hermitages[16] in them in which the sisters may go to pray. But as for a large ornate convent, with a lot of buildings—God preserve us from that! Always remember that these things will all fall down on the Day of Judgment, and who knows how soon that will be?

It would hardly look well if the house of thirteen poor women made a great noise when it fell, for those who are really poor must make no noise: unless they live a noiseless life people will never take pity on them. And how happy my sisters will be if they see someone freed from hell by means of the alms which he has given them; and this is quite possible, since they are strictly bound to offer continual prayer for persons who give them food. It is also God's will that, although the food comes from Him, we should thank the persons by whose means He gives it to us: let there be no neglect of this.

I do not remember what I had begun to say, for I have strayed from my subject. But I think this must have been the Lord's will, for I never intended to write what I have said here. May His Majesty always keep us in His hand so that we may never fall. Amen.

CHAPTER THREE

Continues the subject begun in the first chapter and persuades the sisters to busy themselves constantly in beseeching God to help those who work for the Church. Ends with an exclamatory prayer.

L et us now return to the principal reason for which the Lord has brought us together in this house, for which reason I am most desirous that we may be able to please His Majesty. Seeing how great are the evils of the present day and how no human strength will suffice to quench the fire kindled by these heretics (though attempts have been made to organize opposition to them, as though such a great and rapidly spreading evil could be remedied by force of arms), it seems to me that it is like a war in which the enemy has overrun the whole country, and the Lord of the country, hard pressed, retires into a city, which he causes to be well fortified, and whence from time to time he is able to attack. Those who are in the city are picked men who can do more by themselves than they could do with the aid of many soldiers if they were cowards. Often this method gains the victory; or, if the garrison does not conquer, it is at least not conquered; for, as it contains no traitors, *but picked men,* it can be reduced only by hunger. In our own conflict, however, we cannot be forced to surrender by hunger; we can die but we cannot be conquered.

Now why have I said this? So that you may understand, my sisters, that what we have to ask of God is that, in this little castle of ours, inhabited as it is by good Christians, none of us may go over to the enemy. We must ask God, too, to make the captains in this castle or city—that is, the preachers and theologians—highly proficient in the way of the Lord. And as most of these are religious, we must pray that they may advance in perfection, and in the fulfilment of their vocation, for this is very needful. For, as I have already said, it is the ecclesiastical and not the secular arm which must defend us. And as we can do nothing by either of these means to help our King, let us strive to live in such a way that our prayers may be of avail to help these servants of God, who, at the cost of so much toil, have fortified themselves with learning and virtuous living and have laboured to help the Lord.

You may ask why I emphasize this so much and why I say we must help people who are better than ourselves. I will tell you, for I am not sure if you properly understand as yet how much we owe to the Lord for bringing us to a place where we are so free from business matters, occasions of sin and the society of worldly people. This is a very great favour and one which is not granted to the persons of whom I have been speaking, nor is it fitting that it should be granted to them; it would be less so now, indeed, than at any other time, for it is they who must strengthen the weak and give courage to God's little ones. A fine thing it would be for soldiers if they lost their captains! These preachers and theologians have to live among men and associate with men and stay in palaces and sometimes even behave as people in palaces do in outward matters. Do you think, my daughters, that it is an easy matter to have to do business with the world, to live in the world, to engage in the affairs of the world, and, as I have said, to live as worldly men do, and yet inwardly to be strangers to the world, and enemies of the world, like persons who are in exile—to be, in short, not men but angels? Yet unless these persons act thus, they neither deserve to bear the title of captain nor to be allowed by the Lord to leave their cells, for they would do more harm than good. This is no time for imperfections in those whose duty it is to teach.

And if these teachers are not inwardly fortified by realizing the great importance of spurning everything beneath their feet and by being detached from things which come to an end on earth, and attached to things eternal, they will betray this defect in themselves, however much they may try to hide it. For with whom are they dealing but with the world? They need not fear: the world will not pardon them or fail to observe their imperfections. Of the good things they do many will pass unnoticed, or will even not be considered good at all; but they need not fear that any evil or imperfect thing they do will be overlooked. I am amazed when I wonder from whom they learned about perfection, when, instead of practising it themselves (for they think they have no obligation to do that and have done quite enough by a reasonable observance of the Commandments), they condemn others, and at times mistake virtue for indulgence. Do not think, then, that they need but little Divine favour in this great battle upon which they have entered; on the contrary, they need a great deal.

I beg you to try to live in such a way as to be worthy to obtain two things from God. First, that there may be many of these very learned and religious men who have the qualifications for their task which I have described, and that the Lord may prepare those who are not completely prepared already *and who lack anything,* for a single one who is perfect will do more than many who are not. Secondly, that after they have entered upon this struggle, which, as I say, is not light, *but a very heavy one,* the Lord may have them in His hand so that they may be delivered from all the dangers that are in the world, and, while sailing on this perilous sea, may shut their ears to the song of the sirens. If we can prevail with God in the smallest degree about this, we shall be fighting His battle even while living a cloistered life and I shall consider as well spent all the trouble to which I have gone in founding this retreat,[17] where I have also tried to ensure that this Rule of Our Lady and Empress shall be kept in its original perfection.

Do not think that offering this petition continually is useless. Some people think it a hardship not to be praying all the time for their own souls. Yet what better prayer could there be than this? You may be worried because you think it will do nothing to lessen your pains in Purgatory, but actually praying in this way will relieve you of some of them and anything else that is left—well, let it remain. After all, what does it matter if I am in Purgatory until the Day of Judgment provided a single soul should be saved through my prayer? And how much less does it matter if many souls profit by it and the Lord is honoured! Make no account of any pain which has an end if by means of it any greater service can be rendered to Him Who bore such pains for us. Always try to find out wherein lies the greatest perfection. And for the love of the Lord I beg you to beseech His Majesty to hear us in this; I, miserable creature though I am, beseech this of His Majesty, since it is for His glory and the good of His Church, which are my only wishes.

It seems over-bold of me to think that I can do anything towards obtaining this. But I have confidence, my Lord, in these servants of Thine who are here, knowing that they neither desire nor strive after anything but to please Thee. For Thy sake they have left the little they possessed, wishing they had more so that they might serve Thee with it. Since Thou, my Creator, art not ungrateful, I do not think Thou wilt fail to do what they beseech of Thee, for when Thou wert in the world, Lord, Thou didst not despise women, but didst always help them and show them great compassion.[18] *Thou didst find more faith and no less love in them than in men, and one of them was Thy most sacred Mother, from whose merits we derive merit, and whose habit we wear, though our sins make us unworthy to do so.*[19] *We can do nothing in public that is of any use to Thee, nor dare we speak of some of the truths over which we weep in secret lest Thou shouldst not hear this our just petition. Yet, Lord I cannot believe this of Thy goodness and righteousness, for Thou art a righteous Judge, not like judges in the world, who, being, after all, men and sons of Adam, refuse to consider any woman's virtue as above suspicion. Yes, my King, but the day will come when all will be known. I am not speaking on my own account, for the whole world is already aware of my wickedness, and I am glad that it should become known; but, when I see what the times are like, I feel it is not right to repel spirits which are virtuous and brave, even though they be the spirits of women.*

Hear us not when we ask Thee for honours, endowments, money, or anything that has to do with the world; but why shouldst Thou not hear us, Eternal Father, when we ask only for the honour of Thy Son, when we would forfeit a thousand honours and a thousand lives for Thy sake? Not for ourselves, Lord, for we do not deserve to be heard, but for the blood of Thy Son and for His merits.

Oh, Eternal Father! Surely all these scourgings and insults and grievous tortures will not be forgotten. How, then, my Creator, can a heart so [merciful and] loving as Thine endure that an act which was performed by Thy Son in order to please Thee the more (for He loved Thee most deeply and Thou didst command Him to love us) should be treated as lightly as those heretics treat the Most Holy Sacrament today, in taking it from its resting-place when they destroy the churches? Could it be that [Thy Son and our Redeemer] had failed to do something to please Thee? No: He fulfilled everything. Was it not enough, Eternal Father, that while He lived He had no place to lay His head and had always to endure so many trials? Must they now deprive Him of the places[20] to which He can invite His friends, seeing how weak we are and knowing that those who have to labour need such food to sustain them? Had He not already more than sufficiently paid for the sin of Adam? Has this most loving Lamb to pay once more whenever we relapse into sin? Permit it not, my Emperor; let Thy Majesty be appeased; look not upon our sins but upon our redemption by Thy Most Sacred Son, upon His merits and upon those of His glorious Mother and of all the saints and martyrs who have died for Thee.

Alas, Lord, who is it that has dared to make this petition in the name of all? What a poor mediator am I, my daughters, to gain a hearing for you and to present your petition! When this Sovereign Judge sees how bold I am it may well move Him to anger, as would be both right and just. But behold, Lord, Thou art a God of mercy; have mercy upon this poor sinner, this miserable worm who is so bold with Thee. Behold my desires, my God, and the tears with which I beg this of Thee; forget my deeds, for Thy name's sake, and have pity upon all these souls who are being lost, and help Thy Church. Do not permit more harm to be wrought to Christendom, Lord; give light to this darkness.

For the love of the Lord, my sisters, I beg you to commend this poor sinner[21] to His Majesty and to beseech Him to give her humility, as you are bound to do. I do not charge you to pray particularly for kings and prelates of the Church, especially for our Bishop, for I know that those of you now here are very careful about this and so I think it is needless for me to say more. Let those who are to come remember that, if they have a prelate who is holy, those under him will be holy too, and let them realize how important it is to bring him continually before the Lord. If your prayers and desires and disciplines and fasts are not performed for the intentions of which I have spoken, reflect [and believe] that you are not carrying out the work or fulfilling the object for which the Lord has brought you here.

CHAPTER FOUR

Exhorts the nuns to keep their Rule and names three things which are important for the spiritual life. Describes the first of these three things, which is love of one's neighbour, and speaks of the harm which can be done by individual friendships.

N ow, daughters, you have looked at the great enterprise which we are trying to carry out. What kind of persons shall we have to be if we are not to be considered over-bold in the eyes of God and of the world? It is clear that we need to labour hard and it will be a great help to us if we have sublime thoughts so that we may strive to make our actions sublime also. If we endeavour to observe our Rule and Constitutions in the fullest sense, and with great care, I hope in the Lord that He will grant our requests. I am not asking anything new of you, my daughters—only that we should hold to our profession, which, as it is our vocation, we are bound to do, although there are many ways of holding to it.

Our Primitive Rules tells us to pray without ceasing. Provided we do this with all possible care (and it is the most important thing of all) we shall not fail to observe the fasts, disciplines and periods of silence which the Order commands; for, as you know, if prayer is to be genuine it must be reinforced with these things—prayer cannot be accompanied by self-indulgence.

It is about prayer that you have asked me to say something to you. As an acknowledgment of what I shall say, I beg you to read frequently and with a good will what I have said about it thus far, and to put this into practice. Before speaking of the interior life—that is, of prayer—I shall speak of certain things which those who attempt to walk along the way of prayer must of necessity practise. So necessary are these that, even though not greatly given to contemplation, people who have them can advance a long way in the Lord's service, while, unless they have them, they cannot possibly be great contemplatives, and, if they think they are, they are much mistaken. May the Lord help me in this task and teach me what I must say, so that it may be to His glory. Amen.

Do not suppose, my friends and sisters, that I am going to charge you to do a great many things; may it please the Lord that we do the things which our holy Fathers ordained and practised and by doing which they merited that name. It would be wrong of us to look for any other way or to learn from anyone else. There are only three things which I will explain at some length and which are taken from our Constitution itself. It is essential that we should understand how very important they are to us in helping us to preserve that peace, both inward and outward, which the Lord so earnestly recommended to us. One of these is love for each other; the second, detachment from all created things; the third, true humility, which, although I put it last, is the most important of the three and embraces all the rest.

With regard to the first—namely, love for each other—this is of very great importance; for there is nothing, however annoying, that cannot easily be borne by those who love each other, and anything which causes annoyance must be quite exceptional. If this commandment were kept in the world, as it should be, I believe it would take us a long way towards the keeping of the rest; but, what with having too much love for each other or too little, we never manage to keep it perfectly. It may seem that for us to have too much love for each other cannot be wrong, but I do not think anyone who had not been an eye-witness of it would believe how much evil and how many imperfections can result from this. The devil sets many snares here which the consciences of those who aim only in a rough-and-ready way at pleasing God seldom observe—indeed, they think they are acting virtuously—but those who are aiming at perfection understand what they are very well: little by little they deprive the will of the strength which it needs if it is to employ itself wholly in the love of God.

This is even more applicable to women than to men and the harm which it does to community life is very serious. One result of it is that all the nuns do not love each other equally: some injury done to a friend is resented; a nun desires to have something to give to her friend or tries to make time for talking to her, and often her object in doing this is to tell her how fond she is of her, and other irrelevant things, rather than how much she loves God. These intimate friendships are seldom calculated[22] to make for the love of God; I am more inclined to believe that the devil initiates them so as to create factions within religious Orders. When a friendship has for its object the service of His Majesty, it at once becomes clear that the will is devoid of passion and indeed is helping to conquer other passions.

Where a convent is large I should like to see many friendships of that type; but in this house, where there are not, and can never be, more than thirteen nuns, all must be friends with each other, love each other, be fond of each other and help each other. For the love of the Lord, refrain from making individual friendships, however holy, for even among brothers and sisters such things are apt to be poisonous and I can see no advantage in them; when they are between other relatives,[23] they are much more dangerous and become a pest. Believe me, sisters, though I may seem to you extreme in this, great perfection and great peace come of doing what I say and many occasions of sin may be avoided by those who are not very strong. If our will becomes inclined more to one person than to another (this cannot be helped, because it is natural—it often leads us to love the person who has the most faults if

87

she is the most richly endowed by nature), we must exercise a firm restraint on ourselves and not allow ourselves to be conquered by our affection. Let us love the virtues and inward goodness, and let us always apply ourselves and take care to avoid attaching importance to externals.

Let us not allow our will to be the slave of any, sisters, save of Him Who bought it with His blood. Otherwise, before we know where we are, we shall find ourselves trapped, and unable to move. God help me! The puerilities which result from this are innumerable. And, because they are so trivial that only those who see how bad they are will realize and believe it, there is no point in speaking of them here except to say that they are wrong in anyone, and, in a prioress, pestilential.

In checking these preferences we must be strictly on the alert from the moment that such a friendship begins and we must proceed diligently and lovingly rather than severely. One effective precaution against this is that the sisters should not be together except at the prescribed hours, and that they should follow our present custom in not talking with one another, or being alone together, as is laid down in the Rule: each one should be alone in her cell. There must be no workroom at Saint Joseph's; for, although it is a praiseworthy custom to have one, it is easier to keep silence if one is alone, and getting used to solitude is a great help to prayer. Since prayer must be the foundation on which this house is built, it is necessary for us to learn to like whatever gives us the greatest help in it.

Returning to the question of our love for one another, it seems quite unnecessary to commend this to you, for where are there people so brutish as not to love one another when they live together, are continually in one another's company, indulge in no conversation, association or recreation with any outside their house and believe that God loves us and that they themselves love God since they are leaving everything for His Majesty? More especially is this so as virtue always attracts love, and I hope in God that, with the help of His Majesty, there will always be love in the sisters of this house. It seems to me, therefore, that there is no reason for me to commend this to you any further.

With regard to the nature of this mutual love and what is meant by the virtuous love which I wish you to have here, and how we shall know when we have this virtue, which is a very great one, since Our Lord has so strongly commended it to us and so straitly enjoined it upon His Apostles—about all this I should like to say a little now as well as my lack of skill will allow me; if you find this explained in great detail in other books, take no notice of what I am saying here, for it may be that I do not understand what I am talking about.

There are two kinds of love which I am describing. The one is *purely* spiritual, and apparently has nothing to do with sensuality or the tenderness of our nature, either of which might stain its purity. The other is also spiritual, but mingled with it are our sensuality and weakness;[24] yet it is a worthy love, which, as between relatives and friends, seems lawful. Of this I have already said sufficient.

It is of the first kind of spiritual love that I would now speak. It is untainted by any sort of passion, for such a thing would completely spoil its harmony. If it leads us to treat virtuous people, especially confessors, with moderation and discretion, it is profitable; but, if the confessor is seen to be tending in any way towards vanity, he should be regarded with grave suspicion, and, in such a case, conversation with him, however edifying, should be avoided, and the sister should make her confession briefly and say nothing more. It would be best for her, indeed, to tell the superior that she does not get on with him and go elsewhere; this is the safest way, providing it can be done without injuring his reputation.[25]

In such cases, and in other difficulties with which the devil might ensnare us, so that we have no idea where to turn, the safest thing will be for the sister to try to speak with some learned person; if necessary, permission to do this can be given her, and she can make her confession to him and act in the matter as he directs her. For he cannot fail to give her some good advice about it, without which she might go very far astray. How often people stray through not taking advice, especially when there is a risk of doing someone harm! The course that must on no account be followed is to do nothing at all; for, when the devil begins to make trouble in this way, he will do a great deal of harm if he is not stopped quickly; the plan I have suggested, then, of trying to consult another confessor is the safest one if it is practicable, and I hope in the Lord that it will be so.

Reflect upon the great importance of this, for it is a dangerous matter, and can be a veritable hell, and a source of harm to everyone. I advise you not to wait until a great deal of harm has been done but to take every possible step that you can think of and stop the trouble at the outset; this you may do with a good conscience. But I hope in the Lord that He will not allow persons who are to spend their lives in prayer to have any attachment save to one who is a great servant of God; and I am quite certain He will not, unless they have no love for prayer and for striving after perfection in the way we try to do here. For, unless they see that he understands their language and likes to speak to them of God, they cannot possibly love him, as he is not like them. If he is such a person, he will have very few opportunities of doing any harm, and, unless he is very simple, he will not seek to disturb his own peace of mind and that of the servants of God.

As I have begun to speak about this, I will repeat that the devil can do a great deal of harm here, which will long remain undiscovered, and thus the soul that is striving after perfection can be gradually ruined without knowing how. For, if a confessor gives occasion for vanity through being vain himself, he will be very tolerant with it in [the consciences of] others. May God, for His Majesty's own sake, deliver us from things of this kind. It would be enough to unsettle all the nuns if their consciences and their confessor should give them exactly opposite advice, and, if it is insisted that they must have one confessor only, they will not know what to do, nor how to pacify their minds, since the very person who should be calming them and helping them is the source of the harm. In some places there must be a great deal of trouble of this kind: I always feel very sorry about it and so you must not be surprised if I attach great importance to your understanding this danger.

APPENDIX TO CHAPTER FOUR

The following variant reading of the Escorial Manuscript seems too important to be relegated to a footnote. It occurs the twelfth paragraph of ch. 4 (cf. n. 24) , and deals, as will be seen, with the qualifications and character of the confessor. Many editors substitute it in their text for the corresponding passage in V. As will be seen, however, it is not a pure addition; we therefore reproduce it separately.

The important thing is that these two kinds of mutual love should be untainted by any sort of passion, for such a thing would completely spoil this harmony. If we exercise this love, of which I have spoken, with moderation and discretion, it is wholly meritorious, because what seems to us sensuality is turned into virtue. But the two may be so closely intertwined with one another that it is sometimes impossible to distinguish them, especially where a confessor is concerned. For if persons who are practising prayer find that their confessor is a holy man and understands the way they behave, they become greatly attached to him. And then forthwith the devil lets loose upon them a whole battery of scruples which produce a terrible disturbance within the soul, this being what he is aiming at. In particular, if the confessor is guiding such persons to greater perfection, they become so depressed that they will go so far as to leave him for another and yet another, only to be tormented by the same temptation every time.

What you can do here is not to let your minds dwell upon whether you like your confessor or not, but just to like him if you feel so inclined. For, if we grow fond of people who are kind to our bodies, why should we not love those who are always striving and toiling to help our souls? Actually, if my confessor is a holy and spiritual man and I see that he is taking great pains for the benefit of my soul, I think it will be a real help to my progress for me to like him. For so weak are we that such affection sometimes helps us a great deal to undertake very great things in God's service.

But, if your confessor is not such a person as I have described, there is a possibility of danger, and for him to know that you like him may do the greatest harm, most of all in houses where the nuns are very strictly enclosed. And as it is a difficult thing to get to know which confessors are good, great care and caution are necessary. The best advice to give would be that you should see he has no idea of your affection for him and is not told about it. But the devil is so active that this is not practicable: you feel as if this is the only thing you have to confess and imagine you are obliged to confess it. For this reason I should like you to think that your affection for him is of no importance and to take no more notice of it.

Follow this advice if you find that everything your confessor says to you profits your soul; if you neither see nor hear him indulge in any vanity (and such things are always noticed except by one who is wilfully dull) and if you know him to be a God-fearing man, do not be distressed over any temptation about being too fond of him, and the devil will then grow tired and stop tempting you. But if you notice that the confessor is tending in any way towards vanity in what he says to you, you should regard him with grave suspicion; in such a case conversation with him, even about prayer and about God, should be avoided—the sister should make her confession briefly and say nothing more. It would be best for her to tell the Mother (Superior) that she does not get on with him and go elsewhere. This is the safest way if it is practicable, and I hope in God that it will be, and that you will do all you possibly can to have no relations with him, though this may be very painful for you.

Reflect upon the great importance of this, etc. (pp. 58–9).

CHAPTER FIVE

Continues speaking of confessors. Explains why it is important that they should be learned men.

May the Lord grant, for His Majesty's own sake, that no one in this house shall experience the trials that have been described, or find herself oppressed in this way in soul and body. I hope the superior will never be so intimate with the confessor that no one will dare to say anything about him to her or about her to him. For this will tempt *unfortunate* penitents to leave very grave sins unconfessed because they will feel uncomfortable about confessing them. God help me! What trouble the devil can make here and how dearly people have to pay for their *miserable* worries and concern about honour! If they consult only one confessor, they think they are acting in the interests of their Order and for the *greater* honour of their convent: and that is the way the devil lays his snares for souls when he can find no other. If the *poor* sisters ask for another confessor, they are told that this would mean the *complete* end of all discipline in the convent; and, if he is not a priest of their Order, even though he be a saint, they are led to believe that they would be disgracing their entire Order by consulting him.

Give great praise to God, Daughters, for this liberty that you have, for, though there are not a great many priests whom you can consult, there are a few, other than your ordinary confessors, who can give you light upon everything. I beg every superior,[26] for the love of the Lord, to allow a holy liberty here: let the Bishop or Provincial be approached for leave for the sisters to go from time to time beyond their ordinary confessors and talk about their souls with persons of learning, especially if the confessors, though good men, have no learning; for learning is a great help in giving light upon everything. It should be possible to find a number of people who combine both learning and spirituality, and the more favours the Lord grants you in prayer, the more needful is it that your good works and your prayers should have a sure foundation.

You already know that the first stone of this foundation must be a good conscience and that you must make every effort to free yourselves from even venial sins and follow the greatest possible perfection. You might suppose that any confessor would know this, but you would be wrong: it happened that I had to go about matters of consciences to a man who had taken a complete course in theology; and he did me a great deal of mischief by telling me that certain things were of no importance. I know that he had no intention of deceiving me, or any reason for doing so: it was simply that he knew no better. And in addition to this instance I have met with two or three similar ones.

Everything depends on our having true light to keep the law of God perfectly. This is a firm basis for prayer; but without this strong foundation the whole building will go awry. In making their confessions, then, the nuns must be free to discuss spiritual matters with such persons as I have described. I will even go farther and say that they should sometimes do as I have said even if their confessor has all these good qualities, for he may quite easily make mistakes and it is a pity that he should be the cause of their going astray. They must try, however, never to act in any way against obedience, for they will find ways of getting all the help they need: it is of great importance to them that they should, and so they must make every possible effort to do so.

All this that I have said has to do with the superior. Since there are no consolations but spiritual ones to be had here, I would beg her once again to see that the sisters get these consolations, for God leads [His handmaidens] by different ways and it is impossible that one confessor should be acquainted with them all. I assure you that, if your souls are as they ought to be, there is no lack of holy persons who will be glad to advise and console you, even though you are poor. For He Who sustains our bodies will awaken and encourage someone to give light to our souls, and thus this evil of which I am so much afraid will be remedied. For if the devil should tempt the confessor, with the result that he leads you astray on any point of doctrine he will go slowly and be more careful about all he is doing when he knows that the penitent is also consulting others.

If the devil is prevented from entering convents in this way, I hope in God that he will never get into this house at all; so, for love of the Lord, I beg whoever is Bishop to allow the sisters this liberty and not to withdraw it so long as the confessors are persons both of learning and of good lives, a fact which will soon come to be known in a little place like this.

In what I have said here, I am speaking from experience of things that I have seen and heard *in many convents* and gathered from conversation with learned and holy people who have considered what is most fitting for this house, so that it may advance in perfection. Among the perils which exist everywhere, for as long as life lasts, we shall find that this is the least. No vicar should be free to go in and out of the convent, and no confessor should have this freedom either. They are there to watch over the recollectedness and good living of the house and its progress in both interior and exterior matters, so that they may report to the superior whenever needful, but they are never to be superiors themselves. *As I say, excellent reasons have been found why, everything considered, this is the best course, and why, if any priest hears confessions frequently, it should be the chaplain; but, if the nuns think it necessary, they can make their confessions to such persons as have been described, provided the superior is informed of it, and the prioress is such that the Bishop can trust her discretion. As there are very few nuns here, this will not take up much time.*

This is our present practice; and it is not followed merely on my advice. Our present Bishop, Don Álvaro de Mendoza, under whose obedience we live (since for many reasons we have not been placed under the jurisdiction of the Order), is greatly attached to holiness and the religious life, and, besides being of most noble extraction, is a great servant of God. He is always very glad to help this house in every way, and to this very end he brought together persons of learning, spirituality and experience, and this decision was then come to. It will be only right that future superiors should conform to his opinion, since it has been decided on by such good men, and after so many prayers to the Lord that He would enlighten them in every possible way, which, so far as we can at present see, He has certainly done. May the Lord be pleased to promote the advancement of this to His greater glory. Amen.

CHAPTER SIX

Returns to the subject of perfect love, already begun.

I have digressed a great deal but no one will blame me who understands the importance of what has been said. Let us now return to the love which it is good [and lawful] for us to feel. This I have described as purely spiritual; I am not sure if I know what I am talking about, but it seems to me that there is no need to speak much of it, since so few, I fear, possess it; let any one of you to whom the Lord has given it praise Him fervently, for she must be a person of the greatest perfection. It is about this that I now wish to write. Perhaps what I say may be of some profit, for if you look at a virtue you desire it and try to gain it, and so become attached to it.

God grant that I may be able to understand this, and even more that I may be able to describe it, for I am not sure that I know when love is spiritual and when there is sensuality mingled with it, or how to begin speaking about it. I am like one who hears a person speaking in the distance and, *though he can hear that he is speaking,* cannot distinguish what he is saying. It is just like that with me: sometimes I cannot understand what I am saying, yet the Lord is pleased to enable me to say it well. If at other times what I say is [ridiculous and] nonsensical, it is only natural for me to go completely astray.

Now it seems to me that, when God has brought someone to a clear knowledge of the world, and of its nature, and of the fact that another world *(or, let us say, another kingdom)* exists, and that there is a great difference between the one and the other, the one being eternal and the other only a dream; and of what it is to love the Creator and what to love the creature (this must be discovered by experience, for it is a very different matter from merely thinking about it and believing it); when one understands by sight and experience what can be gained by the one practice and lost by the other, and what the Creator is and what the creature, and many other things which the Lord teaches to those who are willing to devote themselves to being taught by Him in prayer, or whom His Majesty wishes to teach—then one loves very differently from those of us who have not advanced thus far.

It may be, sisters, that you think it irrelevant for me to treat of this, and you may say that you already know everything that I have said. God grant that this may be so, and that you may indeed know it in the only way which has any meaning, and that it may be graven upon your inmost being, *and that you may never for a moment depart from it,* for, if you know it, you will see that I am telling nothing but the truth when I say that he whom the Lord brings thus far possesses this love. Those whom God brings to this state are, *I think,* generous and royal souls; they are not content with loving anything so miserable as these bodies, however beautiful they be and however numerous the graces they possess. If the sight of the body gives them pleasure they praise the Creator, but as for dwelling upon it *for more than just a moment*—no! When I use that phrase "dwelling upon it," I refer to having love for such things. If they had such love, they would think they were loving something insubstantial and were conceiving fondness for a shadow, they would feel shame for themselves and would not have the effrontery to tell God that they love Him, without feeling great confusion.

You will answer me that such persons cannot love or repay the affection shown to them by others. Certainly they care little about having this affection. They may from time to time experience a natural and momentary pleasure at being loved; yet, as soon as they return to their normal condition, they realize that such pleasure is folly save when the persons concerned can benefit their souls, either by instruction or by prayer. Any other kind of affection wearies them, for they know it can bring them no profit and may well do them harm; none the less they are grateful for it and recompense it by commending those who love them to God. They take this affection as something for which those who love them lay the responsibility upon the Lord, from Whom, since they can see nothing lovable in themselves, they suppose the love comes, and think that others love them because God loves them; and so they leave His Majesty to recompense them for this and beg Him to do so, thus freeing themselves and feeling they have no more responsibility. When I ponder it carefully, I sometimes think this desire for affection is sheer blindness, except when, as I say, it relates to persons who can lead us to do good so that we may gain blessings in perfection.

It should be noted here that, when we desire anyone's affection, we always seek it because of some interest, profit or pleasure of our own. Those who are perfect, however, have trodden all these things beneath their feet—[and have despised] the blessings which may come to them in this world, and its pleasures and delights—in such a way that, even if they wanted to, so to say, they could not love anything outside God, or unless it had to do with God. What profit, then, can come to them from being loved themselves?

When this truth is put to them, they laugh at the distress which had been assailing them in the past as to whether their affection was being returned or no. Of course, however pure our affection may be, it is quite natural for us to wish it to be returned. But, when we come to evaluate the return of affection, we realize that it is insubstantial, like a thing of straw, as light as air and easily carried away by the wind. For, however dearly we have been loved, what is there that remains to us? Such persons, then, except for the advantage that the affection may bring to their souls (because they realize that our nature is such that we soon tire of life without love), care nothing whether they are loved or not. Do you think that such persons will love none and delight in none save God? No; they will love others much more than they did, with a more genuine love, with greater passion and with a love which brings more profit; that, in a word, is what love really is. And such souls are always much fonder of giving than of receiving, even in their relations with the Creator Himself. This [holy affection], I say, merits the name of love, which name has been usurped from it by those other base affections.

Do you ask, again, by what they are attracted if they do not love things they see? They do love what they see and they are greatly attracted by what they hear; but the things which they see are everlasting. If they love anyone they immediately look right beyond the body *(on which, as I say, they cannot dwell)*, fix their eyes on the soul and see what there is to be loved in that. If there is nothing, but they see any suggestion or inclination which shows them that, if they dig deep, they will find gold within this mine, they think nothing of the labour of digging, since they have love. There is nothing that suggests itself to them which they will not willingly do for the good of that soul since they desire their love for it to be lasting, and they know quite well that that is impossible unless the loved one has certain good qualities and a great love for God. I really mean that it is impossible, however great their obligations and even if that soul were to die for love of them and do them all the kind actions in its power; even had it all the natural graces joined in one, their wills would not have strength enough to love it nor would they remain fixed upon it. They know and have learned and experienced the worth of all this; no false dice can deceive them. They see that they are not in unison with that soul and that their love for it cannot possibly last; for, unless that soul keeps the law of God, their love will end with life—they know that unless it loves Him they will go to different places.

Those into whose souls the Lord has already infused true wisdom do not esteem this love, which lasts only on earth, at more than its true worth—if, indeed, at so much. Those who like to take pleasure in worldly things, delights, honours and riches, will account it of some worth if their friend is rich and able to afford them pastime *and pleasure* and recreation; but those who already hate all this will care little or nothing for such things. If they have any love for such a person, then, it will be a passion that he may love God so as to be loved by Him; for, as I say, they know that no other kind of affection but this can last, and that this kind will cost them dear, for which reason they do all they possibly can for their friend's profit; they would lose a thousand lives to bring him a small blessing. Oh, precious love, forever imitating the Captain of Love, Jesus, our Good!

Chapter Seven

Treats of the same subject of spiritual love and gives certain counsels for gaining it.

It is strange to see how impassioned this love is; how many tears, penances and prayers it costs; how careful is the loving soul to commend the object of its affection to all who it thinks may prevail with God and to ask them to intercede with Him for it; and how constant is its longing, so that it cannot be happy unless it sees that its loved one is making progress. If that soul seems to have advanced, and is then seen to fall some way back, her friend seems to have no more pleasure in life: she neither eats nor sleeps, is never free from this fear and is always afraid that the soul whom she loves so much may be lost, and that the two may be parted for ever. She cares nothing for physical death, but she will not suffer herself to be attached to something which a puff of wind may carry away so that she is unable to retain her hold upon it. This, as I have said, is love without any degree whatsoever of self-interest; all that this soul wishes and desires is to see the soul [it loves] enriched with blessings from Heaven. This is love, quite unlike our ill-starred earthly affections—to say nothing of illicit affections, from which may God keep us free.

These last affections are a very hell, and it is needless for us to weary ourselves by saying how evil they are, for the least of the evils which they bring are terrible beyond exaggeration. There is no need for us ever to take such things upon our lips, sisters, *or even to think of them,* or to remember that they exist anywhere in the world; you must never listen to anyone speaking of such affections, either in jest or in earnest, nor allow them to be mentioned or discussed in your presence. No good can come from our doing this and it might do us harm even to hear them mentioned. But with regard to the lawful affections which, as I have said, we may have for each other, or for relatives and friends, it is different. Our whole desire is that they should not die: if their heads ache, our souls seem to ache too; if we see them in distress, we are unable (as people say) to sit still under it;[27] and so on.

This is not so with spiritual affection. Although the weakness of our nature may at first allow us to feel something of all this, our reason soon begins to reflect whether our friend's trials are not good for her, and to wonder if they are making her richer in virtue and how she is bearing them, and then we shall ask God to give her patience so that they may win her merit. If we see that she is being patient, we feel no distress—indeed, we are gladdened and consoled. If all the merit and gain which suffering is capable of producing could be made over to her, we should still prefer suffering her trial ourselves to seeing her suffer it, but we are not worried or disquieted.

I repeat once more that this love is a similitude and copy of that which was borne for us by the good Lover, Jesus. It is for that reason that it brings us such immense benefits, for it makes us embrace every kind of suffering, so that others, without having to endure the suffering, may gain its advantages. The recipients of this friendship, then, profit greatly, but their friends should realize that either this intercourse—I mean, this exclusive friendship—must come to an end or that they must prevail upon Our Lord that their friend may walk in the same way as themselves, as Saint Monica prevailed with Him for Saint Augustine.

Their heart does not allow them to practise duplicity: if they see their friend straying from the road, or committing any faults, they will speak to her about it; they cannot allow themselves to do anything else. And if after this the loved one does not amend, they will not flatter her or hide anything from her. Either, then, she will amend or their friendship will cease; for otherwise they would be unable to endure it, nor is it in fact endurable. It would mean continual war for both parties. A person may be indifferent to all other people in the world and not worry whether they are serving God or not, since the person she has to worry about is herself. But she cannot take this attitude with her friends: nothing they do can be hidden from her; she sees the smallest mote in them. This, I repeat, is a very heavy cross for her to bear.

Happy the souls that are loved by such as these! Happy the day on which they came to know them! O my Lord, wilt Thou not grant me the favour of giving me many who have such love for me? Truly, Lord, I would rather have this than be loved by all the kings and lords of the world—and rightly so, for such friends use every means in their power to make us lords of the whole world and to have all that is in it subject to us. When you make the acquaintance of any such persons, sisters, the Mother Prioress should employ every possible effort to keep you in touch with them. Love such persons as much as you like. There can be very few of them, but none the less it is the Lord's will that their goodness should be known. When one of you is striving after perfection, she will at once be told that she has no need to know such people—that it is enough for her to have God. But to get to know God's friends is a very good way of "having" Him; as I have discovered by experience, it is most helpful. For, under the Lord, I owe it to such persons that I am not in hell; I was always very fond of asking them to commend me to God, and so I prevailed upon them to do so.

Let us now return to what we were saying. It is this kind of love which I should like us to have; at first it may not be perfect but the Lord will make it increasingly so. Let us begin with the methods of obtaining it. At first it may be mingled with emotion,[28] but this, as a rule, will do no harm. It is sometimes good and necessary for us to show emotion in our love, and also to feel it, and to be distressed by some of our sisters' trials and weaknesses, however trivial they may be. For on one occasion as much distress may be caused by quite a small matter as would be caused on another by some great trial, and there are people whose nature it is to be very much cast down by small things. If you are not like this, do not neglect to have compassion on others; it may be that Our Lord wishes to spare us these sufferings and will give us sufferings of another kind which will seem heavy to us, though to the person already mentioned they may seem light. In these matters, then, we must not judge others by ourselves, nor think of ourselves as we have been at some time when, perhaps without any effort on our part, the Lord has made us stronger than they; let us think of what we were like at the times when we have been weakest.

Note the importance of this advice for those of us who would learn to sympathize with our neighbours' trials, however trivial these may be. It is especially important for such souls as have been described, for, desiring trials as they do, they make light of them all. They must therefore try hard to recall what they were like when they were weak, and reflect that, if they are no longer so, it is not due to themselves. For otherwise, little by little, the devil could easily cool our charity toward our neighbours and make us think that what is really a failing on our part is perfection. In every respect we must be careful and alert, for the devil never slumbers. And the nearer we are to perfection, the more careful we must be, since his temptations are then much more cunning because there are no others that he dare send us; and if, as I say, we are not cautious, the harm is done before we realize it. In short, we must always watch and pray, for there is no better way than prayer of revealing these hidden wiles of the devil and making him declare his presence.

Contrive always, even if you do not care for it, to take part in your sisters' necessary recreation and to do so for the whole of the allotted time, for all considerate treatment of them is a part of perfect love. It is a very good thing for us to take compassion on each others' needs. See that you show no lack of discretion about things which are contrary to obedience. Though privately you may think the prioress' orders harsh ones, do not allow this to be noticed or tell anyone about it (except that you may speak of it, with all humility, to the prioress herself), for if you did so you would be doing a great deal of harm. Get to know what are the things in your sisters which you should be sorry to see and those about which you should sympathize with them; and always show your grief at any notorious fault which you may see in one of them. It is a good proof and test of our love if we can bear with such faults and not be shocked by them. Others, in their turn, will bear with your faults, which, if you include those of which you are not aware, must be much more numerous. Often commend to God any sister who is at fault and strive for your own part to practise the virtue which is the opposite of her fault with great perfection. Make determined efforts to do this so that you may teach your sister by your deeds what perhaps she could never learn by words nor gain by punishment.

The habit of performing some conspicuously virtuous action through seeing it performed by another is one which very easily takes root. This is good advice: do not forget it. Oh, how true and genuine will be the love of a sister who can bring profit to everyone by sacrificing her own profit to that of the rest! She will make a great advance in each of the virtues and keep her Rule with great perfection. This will be a much truer kind of friendship than one which uses every possible loving expression (such as are not used, and must not be used, in this house): "My life!" "My love!" "My darling!"[29] and suchlike things, one or another of which people are always saying. Let such endearing words be kept for your Spouse, for you will be so often and so much alone with Him that you will want to make use of them all, and this His Majesty permits you. If you use them among yourselves they will not move the Lord so much; and, quite apart from that, there is no reason why you should do so. They are very effeminate; and I should not like you to be that, or even to appear to be that, in any way, my daughters; I want you to be strong men. If you do all that is in you, the Lord will make you so manly that men themselves will be amazed at you. And how easy is this for His Majesty, Who made us out of nothing at all!

It is also a very clear sign of love to try to spare others household work by taking it upon oneself and also to rejoice and give great praise to the Lord if you see any increase in their virtues. All such things, quite apart from the intrinsic good they bring, add greatly to the peace and concord which we have among ourselves, as, through the goodness of God, we can now see by experience. May His Majesty be pleased ever to increase it, for it would be terrible if it did not exist, and very awkward if, when there are so few of us, we got on badly together. May God forbid that.

If one of you should be cross with another because of some hasty word, the matter must at once be put right and you must betake yourselves to earnest prayer. The same applies to the harbouring of any grudge, or to party strife, or to the desire to be greatest, or to any nice point concerning your honour. (My blood seems to run cold, as I write this, at the very idea that this can ever happen, but I know it is the chief trouble in convents.) If it should happen to you, consider yourselves lost. Just reflect and realize that you have driven your Spouse from His home: He will have to go and seek another abode, since you are driving Him from His own house. Cry aloud to His Majesty and try to put things right; and if frequent confessions and communions do not mend them, you may well fear that there is some Judas among you.

For the love of God, let the prioress be most careful not to allow this to occur. She must put a stop to it from the very outset, *and, if love will not suffice, she must use heavy punishments,* for here we have the whole of the mischief and the remedy. If you gather that any of the nuns is making trouble, see that she is sent to some other convent and God will provide them with a dowry for her. Drive away this plague; cut off the branches as well as you can; and, if that is not sufficient, pull up the roots. If you cannot do this, shut up anyone who is guilty of such things and forbid her to leave her cell; far better this than that all the nuns should catch so incurable a plague. Oh, what a great evil is this! God deliver us from a convent into which it enters: I would rather our convent caught fire and we were all burned alive. As this is so important I think I shall say a little more about it elsewhere, so I will not write at greater length here, *except to say that, provided they treat each other equally, I would rather that the nuns showed a tender and affectionate love and regard for each other, even though there is less perfection in this than in the love I have described, than that there were a single note of discord to be heard among them. May the Lord forbid this, for His own sake. Amen.*

CHAPTER EIGHT

Treats of the great benefit of self-detachment, both interior and exterior, from all things created.

Let us now come to the detachment which we must practise, for if this is carried out perfectly it includes everything else. I say "it includes everything else" because, if we care nothing for any created things, but embrace the Creator alone, His Majesty will infuse the virtues into us in such a way that, provided we labour to the best of our abilities day by day, we shall not have to wage war much longer, for the Lord will take our defence in hand against the devils and against the whole world. Do you suppose, daughters, that it is a small benefit to obtain for ourselves this blessing of giving ourselves wholly to Him,[30] and keeping nothing for ourselves? Since, as I say, all blessings are in Him, let us give Him hearty praise, sisters, for having brought us together here, where we are occupied in this alone. I do not know why I am saying this, when all of you here are capable of teaching me, for I confess that, in this important respect, I am not as perfect as I should like to be and as I know I ought to be; and I must say the same about all the virtues and about all that I am dealing with here, for it is easier to write of such things than to practise them. I may not even be able to write of them effectively, for sometimes ability to do this comes only from experience—[that is to say, if I have any success, it must be because] I explain the nature of these virtues by describing the contraries of the qualities I myself possess.

As far as exterior matters are concerned, you know how completely cut off we are from everything. *Oh, my Creator and Lord! When have I merited so great an honour? Thou seemest to have searched everywhere for means of drawing nearer to us. May it please Thy goodness that we lose not this through our own fault.* Oh, sisters, for the love of God, try to realize what a great favour the Lord has bestowed on those of us whom He has brought here. Let each of you apply this to herself, since there are only twelve of us[31] and His Majesty has been pleased for you to be one. How many people—*what a multitude of people!*—do I know who are better than myself and would gladly take this place of mine, yet the Lord has granted it to me who so ill deserve it! Blessed be Thou, my God, and let *the angels and* all created things praise Thee, for I can no more repay this favour than all the others Thou hast shown me. It was a wonderful thing to give me the vocation to be a nun; but I have been so wicked, Lord, that Thou couldst not trust me. In a place where there were many good women living together my wickedness would not *perhaps* have been noticed right down to the end of my life: *I should have concealed it, as I did for so many years.* So Thou didst bring me here, where, as there are so few of us that it would seem impossible for it to remain unnoticed, Thou dost remove occasions of sin from me so that I may walk the more carefully. There is no excuse for me, then, O Lord, I confess it, and so I have need of Thy mercy, that Thou mayest pardon me.

Remember, my sisters, that if we are not good we are much more to blame than others. What I earnestly beg of you is that anyone who knows she will be unable to follow our customs will say so [before she is professed]: there are other convents in which the Lord is also well served and she should not remain here and disturb these few of us whom His Majesty has brought together *for His service.* In other convents nuns are free to have the pleasure of seeing their relatives, whereas here, if relatives are ever admitted, it is only for their own pleasure. A nun who [very much] wishes to see her relatives in order to please herself, *and does not get tired of them after the second visit,* must, unless they are spiritual persons *and do her soul some good,* consider herself imperfect and realize that she is neither detached nor healthy, and will have no freedom of spirit or perfect peace. She needs a physician—and I consider that if this desire does not leave her, and she is not cured, she is not intended for this house.

The best remedy, I think, is that she should not see her relatives again until she feels free in spirit and has obtained this freedom from God by many prayers. When she looks upon such visits as crosses, let her receive them by all means, for then they will do the visitors good and herself no harm. *But if she is fond of the visitors, if their troubles are a great distress to her and if she delights in listening to the stories which they tell her about the world, she may be sure that she will do herself harm and do them no good.*

CHAPTER NINE

Treats of the great blessing that shunning their relatives brings to those who have left the world and shows how by doing so they will find truer friends.

O h, if we religious understood what harm we get from having so much to do with our relatives, how we should shun them! I do not see what pleasure they can give us, or how, quite apart from *the harm they do us as touching* our obligations to God, they can bring us any peace or tranquillity. For we cannot take part in their recreations, as it is not lawful for us to do so; and, though we can certainly share their troubles, we can never help weeping for them, sometimes more than they do themselves. If they bring us any bodily comforts, there is no doubt that our spiritual life *and our poor souls* will pay for it. From this you are [quite] free here; for, as you have everything in common and none of you may accept any private gift, all the alms given us being held by the community, you are under no obligation to entertain your relatives in return for what they give you, since, as you know, the Lord will provide for us all in common.

I am astounded at the harm which intercourse with our relatives does us: I do not think anyone who had not experience of it would believe it. And how our religious Orders nowadays, *or most of them, at any rate,* seem to be forgetting about perfection, *though all, or most, of the saints wrote about it!* I do not know how much of the world we really leave when we say that we are leaving everything for God's sake, if we do not withdraw ourselves from the chief thing of all—namely, our kinsfolk. The matter has reached such a pitch that some people think, when religious are not fond of their relatives and do not see much of them, it shows a want of virtue in them. And they not only assert this but allege reasons for it.

In this house, daughters, we must be most careful to commend our relatives to God, for that is only right. For the rest, we must keep them out of our minds as much as we can, as it is natural that our desires should be attached to them more than to other people. My own relatives were very fond of me, or so they used to say, and I was so fond of them that I would not let them forget me. But I have learned, by my own experience and by that of others, that it is God's servants who have helped me in trouble; my relatives, apart from my parents, have helped me very little. Parents are different, for they very rarely fail to help their children, and it is right that when they need our comfort we should not refuse it them: if we find our main purpose is not harmed by our so doing we can give it them and yet be completely detached; and this also applies to brothers and sisters.

Believe me, sisters, if you serve God as you should, you will find no better relatives than those [of His servants] whom His Majesty sends you. I know this is so, and, if you keep on as you are doing *here,* and realize that by doing otherwise you will be failing your true Friend and Spouse, you may be sure that you will very soon gain this freedom. Then you will be able to trust those who love you for His sake alone more than all your relatives, and they will not fail you, so that you will find parents and brothers and sisters where you had never expected to find them. For these help us and look for their reward only from God; those who look for rewards from us soon grow tired of helping us when they see that we are poor and can do nothing for them. This cannot be taken as a generalization, but it is the most usual thing to happen in the world, for it is the world all over! If anyone tells you otherwise, and says it is a virtue to do such things, do not believe him. I should have to write at great length, *in view of my lack of skill and my imperfection,* if I were to tell you of all the harm that comes from it; as others have written about it who know what they are talking about better than I, what I have said will suffice. If, imperfect as I am, I have been able to grasp as much as this, how much better will those who are perfect do so!

All the advice which the saints give us about fleeing from the world is, of course, good. Believe me, then, attachment to our relatives is, as I have said, the thing which sticks to us most closely and is hardest to get rid of. People are right, therefore, when they flee from their own part of the country[32]—if it helps them, I mean, for I do not think we are helped so much by fleeing from any place in a physical sense as by resolutely embracing the good Jesus, Our Lord, with the soul. Just as we find everything in Him, so for His sake we forget everything. Still, it is a great help, until we have learned this truth, to keep apart from our kinsfolk; later on, it may be that the Lord will wish us to see them again, so that what used to give us pleasure may be a cross to us.

Chapter Ten

Teaches that detachment from the things aforementioned is insufficient if we are not detached from our own selves and that this virtue and humility go together.

Once we have detached ourselves from the world, and from our kinsfolk, and are cloistered here, in the conditions already described, it must look as if we have done everything and there is nothing left with which we have to contend. But, oh, my sisters, do not feel secure and fall asleep, or you will be like a man who goes to bed quite peacefully, after bolting all his doors for fear of thieves, when the thieves are already in the house. And you know there is no worse thief *than one who lives in the house.* We ourselves are always the same;[33] unless we take great care and each of us looks well to it that she renounces her self-will, which is the most important business of all, there will be many things to deprive us of the holy freedom of spirit *which our souls seek* in order to soar to their Maker unburdened by the leaden weight of the earth.

It will be a great help towards this if we keep constantly in our thoughts the vanity of all things and the rapidity with which they pass away, so that we may withdraw our affections from things which are so trivial and fix them upon what will never come to an end. This may seem a poor kind of help but it will have the effect of greatly fortifying the soul. With regard to small things, we must be very careful, as soon as we begin to grow fond of them, to withdraw our thoughts from them and turn them to God. His Majesty will help us to do this. He has granted us the great favour of providing that, in this house, most of it is done already; *but it remains for us to become detached from our own selves* and it is a hard thing to withdraw from ourselves and oppose ourselves, because we are very close to ourselves and love ourselves very dearly.

It is here that true humility can enter,[34] for this virtue and that of detachment from self, I think, always go together. They are two sisters, who are inseparable. These are not the kinsfolk whom I counsel you to avoid: no, you must embrace them, and love them, and never be seen without them. Oh, how sovereign are these virtues, mistresses of all created things, empresses of the world, our deliverers from all the snares and entanglements laid by the devil, so dearly loved by our Teacher, Christ, Who was never for a moment without them! He that possesses them can safely go out and fight all the united forces of hell and the whole world and its temptations. Let him fear none, for his is the kingdom of the Heavens. There is none whom he need fear, for he cares nothing if he loses everything, nor does he count this as loss: his sole fear is that he may displease his God and he begs Him to nourish these virtues within him lest he lose them through any fault of his own.

These virtues, it is true, have the property of hiding themselves from one who possesses them, in such a way that he never sees them nor can believe that he has any of them, even if he be told so. But he esteems them so much that he is for ever trying to obtain them, and thus he perfects them in himself more and more. And those who possess them soon make the fact clear, even against their will, to any with whom they have intercourse. But how inappropriate it is for a person like myself to begin to praise humility and mortification, when these virtues are so highly praised by the King of Glory—a praise exemplified in all the trials He suffered. It is to possess these virtues, then, my daughters, that you must labour if you would leave the land of Egypt, for, when you have obtained them, you will also obtain the manna; all things will taste well to you; and, however much the world may dislike their savour, to you they will be sweet.

The first thing, then, that we have to do, *and that at once,* is to rid ourselves of love for this body of ours—and some of us pamper our natures so much that this will cause us no little labour, *while others* are so concerned about their health that the trouble these things give us (this is especially so of *poor* nuns, but it applies to others as well) is amazing. Some of us, however, seem to think that we embraced the religious life for no other reason than to keep ourselves alive[35] and each nun does all she can to that end. In this house, as a matter of fact, there is very little chance for us to act on such a principle, but I should be sorry if we even wanted to. Resolve, sisters, that it is to die for Christ, and not to practise self-indulgence for Christ, that you have come here. The devil tells us that self-indulgence is necessary if we are to carry out and keep the Rule of our Order, and so many of us, forsooth, try to keep our Rule by looking after our health that we die without having kept it for as long as a month—perhaps even for a day. I really do not know what we are coming to.

No one need be afraid of our committing excesses here, by any chance—for as soon as we do any penances our confessors begin to fear that we shall kill ourselves with them. We are so horrified at our own possible excesses—if only we were as conscientious about everything else! Those who tend to the opposite extreme will, I know, not mind my saying this, nor shall I mind if they say I am judging others by myself, for they will be quite right. *I believe—indeed, I am sure—that more nuns are of my way of thinking than are offended by me because they do just the opposite.* My own belief is that it is for this reason that the Lord is pleased to make us such weakly creatures; at least He has shown me great mercy in making me so; for, as I was sure to be self-indulgent in any case, He was pleased to provide me with an excuse for this. It is really amusing to see how some people torture themselves about it, when the real reason lies in themselves; sometimes they get a desire to do penances, as one might say, without rhyme or reason; they go on doing them for a couple of days; and then the devil puts it into their heads that they have been doing themselves harm and so he makes them afraid of penances, after which they dare not do even those that the Order requires—they have tried them once! They do not keep the smallest points in the Rule, such as silence, which is quite incapable of harming us. Hardly have we begun to imagine that our heads are aching than we stay away from choir, though that would not kill us either. *One day we are absent because we had a headache some time ago; another day, because our head has just been aching again; and on the next three days in case it should ache once more.* Then we want to invent penances of our own, with the result that we do neither the one thing nor the other. Sometimes there is very little the matter with us, yet we think that it should dispense us from all our obligations and that if we ask to be excused from them we are doing all we need.

But why, you will say, does the Prioress excuse us? Perhaps she would not if she knew what was going on inside us; but *she sees one of you wailing about a mere nothing as if your heart were breaking, and you come and ask her to excuse you from keeping the whole of your Rule, saying it is a matter of great necessity, and, when there is any substance in what you say,* there is always a physician at hand to confirm it or some friend or relative weeping at your side. *Sometimes the poor Prioress sees that your request is excessive, but* what can she do? She feels a scruple if she thinks she has been lacking in charity and she would rather the fault were yours than hers: *she thinks, too, that it would be unjust of her to judge you harshly.*

Oh, God help me! That there should be complaining like this among nuns! May He forgive me for saying so, but I am afraid it has become quite a habit. I happened to observe this incident once myself: a nun began complaining about her headaches and she went on complaining to me for a long time. In the end I made enquiries and found she had no headache whatever, but was suffering from some pain or other elsewhere.

These are things which may sometimes happen and I put them down here so that you may guard against them; for if once the devil begins to frighten us about losing our health, we shall never get anywhere. The Lord give us light so that we may act rightly in everything! Amen.

CHAPTER ELEVEN

Continues to treat of mortification and describes how it may be attained in times of sickness.

These continual moanings which we make about trifling ailments, my sisters, seem to me a sign of imperfection: if you can bear a thing, say nothing about it. When the ailment is serious, it proclaims itself; that is quite another kind of moaning, which draws attention to itself immediately. Remember, there are only a few of you, and if one of you gets into this habit she will worry all the rest—that is, assuming you love each other and there is charity among you. On the other hand, if one of you is really ill, she should say so and take the necessary remedies; and, if you have got rid of your self-love, you will so much regret having to indulge yourselves in any way that there will be no fear of your doing so unnecessarily or of your making a moan without proper cause. When such a reason exists, it would be much worse to say nothing about it than to allow yourselves unnecessary indulgence, and it would be very wrong if everybody were not sorry for you.

However, I am quite sure that where there is *prayer and* charity among you, and your numbers are so small *that you will be aware of each other's needs,* there will never be any lack of care in your being looked after. Do not think of complaining about the weaknesses and minor ailments from which women suffer, for the devil sometimes makes you imagine them. They come and go; and unless you get rid of the habit of talking about them and complaining of everything (except to God) you will never come to the end of them. *I lay great stress on this, for I believe myself it is important, and it is one of the reasons for the relaxation of discipline in religious houses.* For this body of ours has one fault: the more you indulge it, the more things it discovers to be essential to it. It is extraordinary how it likes being indulged; and, if there is any reasonable pretext for indulgence, however little necessity for it there may be, the poor soul is taken in and prevented from making progress. Think how many poor people there must be who are ill and have no one to complain to, for poverty and self-indulgence make bad company. Think, too, how many married women—people of position, as I know—have serious complaints and sore trials and yet dare not complain to their husbands about them for fear of annoying them. Sinner that I am! Surely we have not come here to indulge ourselves more than they! Oh, how free you are from the great trials of the world! Learn to suffer a little for the love of God without telling everyone about it. When a woman has made an unhappy marriage she does not talk about it or complain of it, lest it should come to her husband's knowledge, she has to endure a great deal of misery and yet has no one to whom she may relieve her mind. Cannot we, then, keep secret between God and ourselves some of the ailments which He sends us because of our sins? The more so since talking about them does nothing whatever to alleviate them.

In nothing that I have said am I referring to serious illnesses, accompanied by high fever, though as to these, too, I beg you to observe moderation and to have patience: I am thinking rather of those minor indispositions which you may have and still keep going[36] *without worrying everybody else to death over them.* What would happen if these lines should be seen outside this house? What would all the nuns say of me! And how willingly would I bear what they said if it helped anyone to live a better life! For when there is one person of this kind, the thing generally comes to such a pass that *some suffer on account of others, and* nobody who says she is ill will be believed, however serious her ailment. *As this book is meant only for my daughters, they will put up with everything I say.* Let us remember our holy Fathers of past days, the hermits whose lives we attempt to imitate. What sufferings they bore, what solitude, cold, [thirst] and hunger, what burning sun and heat! And yet they had no one to complain to except God. Do you suppose they were made of iron? No: they were as frail as we are. Believe me, daughters, once we begin to subdue these miserable bodies of ours, they give us much less trouble. There will be quite sufficient people to see to what you really need,[37] so take no thought for yourselves except when you know it to be necessary. Unless we resolve to put up with death and ill-health once and for all, we shall never accomplish anything.

Try not to fear these and commit yourselves wholly to God, come what may. What does it matter if we die? How many times have our bodies not mocked us? Should we not occasionally mock them in our turn? And, believe me, *slight as it may seem by comparison with other things,* this resolution is much more important than we may think; for, if we continually make it, day by day, by the grace of the Lord, we shall gain dominion over the body. To conquer such an enemy is a great achievement in the battle of life. May the Lord grant, as He is able, that we may do this. I am quite sure that no one who does not enjoy such a victory, which I believe is a great one, will understand what advantage it brings, and no one will regret having gone through trials in order to attain this tranquillity and self-mastery.

Chapter Twelve

Teaches that the true lover of God must care little for life and honour.

We now come to some other *little* things which are also of very great importance, though they will appear trifling. All this seems a great task, and so it is, for it means warring against ourselves. But once we begin to work, God, too, works in our souls and bestows such favours on them that the most we can do in this life seems to us very little. And we nuns are doing everything we can, by giving up our freedom for the love of God and entrusting it to another, and in putting up with so many trials—fasts, silence, enclosure, service in choir—that however much we may want to indulge ourselves we can do so only occasionally: perhaps, in all the convents I have seen, I am the only nun guilty of self-indulgence. Why, then, do we shrink from interior mortification, since this is the means by which every other kind of mortification may become much more meritorious and perfect, so that it can then be practised with greater tranquillity and ease? This, as I have said, is acquired by gradual progress and by never indulging our own will and desire, even in small things, until we have succeeded in subduing the body to the spirit.

I repeat that this consists mainly or entirely in our ceasing to care about ourselves and our own pleasures, for the least that anyone who is beginning to serve the Lord truly can offer Him is his life. Once he has surrendered his will to Him, what has he to fear? It is evident that if he is a true religious and a real man of prayer and aspires to the enjoyment of Divine consolations, he must not [turn back or] shrink from desiring to die and suffer martyrdom for His sake. And do you not know, sisters, that the life of a good religious, who wishes to be among the closest friends of God, is one long martyrdom? I say "long," for, by comparison with decapitation, which is over very quickly, it may well be termed so, though life itself is short and some lives are short in the extreme. How do we know but that ours will be so short that it may end only one hour or one moment after the time of our resolving to render our entire service to God? This would be quite possible; and so we must not set store by anything that comes to an end, *least of all by life, since not a day of it is secure.* Who, if he thought that each hour might be his last, would not spend it in labour?

Believe me, it is safest to think that this is so; by so doing we shall learn to subdue our wills in everything; for if, as I have said, you are very careful *about your prayer,* you will *soon* find yourselves gradually reaching the summit of the mountain without knowing how. But how harsh it sounds to say that we must take pleasure in nothing, unless we also say what consolations and delights this renunciation brings in its train, and what a great gain it is, even in this life! What security it gives us! Here, as you all practise this, you have done the principal part; each of you encourages[38] and helps the rest; and each of you must try to outstrip her sisters.

Be very careful about your interior thoughts, especially if they have to do with precedence. May God, by His Passion, keep us from expressing, or dwelling upon, such thoughts as these: "But I am her senior [in the Order]"; "But I am older"; "But I have worked harder"; "But that other sister is being better treated than I am." If these thoughts come, you must quickly check them; if you allow yourselves to dwell on them, or introduce them into your conversation, they will spread like the plague and *in religious houses* they may give rise to great abuses. *Remember, I know a great deal about this.* If you have a prioress who allows such things, however trifling, you must believe that God has permitted her to be given to you because of your sins and that she will be the beginning of your ruin. *Cry to Him, and let your whole prayer be that He may come to your aid by sending you either a religious or a person given to prayer; for, if anyone prays with the resolve to enjoy the favours and consolations which God bestows in prayer, it is always well that he should have this detachment.*

You may ask why I lay such stress on this, and think that I am being too severe about it, and say that God grants consolations to persons less completely detached than that. I quite believe He does; for, in His infinite wisdom, He sees that this will enable Him to lead them to leave everything for His sake. I do not mean, by "leaving" everything, entering the religious life, for there may be obstacles to this, and the soul that is perfect can be detached and humble anywhere. It will find detachment harder in the world, however, for worldly trappings will be a great impediment to it. Still, believe me in this: questions of honour and *desires for* property can arise within convents as well as outside them, and the more temptations of this kind are removed from us, the more we are to blame if we yield to them. Though persons who do so may have spent years in prayer, or rather in meditation (for perfect prayer eventually destroys [all] these attachments), they will never make great progress or come to enjoy the real fruit of prayer.

Ask yourselves, sisters, if these things, *which seem so insignificant,* mean anything to you, for the only reason you are here is that you may detach yourselves from them. Nobody honours you any the more for having them and they lose you advantages which might have gained you more honour; the result is that you get both dishonour and loss at the same time. Let each of you ask herself how much humility she has and she will see what progress she has made. If she is really humble, I do not think the devil will dare to tempt her to take even the slightest interest in matters of precedence, for he is so shrewd that he is afraid of the blow she would strike him. If a humble soul is tempted in this way by the devil, that virtue cannot fail to bring her more fortitude and greater profit. For clearly the temptation will cause her to look into her life, to compare the services she has rendered the Lord with what she owes Him and with the marvellous way in which He abased Himself to give us an example of humility, and to think over her sins and remember where she deserves to be on account of them. Exercises like this bring the soul such profit that on the following day Satan will not dare to come back again lest he should get his head broken.

Take this advice from me and do not forget it: you should see to it that your sisters profit by your temptations, not only interiorly (where it would be very wrong if they did not), but exteriorly as well. If you want to avenge yourself on the devil and free yourselves more quickly from temptation, ask the superior, as soon as a temptation comes to you, to give you some lowly office to do, or do some such thing, as best you can, on our own initiative, studying as you do it how to bend your will to perform tasks you dislike. The Lord will show you ways of doing so and this will soon rid you of the temptation.

God deliver us from people who wish to serve Him yet who are mindful of their own honour. Reflect how little they gain from this; for, as I have said, the very act of desiring honour robs us of it, especially in matters of precedence: there is no poison in the world which is so fatal to perfection. You will say that these are little things which have to do with human nature and are not worth troubling about; do not trifle with them, for *in religious houses* they spread like foam on water, and there is no small matter so extremely dangerous as are punctiliousness about honour and sensitiveness to insult. Do you know one reason, apart from many others, why this is so?[39] It may have its root, perhaps, in some trivial slight—hardly anything, in fact—and the devil will then induce someone else to consider it important, so that she will think it a real charity to tell you about it and to ask how you can allow yourself to be insulted so; and she will pray that God may give you patience and that you may offer it to Him, for even a saint could not bear more. The devil is simply putting his deceitfulness into this other person's mouth; and, though you yourself are quite ready to bear the slight, you are tempted to vainglory because you have not resisted something else as perfectly as you should.

This human nature of ours is so *wretchedly* weak that, even while we are telling ourselves that there is nothing for us to make a fuss about, we imagine we are doing something virtuous, and begin to feel sorry for ourselves, particularly when we see that other people are sorry for us too. In this way the soul begins to lose the occasions of merit which it had gained; it becomes weaker; and thus a door is opened to the devil by which he can enter on some other occasion with a temptation worse than the last. It may even happen that, when you yourself are prepared to suffer an insult, your sisters come and ask you if you are a beast of burden, and say you ought to be more sensitive about things. Oh, my sisters, for the love of God, never let charity move you to show pity for another in anything to do with these fancied insults, for that is like the pity shown to holy Job by his wife and friends.

CHAPTER THIRTEEN

Continues to treat of mortification and explains how one must renounce the world's standards of wisdom in order to attain to true wisdom.

I often tell you, sisters, and now I want it to be set down in writing, not to forget that we in this house, and for that matter anyone who would be perfect, must flee a thousand leagues from such phrases as: "I had right on my side"; "They had no right to do this to me"; "The person who treated me like this was not right." God deliver us from such a false idea of right as that! Do you think that it was right for our good Jesus to have to suffer so many insults, and that those who heaped them on Him[40] were right, and that they had any right to do Him those wrongs? I do not know why anyone is in a convent who is willing to bear only the crosses that she has a perfect right to expect: such a person should return to the world, though even there such rights will not be safeguarded. Do you think you can ever possibly have to bear so much that you ought not to have to bear any more? How does right enter into the matter at all? I really do not know.

Before we begin talking about not having our rights, let us wait until we receive some honour or gratification, or are treated kindly, for it is certainly not right that we should have anything in this life like that. When, on the other hand, some offence is done to us (and we do not feel it an offence to us that it should be so described), I do not see what we can find to complain of. Either we are the brides of this great King or we are not. If we are, what wife is there with a sense of honour who does not accept her share in any dishonour done to her spouse, even though she may do so against her will? Each partner, in fact, shares in the honour and dishonour of the other. To desire to share in the kingdom [of our Spouse Jesus Christ], and to enjoy it, and yet not to be willing to have any part in His dishonours and trials, is ridiculous.

God keep us from being like that! Let the sister who thinks that she is accounted the least among all consider herself the [happiest and] most fortunate, as indeed she *really* is, if she lives her life as she should, for in that case she will, *as a rule,* have no lack of honour either in this life or in the next. Believe me when I say this—what an absurdity, though, it is for me to say "Believe me" when the words come from Him Who is true Wisdom, *Who is Truth Itself, and from the Queen of the angels!* Let us, my daughters, in some *small* degree, imitate the great humility of the most sacred Virgin, whose habit we wear and whose nuns we are ashamed to call ourselves. *Let us at least imitate this humility of hers in some degree—I say "in some degree"* because, however much we may seem to humble ourselves, we fall far short of being the daughters of such a Mother, and the brides of such a Spouse. If, then, the habits I have described are not sternly checked, what seems nothing to-day will perhaps be a venial sin to-morrow, and that is so infectious a tendency that, if you leave it alone, the sin will not be the only one for long; and that is a very bad thing for communities.

We who live in a community should consider this very carefully, so as not to harm those who labour to benefit us and to set us a good example. If we realize what great harm is done by the formation of a bad habit of *over-punctiliousness about our honour,* we should rather die *a thousand deaths* than be the cause of such a thing. For only the body would die, whereas the loss of a soul is a great loss which is apparently without end; some of us will die, but others will take our places and perhaps they may all be harmed more by the one bad habit which we started than they are benefited by many virtues. For the devil does not allow a single bad habit to disappear and the very weakness of our mortal nature destroys the virtues in us.

Oh, what a real charity it would be, and what a service would be rendered to God, if any nun who sees that she cannot [endure and] conform to the customs of this house would recognize the fact and go away [before being professed, as I have said elsewhere], *and leave the other sisters in peace! And no convent (at least, if it follows my advice) will take her or allow her to make her profession until they have given her many years' probation to see if she improves. I am not referring to shortcomings affecting penances and fasts, for, although these are wrong, they are not things which do so much harm. I am thinking of nuns who are of such a temperament that they like to be esteemed and made much of; who see the faults of others but never recognize their own; and who are deficient in other ways like these, the true source of which is want of humility. If God does not help such a person by bestowing great spirituality upon her, until after many years she becomes greatly improved, may God preserve you from keeping her in your community. For you must realize that she will neither have peace there herself nor allow you to have any.*

As you do not take dowries, God is very gracious to you in this respect. It grieves me that religious houses should often harbour one who is a thief and robs them of their treasure, either because they are unwilling to return a dowry or out of regard for the relatives. In this house you have risked losing worldly honour and forgone it (for no such honour is paid to those who are poor); do not desire, then, that others should be honoured at such a cost to yourselves. Our honour, sisters, must lie in the service of God, and, if anyone thinks to hinder you in this, she had better keep her honour and stay at home. It was with this in mind that our Fathers ordered a year's probation (which in our Order we are free to extend to four years): personally, I should like it to be prolonged to ten years. A humble nun will mind very little if she is not professed: for she knows that if she is good she will not be sent away, and if she is not, why should she wish to do harm to one of Christ's communities?[41]

By not being good, I do not mean being fond of vanities, which, I believe,

135

with the help of God, will be a fault far removed from the nuns in this house. I am referring to a want of mortification and an attachment to worldly things and to self-interest in the matter which I have described. Let anyone who knows that she is not greatly mortified take my advice and not make her profession if she does not wish to suffer a hell on earth, and God grant there may not be another hell awaiting such a nun in the world to come! There are many reasons why she should fear there may be and possibly neither she nor her sisters may realize this as well as I do.

Believe what I say here; if you will not, I must leave it to time to prove the truth of my words. For the *whole* manner of life we are trying to live is making us, not only nuns, but hermits [like the holy Fathers our predecessors] and leading us to detachment from all things created. I have observed that anyone whom the Lord has specially chosen for this life is granted that favour. She may not have it in full perfection, but that she has it will be evident from the great joy and gladness that such detachment gives her, and she will never have any more to do with worldly things, for her delight will be in all the practices of the religious life. I say once more that anyone who is inclined to things of the world should leave the convent[42] if she sees she is not making progress. If she still wishes to be a nun she should go to another convent; if she does not, she will see what happens to her. She must not complain of me as the foundress of this convent and say I have not warned her.

This house is another Heaven, if it be possible to have Heaven upon earth. Anyone whose sole pleasure lies in pleasing God and who cares nothing for her own pleasure will find our life a very good one; if she wants anything more, she will lose everything, for there is nothing more that she can have. A discontented soul is like a person suffering from severe nausea, who rejects all food, however nice it may be; things which persons in good health delight in eating only cause her *the greater* loathing. Such a person will save her soul better elsewhere than here; she may even gradually reach a degree of perfection which she could not have attained here because we expected too much of her all at once. For although we allow time for the attainment of complete detachment and mortification in interior matters, in externals this has to be practised immediately, *because of the harm which may otherwise befall the rest;* and anyone who sees this being done, and spends all her time in such good company, and yet, at the end of *six months or* a year, has made no progress, will, I fear, make none over a great many years, and will even go backward. I do not say that such a nun must be as perfect as the rest, but she must be sure that her soul is gradually growing healthier—and it will soon become clear if her disease is mortal.

CHAPTER FOURTEEN

I feel sure that the Lord bestows great help on anyone who makes good resolutions, and for that reason it is necessary to enquire into the intentions of anyone who enters [the life of religion]. She must not come, as many nuns [now] do, simply to further her own interests, although the Lord can perfect even this intention if she is a person of intelligence. If not intelligent, a person of this kind should on no account be admitted; for she will not understand her own reasons for coming, nor will she understand others who attempt subsequently to improve her. For, in general, a person who has this fault always thinks she knows better than the wisest what is good for her; and I believe this evil is incurable, for it is rarely unaccompanied by malice. In a convent where there are a great many *nuns* it may be tolerated, but it cannot be suffered among a few.

When an intelligent person begins to grow fond of what is good, she clings to it manfully, for she sees that it is the best thing for her; this course may not bring her great spirituality but it will help her to give profitable advice, and to make herself useful in many ways, without being a trouble to anybody. But I do not see how a person lacking in intelligence can be of any use in community life, and she may do a great deal of harm. This defect, *like others,* will not become obvious immediately; for many people are good at talking and bad at understanding, while others speak in a sharp and none too refined a tone,[43] and yet they have intelligence and can do a great deal of good. There are also simple, holy people who are *quite* unversed in business matters and worldly conventions but have great skill in converse with God. Many enquiries, therefore, must be made before novices are admitted, and the period of probation before profession should be a long one. The world must understand once and for all that you are free to send them away *again,* as it is often necessary to do in a convent where the life is one of austerity; and then if you use this right no one will take offence.

I say this because these times are so unhappy, and our weakness is so great, that we are not content to follow the instructions of our predecessors and disregard the current ideas about honour, lest we should give offence to the novices' relatives. God grant that those of us who admit unsuitable persons may not pay for it in the world to come! Such persons are never without a pretext for persuading us to accept them, *though in a matter of such importance no pretext is valid. If the superior is unaffected by her personal likings and prejudices, and considers what is for the good of the house, I do not believe God will ever allow her to go astray. But if she considers other people's feelings and trivial points of detail, I feel sure she will be bound to err.*

This is something which everyone must think out for herself; she must commend it to God and encourage her superior *when her courage fails her,* of such great importance is it. So I beg God to give you light about it. You do very well not to accept dowries; for, if you were to accept them, it might happen that, in order not to have to give back money which you no longer possess, you would keep a thief in the house who was robbing you of your treasure; and that would be no small pity. So you must not receive dowries from anyone, for to do so may be to harm the very person to whom you desire to bring profit.

CHAPTER FIFTEEN

Treats of the great advantage which comes from our not excusing ourselves, even though we find we are unjustly condemned.

But how disconnectedly I am writing! I am just like a person who does not know what she is doing. It is your fault, sisters, for I am doing this at your command. Read it as best you can, for I am writing it as best I can, and, if it is too bad, burn it. I really need leisure, and, as you see, I have so little opportunity for writing that a week passes without my putting down a word, and so I forget what I have said and what I am going to say next. Now what I have just been doing—namely, excusing myself—is very bad for me, and I beg you not to copy it, for to suffer without making excuses is a habit of great perfection, and very edifying and meritorious; and, though I often teach you this, and by God's goodness you practise it, His Majesty has never granted this favour to me. May He be pleased to bestow it on me before I die.

I am greatly confused as I begin to urge this virtue upon you, for I ought myself to have practised at least something of what I am recommending you with regard to it: but actually I must confess I have made very little progress. I never seem unable to find a reason for thinking I am being virtuous when I make excuses for myself. There are times

141

when this is lawful, and when not to do it would be wrong, but I have not the discretion (or, better, the humility) to do it only when fitting. For, indeed, it takes great humility to find oneself unjustly condemned and be silent, and to do this is to imitate the Lord Who set us free from all our sins. I beg you, then, to study earnestly to do so, for it brings great gain; whereas I can see no gain in our trying to free ourselves from blame: none whatever—save, as I say, in a few cases where hiding the truth might cause offence or scandal. Anyone will understand this who has more discretion than I.

I think it is very important to accustom oneself to practise this virtue and to endeavour to obtain from the Lord the true humility which must result from it. The truly humble person will have a genuine desire to be thought little of, and persecuted, and condemned unjustly, even in serious matters. For, if she desires to imitate the Lord, how can she do so better than in this? And no bodily strength is necessary here, nor the aid of anyone save God.

These are great virtues, my sisters, and I should like us to study them closely, and to make them our penance. As you know, I deprecate [other severe and] excessive penances, which, if practised indiscreetly, may injure the health. Here, however, there is no cause for fear; for, however great the interior virtues may be, they do not weaken the body so that it cannot serve the Order, while at the same time they strengthen the soul; and, furthermore, they can be applied to very little things, and thus, as I have said on other occasions, they accustom one to gain great victories in *very* important matters. I have not, however, been able to test this particular thing myself, for I never heard anything bad said of me which I did not *clearly* realize fell short of the truth. If I had not *sometimes—often, indeed*—offended God in the ways they referred to, I had done so in many others, and I felt they had treated me far too indulgently in saying nothing about these: I much preferred people to blame me for what was not true than to tell the truth about me. *For I disliked hearing things that were true said about me, whereas these other things, however serious they were, I did not mind at all. In small matters I followed my own inclinations, and I still do so, without paying any attection to what is most perfect. So I should like you to begin to realize this at an early stage, and I want each of you to ponder how much there is to be gained in every way by this virtue, and how, so far as I can see, there is nothing to be lost by it. The chief thing we gain is being able, in some degree, to follow the Lord.*

It is a great help to meditate upon the great gain which in any case this is bound to bring us, and to realize how, properly speaking, we can never be blamed unjustly, since we are always full of faults, and a just man falls seven times a day,[44] so that it would be a falsehood for us to say we have no sin. If, then, we are not to blame for the thing that we are accused of, we are never wholly without blame in the way that our good Jesus was.

Oh, my Lord! When I think in how many ways Thou didst suffer, and in all of them undeservedly, I know not what to say for myself, or what I can have been thinking about when I desired not to suffer, or what I am doing when I make excuses for myself. Thou knowest, my Good, that if there is anything good in me it comes from no other hands than Thine own. For what is it to Thee, Lord, to give much instead of little? True, I do not deserve it, but neither have I deserved the favours which Thou hast shown me already. Can it be that I should wish a thing so evil as myself to be thought well of by anyone, when they have said such wicked things of Thee, Who art good above all other good? It is intolerable, my God, it is intolerable; nor would I that Thou shouldst have to tolerate anything displeasing in Thine eyes being found in Thy handmaiden. For see, Lord, mine eyes are blind and very little pleases them. Do Thou give me light and make me truly to desire that all should hate me, since I have so often left Thee, Who hast loved me with such faithfulness.

What is this, my God? What advantage do we think to gain from giving pleasure to creatures? What does it matter to us if we are blamed by them all, provided we are without blame in the sight of the Lord? Oh, my sisters, we shall never succeed in understanding this truth and we shall never attain perfection unless we think and meditate upon what is real and upon what is not. If there were no other gain than the confusion which will be felt by the person who has blamed you when she sees that you have allowed yourselves to be condemned unjustly, that would be a very great thing. Such an experience uplifts the soul more than ten sermons. And we must all try to be preachers by our deeds, since both the Apostle and our own lack of ability forbid us to be preachers in word.

Never suppose that either the evil or the good that you do will remain secret, however strict may be your enclosure. Do you suppose, daughter, that, if you do not make excuses for yourself, there will not be someone else who will defend you? Remember how the Lord took the Magdalen's part in the Pharisee's house and also when her sister blamed her. He will not treat you as rigorously as He treated Himself: it was not until He was on the Cross that He had even a thief to defend Him. His Majesty, then, will put it into somebody's mind to defend you; if He does not, it will be because there is no need. This I have myself seen, and it is a fact, although I should not like you to think too much of it, but rather to be glad when you are blamed, and in due time you will see what profit you experience in your souls. For it is in this way that you will begin to gain freedom; soon you will not care if they speak ill or well of you; it will seem like someone else's business. It will be as if two persons are talking *in your presence* and you are quite uninterested in what they are saying because you are not actually being addressed by them. So here: it becomes such a habit with us not to reply that it seems as if they are not addressing us at all. This may seem impossible to those of us who are very sensitive and not capable of great mortification. It is indeed difficult at first, but I know that, with the Lord's help, the *gradual* attainment of this freedom, and of renunciation and self-detachment, is quite possible.

CHAPTER SIXTEEN

Describes the difference between perfection in the lives of contemplatives and in the lives of those who are content with mental prayer. Explains how it is sometimes possible for God to raise a distracted soul to perfect contemplation and the reason for this. This chapter and that which comes next are to be noted carefully.[45]

I hope you do not think I have written too much about this already; for I have only been placing the board, as they say. You have asked me to tell you about the first steps in prayer; although God did not lead me by them, my daughters, I know no others, and even now I can hardly have acquired these elementary virtues. But you may be sure that anyone who cannot set out the pieces in a game of chess will never be able to play well, and, if he does not know how to give check, he will not be able to bring about a checkmate.[46] Now you will reprove me for talking about games, as we do not play them in this house and are forbidden to do so. That will show you what kind of a mother God has given you—she even knows about vanities like this! However, they say that the game is sometimes legitimate. How legitimate it will be for us to play it in this way, and, if we play it frequently, how quickly we shall give checkmate to this Divine King! He will not be able to move out of our check nor will He desire to do so.

It is the queen which gives the king most trouble in this game and all the other pieces support her. There is no queen who can beat this King as well as humility can; for humility brought Him down from Heaven into the Virgin's womb and with humility we can draw Him into our souls by a single hair. Be sure that He will give most humility to him who has most already and least to him who has least. I cannot understand how humility exists, or can exist, without love, or love without humility, and it is impossible for these two virtues to exist save where there is great detachment from all created things.

You will ask, my daughters, why I am talking to you about virtues when you have more than enough books to teach you about them and when you want me to tell you only about contemplation. My reply is that, if you had asked me about meditation, I could have talked to you about it, and advised you all to practise it, even if you do not possess the virtues. For this is the first step to be taken towards the acquisition of the virtues and the very life of all Christians depends upon their beginning it. No one, however lost a soul he may be, should neglect so great a blessing if God inspires him to make use of it. All this I have already written elsewhere, and so have many others who know what they are writing about, which I certainly do not: God knows that.

But contemplation, daughters, is another matter. This is an error which we all make: if a person gets so far as to spend a short time each day in thinking about his sins, as he is bound to do if he is a Christian in anything more than name, people at once call him a great contemplative; and then they expect him to have the rare virtues which a great contemplative is bound to possess; he may even think he has them himself, but he will be quite wrong. In his early stages he did not even know how to set out the chess-board, and thought that, in order to give checkmate, it would be enough to be able to recognize the pieces. But that is impossible, for this King does not allow Himself to be taken except by one who surrenders wholly to Him.

Therefore, daughters, if you want me to tell you the way to attain to contemplation, do allow me to speak at some length about these things, even if at the time they do not seem to you very important, for I think myself that they are. If you have no wish either to hear about them or to practise them, continue your mental prayer all your life; but in that case I assure you, and all persons who desire this blessing, that *in my opinion* you will not attain true contemplation. I may, of course, be wrong about this, as I am judging by my own experience, but I have been striving after contemplation for twenty years.

I will now explain what mental prayer is, as some of you will not understand this. God grant that we may practise it as we should! I am afraid, however, that, if we do not achieve the virtues, this can only be done with great labour, although the virtues are not necessary here in such a high degree as they are for contemplation. I mean that the King of glory will not come to our souls—that is, so as to be united with them—unless we strive to gain the greatest virtues.[47] I will explain this, for if you once catch me out in something which is not the truth, you will believe nothing I say—and if I were to say something untrue intentionally, from which may God preserve me, you would be right; but, if I did, it would be because I knew no better or did not understand what I said. I will tell you, then, that God is sometimes pleased to show great favour to persons who are in an evil state [and to raise them to perfect contemplation], so that by this means He may snatch them out of the hands of the devil. *It must be understood, I think, that such persons will not be in mortal sin at the time. They may be in an evil state, and yet the Lord will allow them to see a vision, even a very good one, in order to draw them back to Himself. But I cannot believe that He would grant them contemplation. For that is a Divine union, in which the Lord takes His delight in the soul and the soul takes its delight in Him; and there is no way in which the Purity of the Heavens can take pleasure in a soul that is unclean, nor can the Delight of the angels have delight in that which is not His own. And we know that, by committing mortal sin, a soul becomes the property of the devil, and must take its delight in him, since it has given him pleasure; and, as we know, his delights, even in this life, are continuous torture. My Lord will have no lack of children of His own in whom He may rejoice without going and taking the children of others. Yet His Majesty will do what He often does—namely, snatch them out of the devil's hands.*[48]

Oh, my Lord! How often do we cause Thee to wrestle with the devil! Was it not enough that Thou shouldst have allowed him to bear Thee in his arms when he took Thee to the pinnacle of the Temple in order to teach us how to vanquish him? What a sight it would have been, daughters, to see this Sun by the side of the darkness, and what fear that wretched creature must have felt, though he would not have known why, since God did not allow him to understand!

Blessed be such great pity and mercy; we Christians ought to feel great shame at making Him wrestle daily, in the way I have described, with such an unclean beast. Indeed, Lord, Thine arms had need to be strong, but how was it that they were not weakened by the many [trials and] tortures which Thou didst endure upon the Cross? Oh, how quickly all that is borne for love's sake heals again! I really believe that, if Thou hadst lived longer, the very love which Thou hast for us would have healed Thy wounds again and Thou wouldst have needed no other medicine. Oh, my God, who will give me such medicine for all the things which grieve and try me? How eagerly should I desire them if it were certain that I could be cured by such a health-giving ointment!

Returning to what I was saying, there are souls whom God knows He may gain for Himself by this means; seeing that they are completely lost, His Majesty wants to leave no stone unturned to help them; and therefore, though they are in a sad way and lacking in virtues, He gives them consolations, favours and emotions[49] which begin to move their desires, and occasionally even brings them to a state of contemplation, though rarely and not for long at a time. And this, as I say, He does because He is testing them to see if that favour will not make them anxious to prepare themselves to enjoy it often; if it does not, may they be pardoned; pardon Thou us, Lord, for it is a dreadful thing that a soul whom Thou hast brought near to Thyself should approach any earthly thing and become attached to it.

For my own part I believe there are many souls whom God our Lord tests in this way, and few who prepare themselves to enjoy this favour. When the Lord does this and we ourselves leave nothing undone either, I think it is certain that He never ceases from giving until He has brought us to a very high degree of prayer. If we do not give ourselves to His Majesty as resolutely as He gives Himself to us, He will be doing more than enough for us if He leaves us in mental prayer and from time to time visits us as He would visit servants in His vineyard. But these others are His beloved children, whom He would never want to banish from His side; and, as they have no desire to leave Him, He never does so. He seats them at His table, and feeds them with His own food, almost taking the food from His mouth in order to give it them.

Oh, what blessed care of us is this, my daughters! How happy shall we be if by leaving these few, petty[50] things we can arrive at so high an estate! Even if the whole world should blame you, *and deafen you with its cries,* what matter so long as you are in the arms of God? He is powerful enough to free you from everything; for only once did He command the world to be made and it was done; with Him, to will is to do. Do not be afraid, then, if He is pleased to speak with you, for He does this for the greater good of those who love Him. His love for those to whom He is dear is by no means so weak: *He shows it in every way possible.* Why, then, my sisters, do we not show Him love in so far as we can? Consider what a wonderful exchange it is if we give Him our love and receive His. Consider that He can do all things, and we can do nothing here below save as He enables us. And what is it that we do for Thee, O Lord, our Maker? We do hardly anything [at all]—just make some poor weak resolution. And, if His Majesty is pleased that by doing a mere nothing we should win everything, let us not be so foolish as to fail to do it.

O Lord! All our trouble comes to us from not having our eyes fixed upon Thee. If we only looked at the way along which we are walking, we should soon arrive; but we stumble and fall a thousand times and stray from the way because, as I say, we do not set our eyes on the true Way. One would think that no one had ever trodden it before, so new is it to us. It is indeed a pity that this should sometimes happen. *I mean, it hardly seems that we are Christians at all or that we have ever in our lives read about the Passion. Lord help us—that we should be hurt about some small point of honour! And then, when someone tells us not to worry about it, we think he is no Christian. I used to laugh—or sometimes I used to be distressed—at the things I heard in the world, and sometimes, for my sins, in religious Orders. We refuse* to be thwarted over the very smallest matter of precedence: apparently such a thing is quite intolerable. We cry out at once: "Well, I'm no saint"; *I used to say that myself.*

God deliver us, sisters, from saying "We are not angels," or "We are not saints," whenever we commit some imperfection. We may not be; but what a good thing it is for us to reflect that we can be if we will only try and if God gives us His hand! Do not be afraid that He will fail to do His part if we do not fail to do ours. And since we come here for no other reason, let us put our hands to the plough, as they say. Let there be nothing we know of which it would be a service to the Lord for us to do, and which, with His help, we would not venture to take in hand. I should like that kind of venturesomeness to be found in this house, as it always increases humility. We must have a holy boldness, for God helps the strong, being no respecter of persons;[51] *and He will give courage to you and to me.*

I have strayed far from the point. I want to return to what I was saying—that is, to explain the nature of mental prayer and contemplation. It may seem irrelevant, but it is all done for your sakes; you may understand it better as expressed in my rough style than in other books which put it more elegantly. May the Lord grant me His favour, so that this may be so. Amen.

CHAPTER SEVENTEEN

*How not all souls are fitted for contemplation and how some take
long to attain it. True humility will walk happily along the road
by which the Lord leads it.*

I seem now to be beginning my treatment of prayer, but there still remains a little for me to say, which is of great importance because it has to do with humility, and in this house that is necessary. For humility is the principal virtue which must be practised by those who pray, and, as I have said, it is very fitting that you should try to learn how to practise it often: that is one of the chief things to remember about it and it is very necessary that it should be known by all who practise prayer. How can anyone who is truly humble think herself as good as those who become contemplatives? God, it is true, by His goodness and mercy, can make her so; but my advice is that she should always sit down in the lowest place, for that is what the Lord instructed us to do and taught us by His own example.[52] Let such a one make herself ready for God to lead her by this road if He so wills; if He does not, the whole point of *true* humility is that she should consider herself happy in serving the servants of the Lord and in praising Him. For she deserves to be a slave of the devils in hell; yet His Majesty has brought her here to live among His servants.

I do not say this without good reason, for, as I have said, it is very important for us to realize that God does not lead us all by the same road, and perhaps she who believes herself to be going along the lowest of roads is the highest in the Lord's eyes. So it does not follow that, because all of us in this house practise prayer, we are all *perforce* to be contemplatives. That is impossible; and those of us who are not would be greatly discouraged if we did not grasp the truth that contemplation is something given by God, and, as it is not necessary for salvation and God does not ask it of us before He gives us our reward, we must not suppose that anyone else will require it of us. We shall not fail to attain perfection if we do what has been said here; we may, in fact, gain much more merit, because what we do will cost us more labour; the Lord will be treating us like those who are strong and will be laying up for us all that we cannot enjoy in this life. Let us not be discouraged, then, and give up prayer or cease doing what the rest do; for the Lord sometimes tarries long, and gives us as great rewards all at once as He has been giving to others over many years.

I myself spent over fourteen years without ever being able to meditate except while reading. There must be many people like this, and others who cannot meditate even after reading, but can only recite vocal prayers, in which they chiefly occupy themselves *and take a certain pleasure.* Some find their thoughts wandering so much that they cannot concentrate upon the same thing, but are always restless, to such an extent that, if they try to fix their thoughts upon God, they are attacked by a thousand foolish ideas and scruples and doubts *concerning the Faith.* I know a very old woman, leading a most excellent life—*I wish mine were like hers*— a penitent and a great servant of God, who for many years has been spending hours and hours in vocal prayer, but from mental prayer can get no help at all; the most she can do is to dwell upon each of her vocal prayers as she says them. There are a great many other people *just* like this; if they are humble, they will not, I think, be any the worse off in the end, but very much in the same state as those who enjoy numerous consolations. In one way they may feel safer, for we cannot tell if consolations come from God or are sent by the devil. If they are not of God, they are the more dangerous; for the chief object of the devil's work on earth is to fill us with pride. If they are of God, there is no reason for fear, for they bring humility with them, as I explained in my other book at great length.

Others[53] walk in humility, and *always* suspect that if they fail to receive consolations the fault is theirs, and are always most anxious to make progress. They never see a person shedding a tear without thinking themselves very backward in God's service unless they are doing the same, whereas they may perhaps be much more advanced. For tears, though good, are not invariably signs of perfection; there is always greater safety in humility, mortification, detachment and other virtues. There is no reason for fear, and you must not be afraid that you will fail to attain the perfection of the greatest contemplatives.

Saint Martha was holy, but we are not told that she was a contemplative. What more do you want than to be able to grow to be like that blessed woman, who was worthy to receive Christ our Lord so often in her house, and to prepare meals for Him, and to serve Him and *perhaps* to eat at table with Him? If she had been absorbed in devotion [all the time], as the Magdalen was, there would have been no one to prepare a meal for this Divine Guest. Now remember that this *little* community is Saint Martha's house and that there must be people of all kinds here. Nuns who are called to the active life must not murmur at others who are very much absorbed in contemplation, for contemplatives know that, though they themselves may be silent, the Lord will speak for them, and this, as a rule, makes them forget themselves and everything else.

Remember that there must be someone to cook the meals and count yourselves happy in being able to serve like Martha. Reflect that true humility consists to a great extent in being ready for what the Lord desires to do with you and happy that He should do it, and in always considering yourselves unworthy to be called His servants. If contemplation and mental and vocal prayer and tending the sick and serving in the house and working at even the lowliest tasks are of service to the Guest who comes to stay with us and to eat and take His recreation with us, what should it matter to us if we do one of these things rather than another?

I do not mean that it is for us to say what we shall do, but that we must do our best in everything, for the choice is not ours but the Lord's. If after many years He is pleased to give each of us her office, it will be a curious kind of humility for you to wish to choose; let the Lord of the house do that, for He is wise and powerful and knows what is fitting for you and for Himself as well. Be sure that, if you do what lies in your power and prepare yourself for *high* contemplation with the perfection aforementioned, then, if He does not grant it you (and I think He will not fail to do so if you have true detachment and humility), it will be because He has laid up this joy for you so as to give it you in Heaven, and because, as I have said elsewhere, He is pleased to treat you like people who are strong and give you a cross to bear on earth like that which His Majesty Himself always bore.

What better sign of friendship is there than for Him to give you what He gave Himself? It might well be that you would not have had so great a reward from contemplation. His judgments are His own; we must not meddle in them. It is indeed a good thing that the choice is not ours; for, if it were, we should think it the more restful life and all become great contemplatives. Oh, how much we gain if we have no desire to gain what seems to us best and so have no fear of losing, since God never permits a truly mortified person to lose anything except when such loss will bring him greater gain!

CHAPTER EIGHTEEN

Continues the same subject and shows how much greater are the trials of contemplatives than those of actives. This chapter offers great consolation to actives.

I tell you, then, daughters—those of you whom God is not leading by this road [of contemplation]—that, as I know from what I have seen and been told by those who are following this road, they are not bearing a lighter cross than you; you would be amazed at all the ways and manners in which God sends them crosses. I know about both types of life and I am well aware that the trials given by God to contemplatives are intolerable; and they are of such a kind that, were He not to feed them with consolations, they could not be borne. It is clear that, since God leads those whom He most loves by the way of trials, the more He loves them, the greater will be their trials; and there is no reason to suppose that He hates contemplatives, since with His own mouth He praises them and calls them friends.

To suppose that He would admit to His close friendship pleasure-loving people who are free from all trials is ridiculous. I feel quite sure that God gives them much greater trials; and that He leads them by a hard and rugged road, so that they sometimes think they are lost and will have to go back and begin again. Then His Majesty is obliged to give them sustenance—not water, but wine, so that they may become inebriated by it and not realize what they are going through and what they are capable of bearing. Thus I find few true contemplatives who are not courageous and resolute in suffering; for, if they are weak, the first thing the Lord does is to give them courage so that they may fear no trials *that may come to them*.

I think, when those who lead an active life occasionally see contemplatives receiving consolations, they suppose that they never experience anything else. But I can assure you that you might not be able to endure their sufferings for as long as a day. The point is that the Lord knows everyone as he really is and gives each his work to do—according to what He sees to be most fitting for his soul, and for His own Self, and for the good of his neighbour. Unless you have omitted to prepare yourselves for your work you need have no fear that it will be lost. Note that I say we must all strive to do this, for we are here for no other purpose; and we must not strive merely for a year, or for two years or ten years, or it will look as if we are abandoning our work like cowards. It is well that the Lord should see we are not leaving anything undone. We are like soldiers who, however long they have served, must always be ready for their captain to send them away on any duty which he wants to entrust to them, since it is he who is paying them. And how much better is the payment given by our King than by people on this earth! *For the unfortunate soldiers die, and God knows who pays them after that!*

When their captain sees they are all present, and anxious for service, he assigns duties to them according to their fitness, *though not so well as our Heavenly Captain*. But if they were not present, He would give them neither pay[54] nor service orders. So practise mental prayer, sisters; or, if any of you cannot do that, vocal prayer, reading and colloquies with God, as I shall explain to you later. Do not neglect the hours of prayer which are observed by all the nuns; you never know when the Spouse will call you (do not let what happened to the foolish virgins happen to you) and if He will give you fresh trials under the disguise of consolations. If He does not, you may be sure that you are not fit for them and that what you are doing is suitable for you. That is where both merit and humility come in, when you really think that you are not fit for what you are doing.

Go cheerfully about whatever services you are ordered to do, as I have said; if such a servant is truly humble she will be blessed in her active life and will never make any complaint save of herself. *I would much rather be like her than like some contemplatives.* Leave others to wage their own conflicts, which are not light ones. The standard-bearer is not a combatant, yet none the less he is exposed to great danger, and, inwardly, must suffer more than anyone, for he cannot defend himself, as he is carrying the standard, which he must not allow to leave his hands, even if he is cut to pieces. Just so contemplatives have to bear aloft the standard of humility and must suffer all the blows which are aimed at them without striking any themselves. Their duty is to suffer as Christ did, to raise the Cross on high, not to allow it to leave their hands, whatever the perils in which they find themselves, and not to let themselves be found backward in suffering. It is for this reason that they are given such an honourable duty. Let the contemplative consider what he is doing; for, if he lets the standard fall, the battle will be lost. Great harm, I think, is done to those who are not so far advanced if those whom they consider as captains and friends of God let them see them acting in a way unbefitting to their office.

The other soldiers do as best they can; at times they will withdraw from some position of extreme danger, and, as no one observes them, they suffer no loss of honour. But these others have all eyes fixed on them and cannot move. Their office, then, is a noble one, and the King confers great honour and favour upon anyone to whom He gives it, and who, in receiving it, accepts no light obligation. So, sisters, as we *do not understand ourselves and* know not what we ask, let us leave everything to the Lord, *Who knows us better than we know ourselves. True humility consists in our being satisfied with what is given us.* There are some people who seem to want to ask favours from God as a right. A pretty kind of humility that is! He Who knows us all does well in seldom giving things to such persons, He sees clearly that they are unable to drink of His chalice.

If you want to know whether you have made progress or not, sisters, you may be sure that you have if each of you thinks herself the worst of all and shows that she thinks this by acting for the profit and benefit of the rest. Progress has nothing to do with enjoying the greatest number of consolations in prayer, or with raptures, visions or favours [often] given by the Lord, the value of which we cannot estimate until we reach the world to come. The other things I have been describing are current coin, an unfailing source of revenue and a perpetual inheritance—not payments liable at any time to cease, like those favours which are given us and then come to an end. I am referring to the great virtues of humility, mortification and an obedience so *extremely* strict that we never go an inch beyond the superior's orders, knowing that these orders come from God since she is in His place. It is to this duty of obedience that you must attach the greatest importance. It seems to me that anyone who does not have it is not a nun at all, and so I am saying no more about it, as I am speaking to nuns whom I believe to be good, or, at least, desirous of being so. So well known is the matter, and so important, that a single word will suffice to prevent you from forgetting it.

I mean that, if anyone is under a vow of obedience and goes astray through not taking the greatest care to observe these vows with the highest degree of perfection, I do not know why she is in the convent. I can assure her, in any case, that, for so long as she fails in this respect, she will never succeed in leading the contemplative life, or even in leading a good active life: of that I am absolutely certain.[55] And even a person who has not this obligation, but who wishes or tries to achieve contemplation, must, if she would walk safely, be fully resolved to surrender her will to a confessor who is himself a contemplative[56] *and will understand her*. It is a well-known fact that she will make more progress in this way in a year than in a great many years if she acts otherwise. As this does not affect you, however, I will say no more about it.

I conclude, my daughters, [by saying] that these are the virtues which I desire you to possess and to strive to obtain and of which you should cherish a holy envy. Do not be troubled because you have no experience of those other kinds of devotion: they are very unreliable. It may be that to some people they come from God, and yet that if they came to you it might be because His Majesty had permitted you to be deceived and deluded by the devil, as He has permitted others: *there is danger in this for women.* Why do you want to serve the Lord in so doubtful a way when there are so many ways of [serving Him in] safety? Who wants to plunge you into these perils? I have said a great deal about this, because I am sure it will be useful, for this nature of ours is weak, though His Majesty will strengthen those on whom He wishes to bestow contemplation. With regard to the rest, I am glad to have given them this advice, which will teach contemplatives humility also. *If you say you have no need of it, daughters, some of you may perhaps find it pleasant reading.* May the Lord, for His own sake, give us light to follow His will in all things and we shall have no cause for fear.

CHAPTER NINETEEN

Begins to treat of prayer. Addresses souls who cannot reason with the understanding.

I t is a long time[57] since I wrote the last chapter and I have had no chance of returning to my writing, so that, without reading through what I have written, I cannot remember what I said. However, I must not spend too much time at this, so it will be best if I go right on[58] without troubling about the connection. For those with orderly minds, and for souls who practise prayer and can be a great deal in their own company, many books have been written, and these are so good and are the work of such competent people that you would be making a mistake if you paid heed to anything about prayer that you learned from me. There are books, as I say, in which the mysteries of the life of the Lord and of His *sacred* Passion are described in short passages, one for each day of the week; there are also meditations on the Judgment, on hell, on our own nothingness and on all that we owe to God, and these books are excellent both as to their teaching and as to the way in which they plan the beginning and the end of the time of prayer.[59] There is no need to tell anyone who is capable of practising prayer in this way, and has already formed the habit of doing so, that by this good road the Lord will bring her to the harbour of light. If she begins so well, her end will be good also; and all who can walk along this road will walk restfully and securely, for one always walks restfully when the understanding is kept in restraint. It is something else that I wish to treat of and help you about if the Lord is pleased to enable me to do so; if not, you will at least realize that there are many souls who suffer this trial, and you will not be so much distressed at undergoing it yourselves at first, *but will find some comfort in it.*

There are some souls, and some minds, as unruly as horses not yet broken in. No one can stop them: now they go this way, now that way; they are never still. *Although a skilled rider mounted on such a horse may not always be in danger, he will be so sometimes; and, even if he is not concerned about his life, there will always be the risk of his stumbling,*[60] *so that he has to ride with great care.* Some people are either like this by nature or God permits them to become so. I am very sorry for them; they seem to me like people who are very thirsty and see water a long way off, yet, when they try to go to it, find someone who all the time is barring their path— at the beginning of their journey, in the middle and at the end. And when, after all their labour—and the labour is tremendous—they have conquered the first of their enemies, they allow themselves to be con- quered by the second, and they prefer to die of thirst rather than drink water which is going to cost them so much trouble. Their strength has come to an end; their courage has failed them; and, though some of them are strong enough to conquer their second enemies as well as their first, when they meet the third group their strength comes to an end, though perhaps they are only a couple of steps from the fountain of living water, of which the Lord said to the Samaritan woman that whoso- ever drinks of it shall not thirst again.[61] How right and *how very* true is that which comes from the lips of Truth Himself! In this life the soul will never thirst for anything more, although its thirst for things in the life to come will exceed any natural thirst that we can imagine here below. How the soul thirsts to experience this thirst! For it knows how very precious it is, and, grievous though it be and exhausting, it creates the very satisfaction by which this thirst is allayed. It is therefore a thirst which quenches nothing but desire for earthly things, and, when God slakes it, satisfies in such a way that one of the greatest favours He can bestow on the soul is to leave it with this longing, so that it has an even greater desire to drink of this water again.

Water has three properties—three relevant properties which I can remember, that is to say, for it must have many more. One of them is that of cooling things; however hot we are, water tempers the heat, and it will even put out a large fire, except when there is tar in the fire, in which case, *they say,* it only burns the more. God help me! What a marvellous thing it is that, when this fire is strong and fierce and subject to none of the elements, water should make it grow fiercer, and, though its contrary element, should not quench it but only cause it to burn the more! It would be very useful to be able to discuss this with someone who understands philosophy; if I knew the properties of things I could explain it myself; but, though I love thinking about it, I cannot explain it—perhaps I do not even understand it.

You will be glad, sisters, if God grants you to drink of this water, as are those who drink of it now, and you will understand how a genuine love of God, if it is really strong, and completely free from earthly things, and able to rise above them, is master of all the elements and of the whole world. And, as water proceeds from the earth, there is no fear of its quenching this fire, which is the love of God; though the two elements are contraries, it has no power over it. The fire is absolute master, and subject to nothing. You will not be surprised, then, sisters, at the way I have insisted in this book that you should strive to obtain this freedom. Is it not a funny thing that a poor *little* nun of Saint Joseph's should attain mastery over the whole earth and all the elements? What wonder that the saints did as they pleased with them by the help of God? Fire and water obeyed Saint Martin; even birds and fishes were obedient to Saint Francis; and similarly with many other saints. *Helped as they were by God, and themselves doing all that was in their power, they could almost have claimed this as a right.* It was clear that they were masters over everything in the world, because they had striven so hard to despise it and subjected themselves to the Lord of the world with all their might. So, as I say, the water, which springs from the earth, has no power over this fire. Its flames rise high and its source is in nothing so base as the earth. There are other fires of love for God—small ones, which may be quenched by the least little thing. But this fire will most certainly not be so quenched.[62] Even should a whole sea of temptations assail it, they will not keep it from burning or prevent it from gaining the mastery over them.

Water which comes down as rain from Heaven will quench the flames even less, for in that case the fire and the water are not contraries, but have the same origin. Do not fear that the one element may harm the other; each helps the other and they produce the same effect. For the water of genuine tears—that is, tears which come from true prayer—is a good gift from the King of Heaven; it fans the flames and keeps them alight, while the fire helps to cool the water. God bless me! What a beautiful and wonderful thing it is that fire should cool water! But it does; and it even freezes all worldly affections, when it is combined with the living water which comes from Heaven, the source of the above-mentioned tears, which are given us, and not acquired by our diligence. Certainly, then, nothing worldly has warmth enough left in it to induce us to cling to it unless it is something which increases this fire, the nature of which is not to be easily satisfied, but, if possible, to enkindle the entire world.

The second property of water is that it cleanses things that are not clean already. What would become of the world if there were no water for washing? Do you know what cleansing properties there are in this living water, this heavenly water, this clear water, when it is unclouded, and free from mud, and comes down from Heaven? Once the soul has drunk of it I am convinced that it makes it pure and clean of all its sins; for, as I have written, God does not allow us to drink of this water *of perfect contemplation* whenever we like: the choice is not ours; this Divine union is something quite supernatural, given that it may cleanse the soul and leave it pure and free from the mud and misery in which it has been plunged because of its sins. Other consolations, excellent as they may be, which come through the intermediacy of the understanding, are like water running all over the ground. This cannot be drunk directly from the source; and its course is never free from clogging impurities, so that it is neither so pure nor so clean as the other. I should not say that this prayer I have been describing, which comes from reasoning with the intellect, is living water—I mean so far as my understanding of it goes. For, despite our efforts, there is always something clinging to the soul, through the influence of the body and of the baseness of our nature, which we should prefer not to be there.

I will explain myself further. We are meditating on the nature of the world, and on the way in which everything will come to an end, so that we may learn to despise it, when, almost without noticing it, we find ourselves ruminating on things in the world that we love. We try to banish these thoughts, but we cannot help being slightly distracted by thinking of things that have happened, or will happen, of things we have done and of things we are going to do. Then we begin to think of how we can get rid of these thoughts; and that sometimes plunges us once again into the same danger. It is not that we ought to omit such meditations; but we need to retain our misgivings about them and not to grow careless. In contemplation the Lord Himself relieves us of this care, for He will not trust us to look after ourselves. So dearly does He love our souls that He prevents them from rushing into things which may do them harm just at this time when He is anxious to help them. So He calls them to His side at once, and in a single moment reveals more truths to them and gives them a clearer insight into the nature of everything than they could otherwise gain in many years. For our sight is poor and the dust which we meet on the road blinds us; but in contemplation the Lord brings us to the end of the day's journey without our understanding how.

The third property of water is that it satisfies and quenches thirst. Thirst, I think, means the desire for something which is very necessary for us—so necessary that if we have none of it we shall die. It is a strange thing that if we have no water we die, and that we can also lose our lives through having too much of it, as happens to many people who get drowned. Oh, my Lord, if only one could be plunged so deeply into this living water that one's life would end! Can that be? Yes: this love and desire for God can increase so much that human nature is unable to bear it, and so there have been persons who have died of it. I knew one person[63] who had this living water in such great abundance that she would almost have been drawn out of herself by raptures if God had not quickly succoured her. *She had such a thirst, and her desire grew so greatly, that she realized clearly that she might quite possibly die of thirst if something were not done for her.* I say that she would almost have been drawn out of herself because in this state the soul is in repose. So intolerable does such a soul find the world that it seems to be overwhelmed,[64] but it comes to life again in God; and in this way His Majesty enables it to enjoy experiences which, if it had remained within itself, would perforce have cost it its life.

Let it be understood from this that, as there can be nothing in our supreme Good which is not perfect, all that He gives is for our welfare; and, however abundant this water which He gives may be, in nothing that He gives can there be superfluity. For, if His gift is abundant, He also bestows on the soul, as I have said, an abundant capacity for drinking; just as a glassmaker moulds his vessels to the size he thinks necessary, so that there is room for what he wishes to pour into them. As our desires for this water come from ourselves, they are never free from fault; any good that there may be in them comes from the help of the Lord. But we are so indiscreet that, as the pain is sweet and pleasant, we think we can never have too much of it. We have an immeasurable longing for it,[65] and, so far as is possible on earth, we stimulate this longing: sometimes this goes so far as to cause death. How happy is such a death! And yet by living one might perhaps have helped others to die of the desire for it. I believe the devil has something to do with this: knowing how much harm we can do him by living, he tempts us to be indiscreet in our penances and so to ruin our health, which is a matter of no small moment to him.

I advise anyone who attains to an experience of this fierce thirst to watch herself carefully, for I think she will have to contend with this temptation. She may not die of her thirst, but her health will be ruined, and she will involuntarily give her feelings outward expression, which ought at all costs to be avoided. Sometimes, however, all our diligence in this respect is unavailing and we are unable to hide our emotions as much as we should like. Whenever we are assailed by these strong impulses stimulating the increase of our desire, let us take great care not to add to them ourselves but to check them gently[66] by thinking of something else. For our own nature may be playing as great a part in producing these feelings as our love. There are some people *of this type* who have keen desires for all kinds of things, even for bad things, but I do not think such people can have achieved great mortification, for mortification is always profitable. It seems foolish to check so good a thing as this desire, but it is not. I am not saying that the desire should be uprooted—only checked; one may be able to do this by stimulating some other desire which is equally praiseworthy.

In order to explain myself better I will give an illustration. A man has a great desire to be with God, as Saint Paul had, and to be loosed from this prison.[67] This causes him pain which yet is in itself a great joy, and no small degree of mortification will be needed if he is to check it—in fact, he will not always be able to do so. But when he finds it oppressing him so much he may almost lose his reason. I saw this happen to someone not long ago; she was of an impetuous nature, but so accustomed to curbing her own will that, from what I had seen at other times, I thought her will was completely annihilated; yet, when I saw her for a moment, the great stress and strain caused by her efforts to hide her feelings had all but destroyed her reason.[68] In such an extreme case, I think, even did the desire come from the Spirit of God, it would be true humility to be afraid; for we must not imagine that we have sufficient charity to bring us to such a state of oppression.

I shall not think it at all wrong (if it be possible, I mean, for it may not always be so) for us to change our desire by reflecting that, if we live, we have more chance of serving God, and that we might do this by giving light to some soul which otherwise would be lost; as well as that, if we serve Him more, we shall deserve to enjoy Him more, and grieve that we have served Him so little. These are consolations appropriate to such great trials: they will allay our pain and we shall gain a great deal by them if in order to serve the Lord Himself we are willing to spend a long time here below and to live with our grief. It is as if a person were suffering a great trial or a grievous affliction and we consoled him by telling him to have patience and leave himself in God's hands so that His will might be fulfilled in him: it is always best to leave ourselves in God's hands.

And what if the devil had anything to do with these strong desires? This might be possible, as I think is suggested in Cassian's story of a hermit, leading the austerest of lives, who was persuaded by the devil to throw himself down a well so that he might see God the sooner.[69] I do not think this hermit can have served God either humbly or efficiently, for the Lord is faithful and His Majesty would never allow a servant of His to be blinded in a matter in which the truth was so clear. But, of course, if the desire had come from God, it would have done the hermit no harm; for such desires bring with them illumination, moderation and discretion. This is fitting, but our enemy and adversary seeks to harm us wherever he can; and, as he is not unwatchful, we must not be so either. This is an important matter in many respects: for example, we must shorten our time of prayer, however much joy it gives us, if we see our bodily strength waning or find that our head aches: discretion is most necessary in everything.

Why do you suppose, daughters, that I have tried, *as people say,* to describe the end of the battle before it has begun and to point to its reward by telling you about the blessing which comes from drinking of the heavenly source of this living water? I have done this so that you may not be distressed at the trials and annoyances of the road, and may tread it with courage and not grow weary; for, as I have said, it may be that, when you have arrived, and have only to stoop and drink of the spring, you may fail to do so and lose this blessing, thinking that you have not the strength to attain it and that it is not for you.

Remember, the Lord invites us all; and, since He is Truth Itself, we cannot doubt Him. If His invitation were not a general one, He would not have said: "I will give you to drink." He might have said: "Come, all of you, for after all you will lose nothing by coming; and I will give drink to those whom I think fit for it." But, as He said we were all to come, without making this condition, I feel sure that none will fail to receive this living water unless they cannot keep to the path.[70] May the Lord, Who promises it, give us grace, for His Majesty's own sake, to seek it as it must be sought.

CHAPTER TWENTY

Describes how, in one way or another, we never lack consolation on the road of prayer. Counsels the sisters to include this subject continually in their conversation.

In this last chapter I seem to have been contradicting what I had previously said, as, in consoling those who had not reached the contemplative state, I told them that the Lord had different roads by which they might come to Him, just as He also had many mansions.[71] I now repeat this: His Majesty, being Who He is and understanding our weakness, has provided for us. But He did not say: "Some must come by this way and others by that." His mercy is so great that He has forbidden none to strive to come and drink of this fountain of life. Blessed be He for ever! What good reasons there would have been for His forbidding me!

But as He did not order me to cease from drinking when I had begun to do so, but caused me to be plunged into the depths of the water, it is certain that He will forbid no one to come: indeed, He calls us publicly, and in a loud voice, to do so.[72] Yet, as He is so good, He does not force us to drink, but enables those who wish to follow Him to drink in many ways so that none may lack comfort or die of thirst. For from this rich spring flow many streams—some large, others small, and also little pools for children, which they find quite large enough, for the sight of a great deal of water would frighten them: by children, I mean those who are in the early stages.[73] Therefore, sisters, have no fear that you will die of thirst on this road; you will never lack so much of the water of comfort that your thirst will be intolerable; so take my advice and do not tarry on the way, but strive like strong men until you die in the attempt, for you are here for nothing else than to strive. If you always pursue this determination to die rather than fail to reach the end of the road, the Lord may bring you through this life with a certain degree of thirst, but in the life which never ends He will give you great abundance to drink and you will have no fear of its failing you. May the Lord grant us never to fail Him. Amen.

Now, in order to set out upon this aforementioned road so that we do not go astray at the very start, let us consider for a moment how the first stage of our journey is to be begun, for that is the most important thing—or rather, every part of the journey is of importance to the whole. I do not mean to say that no one who has not the resolution that I am going to describe should set out upon the road, for the Lord will gradually bring her nearer to perfection. And even if she did no more than take one step, this alone has such virtue that there is no fear of her losing it or of failing to be very well rewarded. We might compare her to someone who has a rosary with a bead specially indulgenced:[74] one prayer in itself will bring her something, and the more she uses the bead the more she will gain; but if she left it in a box and never took it out it would be better for her not to have it. So, although she may never go any farther along the same road, the short distance she has progressed will give her light and thus help her to go along other roads, and the farther she goes the more light she will gain. In fact, she may be sure that she will do herself no kind of harm through having started on the road, even if she leaves it, for good never leads to evil. So, daughters, whenever you meet people and find them well-disposed and even attracted to the life of prayer, try to remove from them all fear of beginning a course which may bring them such great blessings.[75] For the love of God, I beg you always to see to it that your conversation is benefiting those with whom you speak. For your prayers must be for the profit of their souls; and, since you must always pray to the Lord for them, sisters, you would seem to be doing ill if you did not strive to benefit them in every possible way.

If you would be a good kinswoman, this is true friendship; if you would be a good friend, you may be sure that this is the only possible way. Let the truth be in your hearts, as it will be if you practise meditation, and you will see clearly what love we are bound to have for our neighbours. This is no time for child's play, sisters, and these worldly friendships, good though they may be, seem no more than that. Neither with your relatives nor with anyone else must you use such phrases as "If you love me," or "Don't you love me?" unless you have in view some noble end and the profit of the person to whom you are speaking. It may be necessary, in order to get a relative—a brother or some such person—to listen to the truth and accept it, to prepare him for it by using such phrases and showing him signs of love, which are always pleasing to sense. He may possibly be more affected, and influenced, by one kind word, as such phrases are called, than by a great deal which you might say about God, and then there would be plenty of opportunities for you to talk to him about God afterwards. I do not forbid such phrases, therefore, provided you use them in order to bring someone profit. But for no other reason can there be any good in them and they may even do harm without your being aware of it. Everybody knows that you are nuns and that your business is prayer. Do not say to yourselves: "I have no wish to be considered good," for what people see in you is bound to bring them either profit or harm. People like nuns, on whom is laid the obligation to speak of nothing save in the spirit of God,[76] act very wrongly if they dissemble in this way, except occasionally for the purpose of doing greater good. Your intercourse and conversation must be like this: let any who wish to talk to you learn your language; and, if they will not, be careful never to learn theirs: it might lead you to hell.

It matters little if you are considered ill-bred and still less if you are taken for hypocrites: indeed, you will gain by this, because only those who understand your language will come to see you. If one knows no Arabic, one has no desire to talk a great deal with a person who knows no other language. So worldly people will neither weary you nor do you harm—and it would do you no small harm to have to begin to *learn and* talk a new language; you would spend all your time learning it. You cannot know as well as I do, for I have found it out by experience, how very bad this is for the soul; no sooner does it learn one thing than it has to forget another and it never has any rest. This you must at all costs avoid; for peace and quiet in the soul are of great importance on the road which we are about to tread.

If those with whom you converse wish to learn your language, it is not for you to teach it to them, but you can tell them what wealth they will gain by learning it. Never grow tired of this, but do it piously, lovingly and prayerfully, with a view to helping them; they will then realize what great gain *it brings,* and will go and seek a master to teach it them. Our Lord would be doing you no light favour if through your agency He were to arouse some soul to obtain this blessing. When once one begins to describe this road, what a large number of things there are to be said about it, even by those who have trodden it as unsuccessfully as I have! *I only wish I could write with both hands, so as not to forget one thing while I am saying another.* May it please the Lord, sisters, that you may be enabled to speak of it better than I have done.

CHAPTER TWENTY-ONE

Describes the great importance of setting out upon the practice of prayer with firm resolution and of heeding no difficulties put in the way by the devil.

D o not be dismayed, daughters, at the number of things which you have to consider before setting out on this Divine journey, which is the royal road to Heaven.[77] By taking this road we gain such precious treasures that it is no wonder if the cost seems to us a high one. The time will come when we shall realize that all we have paid has been nothing at all by comparison with the greatness of our prize.

Let us now return to those who wish to travel on this road, and will not halt until they reach their goal, which is the place where they can drink of this water of life. *Although in some book or other—in several, in fact—I have read what a good thing it is to begin in this way, I do not think anything will be lost if I speak of it here.* As I say, it is most important—all-important, indeed—that they should begin well by making an earnest and most determined resolve[78] not to halt until they reach their goal, whatever may come, whatever may happen to them, however hard they may have to labour, whoever may complain of them, whether they reach their goal or die on the road or have no heart to confront the trials which they meet, whether the very world dissolves before them. Yet again and again people will say to us: "It is dangerous," "So-and-so was lost through doing this," "Someone else got into wrong ways," "Some other person, who was always praying, fell just the same," "It is bad for virtue," "It is not meant for women; it may lead them into delusions," "They would do better to stick to their spinning," "These subtleties are of no use to them," "It is quite enough for them to say their Paternoster and Ave Maria."

With this last remark, sisters, I quite agree. Of course it is enough! It is always a great thing to base your prayer on prayers which were uttered by the very lips of the Lord. People are quite right to say this, and, were it not for our great weakness and the lukewarmness of our devotion, there would be no need for any other systems of prayer or for any other books at all. I am speaking to souls who are unable to recollect themselves by meditating upon other mysteries, and who think they need special methods of prayer; some people have such ingenious minds[79] that nothing is good enough for them! So I think I will start to lay down some rules for each part of our prayer—beginning, middle and end—although I shall not spend long on the higher stages. They cannot take books from you, and, if you are studious and humble, you need nothing more.

I have always been fond of the words of the Gospels and have found more recollection in them than in the most carefully planned books—especially books of which the authors were not fully approved, and which I never wanted to read. If I keep close to this Master of wisdom, He may perhaps give me some thoughts[80] which will help you. I do not say that I will explain these Divine prayers, for that I should not presume to do, and there are a great many explanations of them already. Even were there none, it would be ridiculous for me to attempt any. But I will write down a few thoughts on the words of the Paternoster; for sometimes, when we are most anxious to nurture our devotion, consulting a great many books will kill it. When a master is himself giving a lesson, he treats his pupil kindly and likes him to enjoy being taught and does his utmost to help him learn. Just so will this heavenly Master do with us.

Pay no heed, then, to anyone who tries to frighten you or depicts to you the perils of the way. What a strange idea that one could ever expect to travel on a road infested by thieves, for the purpose of gaining some great treasure, without running into danger! Worldly people like to take life peaceably; but they will deny themselves sleep, *perhaps* for nights on end, in order to gain a farthing's profit, and they will leave you no peace either of body or of soul. If, when you are on the way to gaining this treasure, or to taking it by force (as the Lord says the violent do) and are travelling by this royal road—this safe road trodden by our King and by His elect and His saints—if even then they tell you it is full of danger and make you so afraid, what will be the dangers encountered by those who think they will be able to gain this treasure and yet are not on the road to it?

Oh, my daughters, how incomparably greater must be the risks they run! And yet they have no idea of this until they fall headlong into some real danger. Having *perhaps* no one to help them, they lose this water altogether, and drink neither much nor little of it, either from a pool or from a stream. How do you suppose they can do without a drop of this water and yet travel along a road on which there are so many adversaries to fight? Of course, sooner or later, they will die of thirst; for we must all journey to this fountain, my daughters, whether we will or no, though we may not all do so in the same way. Take my advice, then, and let none mislead you by showing you any other road than that of prayer.

I am not now discussing whether or no everyone must practise mental or vocal prayer; but I do say that you yourselves require both. For prayer is the duty of religious. If anyone tells you it is dangerous, look upon that person himself as your principal danger and flee from his company. Do not forget this, for it is advice that you may possibly need. It will be dangerous for you if you do not possess humility and the other virtues; but God forbid that the way of prayer should be a way of danger! This fear seems to have been invented by the devil, who has apparently been very clever in bringing about the fall of some who practise prayer.

See how blind the world is! It never thinks of all the thousands who have fallen into heresies and other great evils through yielding to distractions and not practising prayer. As against these multitudes there are a few who did practise prayer and whom the devil has been successful enough at his own trade to cause to fall: in doing this he has also caused some to be very much afraid of virtuous practices. Let those who make use of this pretext to absolve themselves from such practices take heed, for in order to save themselves from evil they are fleeing from good. I have never heard of such a wicked invention; it must indeed come from the devil. Oh, my Lord, defend Thyself. See how Thy words are being misunderstood. Permit no such weakness in Thy servants.

There is one great blessing—you will always find a few people ready to help you. For it is a characteristic of the true servant of God, to whom His Majesty has given light to follow the true path, that, when beset by these fears, his desire not to stop only increases. He sees clearly whence the devil's blows are coming, but he parries each blow and breaks his adversary's head. The anger which this arouses in the devil is greater than all the satisfaction which he receives from the pleasures given him by others. When, in troublous times, he has sown his tares, and seems to be leading men everywhere in his train, half-blinded, and [deceiving them into] believing themselves to be zealous for the right, God raises up someone to open their eyes and bid them look at the fog with which the devil has obscured their path. (How great God is! To think that just one man, or perhaps two, can do more by telling the truth than can a great many men all together!) And then they gradually begin to see the path again and God gives them courage. If people say there is danger in prayer, this servant of God, by his deeds if not by his words, tries to make them realize what a good thing it is. If they say that frequent communion is inadvisable, he only practises it the more. So, because just one or two are fearlessly following the better path, the Lord gradually regains what He had lost.

Cease troubling about these fears, then, sisters; and never pay heed to such matters of popular opinion. This is no time for believing everyone; believe only those whom you see modelling their lives on the life of Christ. Endeavour always to have a good conscience; practise humility; despise all worldly things; and believe firmly in the teaching of our Holy Mother [the Roman] Church. You may then be quite sure that you are on a [very] good road. Cease, as I have said, to have fear where no fear is; if any one attempts to frighten you, point out the road to him in all humility. Tell him that you have a Rule which commands you, as it does, to pray without ceasing, and that that rule you must keep. If they tell you that you should practise only vocal prayer, ask whether your mind and heart ought not to be in what you say. If they answer "Yes"— and they cannot do otherwise—you see they are admitting that you are bound to practise mental prayer, and even contemplation, if God should grant it you. [Blessed be He for ever.]

CHAPTER TWENTY-TWO

Explains the meaning of mental prayer.

You must know, daughters, that whether or no you are practising mental prayer has nothing to do with keeping the lips closed. If, while I am speaking with God, I have a clear realization and full consciousness that I am doing so, and if this is more real to me than the words I am uttering, then I am combining mental and vocal prayer. When people tell you that you are speaking with God by reciting the Paternoster and thinking of worldly things—well, words fail me. When you speak, as it is right for you to do, with so great a Lord, it is well that you should think of Who it is that you are addressing, and what you yourself are, if only that you may speak to Him with proper respect. How can you address a king with the deference due to him, or how can you know what ceremonies have to be used when speaking to a grandee, unless you are clearly conscious of the nature of his position and of yours? It is because of this, and because it is the custom to do so, that you must behave respectfully to him, and must learn *what the custom is, and not be careless about such things,* or you will be dismissed as a simpleton and obtain none of the things you desire. *And furthermore, unless you are quite conversant with it, you must get all necessary information, and have what you are going to say written down for you. It once happened to me, when I was not accustomed to addressing aristocrats, that I had to go on a matter of urgent business to see a lady who had to be addressed as "Your Ladyship."*[81] *I was shown that word in writing; but I am stupid, and had never used such a term before; so when I arrived I got it wrong. So I decided to tell her about it and she laughed heartily and told me to be good enough to use the ordinary form of polite address,*[82] *which I did.*

How is it, my Lord, how is it, my Emperor, that Thou canst suffer this, *Prince of all Creation?* For Thou, my God, art a King without end, and Thine is no borrowed Kingdom, *but Thine own, and it will never pass away.* When the Creed says "Whose Kingdom shall have no end" the phrase nearly always makes me feel particularly happy. I praise Thee, Lord, and bless Thee, *and all things praise Thee* for ever—for Thy Kingdom will endure for ever. Do Thou never allow it to be thought right, Lord, for those who *praise Thee and* come to speak with Thee to do so with their lips alone. What do you mean, Christians, when you say that mental prayer is unnecessary? Do you understand what you are saying? I really do not think you can. And so you want us all to go wrong: you cannot know what mental prayer is, or how vocal prayers should be said, or what is meant by contemplation. For, if you knew this, you would not condemn on the one hand what you praise on the other.

Whenever I remember to do so, I shall always speak of mental and vocal prayer together, daughters, so that you may not be alarmed. I know what such fears lead to,[83] for I have suffered a certain number of trials in this respect, and so I should be sorry if anyone were to unsettle you, for it is very bad for you to have misgivings while you are walking on this path. It is most important that you should realize you are making progress; for if a traveller is told that he has taken the wrong road, and has lost his way, he begins to wander to and fro and the constant search for the right road tires him, wastes his time and delays his arrival. Who can say that it is wrong if, before we begin reciting the Hours or the Rosary, we think Whom we are going to address, and who we are that are addressing Him, so that we may do so in the way we should? I assure you, sisters, that if you gave all due attention to a consideration of these two points before beginning the vocal prayers which you are about to say you would be engaging in mental prayer for a very long time. For we cannot approach a prince and address him in the same careless way that we should adopt in speaking to a peasant or to some poor woman like ourselves, whom we may address however we like.

The reason we sometimes do so is to be found in the humility of this King, Who, unskilled though I am in speaking with Him, does not refuse to hear me or forbid me to approach Him, or command His guards to throw me out. For the angels in His presence know well that their King is such that He prefers the unskilled language of a humble peasant boy, knowing that he would say more if he had more to say, to the speech of the wisest and most learned men, however elegant may be their arguments, if these are not accompanied by humility. But we must not be unmannerly because He is good. If only to show our gratitude to Him for enduring our foul odour and allowing such a one as myself to come near Him, it is well that we should try to realize His purity and His nature. It is true that we recognize this at once when we approach Him, just as we do when we visit the lords of the earth. Once we are told about their fathers' names and their incomes and dignities, there is no more for us to know about them; for on earth one makes account of persons, and honours them, not because of their merits but because of their possessions.

O miserable world! Give hearty praise to God, daughters, that you have left so wretched a place,[84] where people are honoured, not for their own selves, but for what they get from their tenants and vassals: if these fail them, they have no honour left. It is a curious thing, and when you go out to recreation together you should laugh about it, for it is a good way of spending your time to reflect how blindly people in the world spend theirs.

O Thou our Emperor! Supreme Power, Supreme Goodness, Wisdom Itself, without beginning, without end and without measure in Thy works: infinite are these and incomprehensible, a fathomless ocean of wonders, O Beauty[85] containing within Thyself all beauties. O Very Strength! God help me! Would that I could command all the eloquence of mortals and all wisdom, so as to understand, as far as is possible here below, that to know nothing is everything, and thus to describe some of the many things on which we may meditate in order to learn something of the nature of this our Lord and Good.

When you approach God, then, try[86] to think and realize Whom you are about to address and continue to do so while you are addressing Him. If we had a thousand lives, we should never fully understand how this Lord merits that we behave toward Him, before Whom even the angels tremble. He orders all things and He can do all things: with Him to will is to perform. It will be right, then, daughters, for us to endeavour to rejoice in these wondrous qualities of our Spouse and to know Whom we have wedded and what our lives should be. Why, God save us, when a woman in this world is about to marry, she knows beforehand whom she is to marry, what sort of a person he is and what property he possesses. Shall not we, then, who are already betrothed, think about our Spouse,[87] before we are wedded to Him and He takes us home to be with Him? If these thoughts are not forbidden to those who are betrothed to men on earth, how can we be forbidden to discover Who this Man is, Who is His Father, what is the country to which He will take me, what are the riches with which He promises to endow me, what is His rank, how I can best make Him happy, what I can do that will give Him pleasure, and how I can bring my rank into line with His. If a woman is to be happy in her marriage, it is just those things that she is advised to see about, even though her husband be a man of very low station.

Shall less respect be paid to Thee, then, my Spouse, than to men? If they think it unfitting to do Thee honour, let them at least leave Thee Thy brides, who are to spend their lives with Thee. A woman is indeed fortunate in her life if her husband is so jealous that he will allow her to speak with no one but himself; it would be a pretty pass if she could not resolve to give him this pleasure, for it is reasonable enough that she should put up with this and not wish to converse with anyone else, since in him she has all that she can desire. To understand these truths, my daughters, is to practise mental prayer. If you wish to learn to understand them, and at the same time to practise vocal prayer, well and good. But do not, I beg you, address God while you are thinking of other things, for to do that is the result of not understanding what mental prayer is. I think I have made this clear. May the Lord grant us to learn how to put it into practice. Amen.

Chapter Twenty-Three

Describes the importance of not turning back when one has set out upon the way of prayer. Repeats how necessary it is to be resolute.

Now, as I have said, it is most important that from the first we should be very resolute, and for this there are so many reasons that if I were to give them all I should have to write at great length. *Some of them are given in other books.* I will tell you just two or three of them, sisters. One is that when we decide to give anything—such as this slight effort of recollection[88]—to Him Who has given us so much, and Who is continually giving, it would be wrong for us not to be entirely resolute in doing so and to act like a person who lends something and expects to get it back again. (Not that we do not receive interest: on the contrary, we gain a great deal.) I do not call this "giving." Anyone who has been lent something always feels slightly displeased when the lender wants it back again, especially if he is using it himself and has come to look upon it as his own. If the two are friends and the lender is indebted to the recipient for many things of which he has made him free gifts, he will think it meanness and a great lack of affection if he will leave not even the smallest thing in his possession, merely as a sign of love.

What wife is there who, after receiving many valuable jewels from her husband, will not give him so much as a ring—which he wants, not because of its value, for all she has is his, but as *a sign of love and* a token that she will be his until she dies? Does the Lord deserve less than this that we should mock Him by taking away the worthless gift[89] which we have given Him? Since we have resolved to devote to Him this very brief period of time—only a small part of what we spend upon ourselves and upon people who are not particularly grateful to us for it—let us give it Him freely, with our minds unoccupied by other things and entirely resolved never to take it back again, whatever we may suffer through trials, annoyances or aridities. Let me realize that this time is being lent me and is not my own, and feel that I can rightly be called to account for it if I am not prepared to devote it wholly to God.

I say "wholly," but we must not be considered as taking it back if we should fail to give it Him for a day, or for a few days, because of legitimate occupations or through some indisposition. Provided the intention remains firm, my God is not in the least meticulous;[90] He does not look at trivial details; and, if you are trying to please Him in any way, He will assuredly accept that as your gift. The other way is suitable for ungenerous souls, so mean that they are not large-hearted enough to give but find it as much as they can do to lend. Still, let them make some effort, for this Lord of ours will reckon everything we do to our credit and accept everything we want to give Him. In drawing up our reckoning, He is not in the least exacting, but generous; however large the amount we may owe Him, it is a small thing for Him to forgive us. And, as to paying us, He is so careful about this that you need have no fear He will leave us without our reward if only we raise our eyes to Heaven and remember Him.

A second reason why we should be resolute is that this will give the devil less opportunity to tempt us. He is very much afraid of resolute souls, knowing by experience that they inflict great injury upon him, and, when he plans to do them harm, he only profits them and others and is himself the loser. We must not become unwatchful, or count upon this, for we have to do with treacherous folk, who are great cowards and dare not attack the wary, but, if they see we are careless, will work us great harm. And if they know anyone to be changeable, and not resolute in *doing* what is good and firmly determined to persevere, they will not leave him alone either by night or by day and will suggest to him endless misgivings and difficulties. This I know very well by experience and so I have been able to tell you about it: I am sure that none of us realize its great importance.

Another reason, very much to the point, is that a resolute person fights more courageously. He knows that, come what may, he must not retreat. He is like a soldier in battle who is aware that if he is vanquished his life will not be spared and that if he escapes death in battle he must die afterwards. *It has been proved, I think, that* such a man will fight more resolutely and will try, as they say, to sell his life dearly, fearing the enemy's blows the less because he understands the importance of victory and knows that his very life depends upon his gaining it. We must also be *firmly* convinced from the start that, if we *fight courageously and* do not allow ourselves to be beaten, we shall get what we want, and there is no doubt that, however small our gains may be, they will make us very rich. Do not be afraid that the Lord Who has called us to drink of this spring will allow you to die of thirst. This I have already said and I should like to repeat it; for people are often timid when they have not learned by experience of the Lord's goodness, even though they know of it by faith. It is a great thing to have experienced what friendship and joy He gives to those who walk on this road and how He takes almost the whole cost of it upon Himself.

I am not surprised that those who have never made this test should want to be sure that they will receive some interest on their outlay. But you already know that even in this life we shall receive a hundredfold, and that the Lord says: "Ask and it shall be given you."[91] If you do not believe His Majesty in those passages of His Gospel where He gives us this assurance, it will be of little help to you, sisters, for me to weary my brains by telling you of it. Still, I will say to anyone who is in doubt that she will lose little by putting the matter to the test; for this journey has the advantage[92] of giving us *very much* more than we ask or shall even get so far as to desire. This is a never-failing truth: I know it; *though, if you do not find it so, do not believe any of the things I tell you.* I can call as witnesses those of you who, by God's goodness, know it from experience.

CHAPTER TWENTY-FOUR

Describes how vocal prayer may be practised with perfection
and how closely allied it is to mental prayer.

L et us now return to speak of those souls I have mentioned who cannot practise recollection or tie down their minds to mental prayer or make a meditation. We must not talk to them of either of those two things—they will not hear of them; as a matter of fact, there are a great many people who seem terrified at the very name of contemplation or mental prayer.

In case any such person should come to this house (for, as I have said, not all are led by the same path), I want to advise you, or, I might even say, to teach you (for, as your mother, and by the office of prioress which I hold, I have the right to do so) how you must practise vocal prayer, for it is right that you should understand what you are saying. Anyone unable to think of God may find herself wearied by long prayers, and so I will not begin to discuss these, but will speak simply of prayers which, as Christians, we must perforce recite—namely, the Paternoster and the Ave Maria—and then no one will be able to say of us that we are repeating words without understanding what we are saying. We may, of course, consider it enough to say our prayers as a mere habit, repeating the words and thinking that this will suffice. Whether it suffices or no I will not now discuss.[93] Learned men must decide: *they will instruct people to whom God gives light to consult them, and I will not discuss the position of those who have not made a profession like our own.* But what I should like, daughters, is for us not to be satisfied with that alone: when I say the Creed, it seems to me right, *and indeed obligatory,* that I should understand and know what it is that I believe; and, when I repeat the "Our Father," my love should make me want to understand Who this Father of ours is and Who the Master is that taught us this prayer.

If you assert that you know Who He is already, and so there is no need for you to think about Him, you are not right; there is a great deal of difference between one master and another, and it would be very wrong of us not to think about those who teach us, even on earth; if they are holy men and spiritual masters, and we are good pupils, it is impossible for us *not to have great love for them, and indeed to hold them in honour and often to talk about them.* And when it comes to the Master Who taught us this prayer, and Who loves us so much and is so anxious for us to profit by it, may God forbid that we should fail to think of Him often when we repeat it, although our own weakness may prevent us from doing so every time.

Now, in the first place, you know that His Majesty teaches that this prayer must be made when we are alone, just as He was often alone when He prayed, not because this was necessary for Him, but for our edification. It has already been said that it is impossible to speak to God and to the world at the same time; yet this is just what we are trying to do when we are saying our prayers and at the same time listening to the conversation of others or letting our thoughts wander on any matter that occurs to us, without making an effort to control them. There are occasions when one cannot help doing this: times of ill-health (especially in persons who suffer from melancholia); or times when our heads are tired, and, however hard we try, we cannot concentrate; or times when, for their own good, God allows His servants for days on end to go through great storms. And, although they are distressed and strive to calm themselves, they are unable to do so and incapable of attending to what they are saying, however hard they try, nor can they fix their understanding on anything: they seem to be in a frenzy, so distraught are they.

The very suffering of anyone in this state will show her that she is not to blame, and she must not worry, for that only makes matters worse, nor must she weary herself by trying to put sense into something—namely, her mind—which for the moment is without any. She should pray as best she can: indeed, she need not pray at all, but may try to rest her spirit as though she were ill and busy herself with some other virtuous action. These directions are meant for persons who keep careful guard over themselves and know that they must not speak to God and to the world at the same time. What we can do ourselves is to try to be alone—and God grant that this may suffice, as I say, to make us realize in Whose presence we are and how the Lord answers our petitions. Do you suppose that, because we cannot hear Him, He is silent? He speaks clearly to the heart when we beg Him from our hearts to do so. It would be a good idea for us to imagine[94] that He has taught this prayer to each one of us individually, and that He is continually expounding it to us. The Master is never so far away that the disciple needs to raise his voice in order to be heard: He is always right at his side. I want you to understand that, if you are to recite the Paternoster well, one thing is needful: you must not leave the side of the Master Who has taught it you.

You will say *at once* that this is meditation, and that you are not capable of it, and do not even wish to practise it, but are content with vocal prayer. For there are impatient people who dislike giving themselves trouble, and it is troublesome at first to practise recollection of the mind when one has not made it a habit. So, in order not to make themselves the least bit tired, they say they are incapable of anything but vocal prayer and do not know how to do anything further. You are right to say that what we have described is mental prayer; but I assure you that I cannot distinguish it from vocal prayer faithfully recited with a realization of Who it is that we are addressing. Further, we are under the obligation of trying to pray attentively: may God grant that, by using these means, we may learn to say the Paternoster well and not find ourselves thinking of something irrelevant. I have sometimes experienced this myself, and the best remedy I have found for it is to try to fix my mind on the Person by Whom the words were first spoken. Have patience, then, and try to make this necessary practice into a habit, *for necessary it is, in my opinion, for those who would be nuns, and indeed for all who would pray like good Christians.*

CHAPTER TWENTY-FIVE

*Describes the great gain which comes to a soul when it practises
vocal prayer perfectly. Shows how God may raise it thence
to things supernatural.*

I n case you should think there is little gain to be derived from practising vocal prayer perfectly, I must tell you that, while you are repeating the Paternoster or some other vocal prayer, it is quite possible for the Lord to grant you perfect contemplation. In this way His Majesty shows that He is listening to the person who is addressing Him, and that, in His greatness, He is addressing her,[95] by suspending the understanding, putting a stop to all thought, and, as we say, taking the words out of her mouth, so that even if she wishes to speak she cannot do so, or at any rate not without great difficulty.

Such a person understands that, without any sound of words, she is being taught by this Divine Master, Who is suspending her faculties, which, if they were to work, would be causing her harm rather than profit. The faculties rejoice without knowing how they rejoice; the soul is enkindled in love without understanding how it loves; it knows that it is rejoicing in the object of its love, yet it does not know how it is rejoicing in it. It is well aware that this is not a joy which can be attained by the understanding; the will embraces it, without understanding how; but, in so far as it can understand anything, it perceives that this is a blessing which could not be gained by the merits of all the trials suffered on earth put together. It is a gift of the Lord of earth and Heaven, Who gives it like the God He is. This, daughters, is perfect contemplation.

You will now understand how different it is from mental prayer, which I have already described, and which consists in thinking of what we are saying, understanding it, and realizing Whom we are addressing, and who we are that are daring to address so great a Lord. To think of this and other similar things, such as how little we have served Him and how great is our obligation to serve Him, is mental prayer. Do not think of it as one more thing with an outlandish name[96] and do not let the name frighten you. To recite the Paternoster and the Ave Maria, or any other petition you like, is vocal prayer. But think how harsh your music will be without what must come first; sometimes even the words will get into the wrong order. In these two kinds of prayer, with God's help, we may accomplish something ourselves. In the contemplation which I have just described we can do nothing. It is His Majesty Who does everything; the work is His alone and far transcends human nature.

I described this as well as I was able in the relation which I made of it, as I have said, so that my confessors should see it when they read the account of my life which they had ordered me to write. As I have explained all this about contemplation at such length, therefore, I shall not repeat myself here and I am doing no more than touch upon it. If those of you who have experienced the happiness of being called by the Lord to this state of contemplation can get this book, you will find in it points and counsels which the Lord was pleased to enable me to set down. These should bring you great comfort and profit—in my opinion, at least, and in the opinion of several people who have seen it and who keep it at hand in order to make frequent use of it. I am ashamed to tell you that anything of mine is made such use of and the Lord knows with what confusion I write a great deal that I do. Blessed be He for thus bearing with me. Those of you who, as I say, have experience of supernatural prayer should procure the book after my death; those who have not have no need to do so but they should try to carry out what has been said in this one. Let them leave everything to the Lord, to Whom it belongs to grant this gift, and He will not deny it you if you do not tarry on the road but press forward so as to reach the end of your journey.

CHAPTER TWENTY-SIX

Continues the description of a method for recollecting the thoughts.
Describes means of doing this. This chapter is very profitable
for those who are beginning prayer.

L et us now return to our vocal prayer, so that we may learn to pray in such a way that, without our understanding how, God may give us everything at once: if we do this, as I have said, we shall pray as we ought. As you know, the first things must be examination of conscience, confession of sin and the signing of yourself with the Cross. Then, daughter, as you are alone, you must look for a companion—and who could be a better Companion than the very Master Who taught you the prayer that you are about to say? Imagine that this Lord Himself is at your side and see how lovingly and how humbly He is teaching you—and, believe me, you should stay with so good a Friend for as long as you can before you leave Him. If you become accustomed to having Him at your side, and if He sees that you love Him to be there and are always trying to please Him, you will never be able, as we put it, to send Him away, nor will He ever fail you. He will help you in all your trials and you will have Him everywhere. Do you think it is a small thing to have such a Friend as that beside you?

O sisters, those of you whose minds cannot reason for long or whose thoughts cannot dwell *upon* God but are *constantly* wandering must at all costs form this habit. I know quite well that you are capable of it—for many years I endured this trial of being unable to concentrate on one subject, and a very sore trial it is. But I know the Lord does not leave us so devoid of help that if we approach Him humbly and ask Him to be with us He will not grant our request. If a whole year passes without our obtaining what we ask, let us be prepared to try for longer. Let us never grudge time so well spent. Who, after all, is hurrying us? I am sure we can form this habit and strive to walk at the side of this true Master.

I am not asking you now to think of Him, or to form numerous conceptions of Him, or to make long and subtle meditations with your understanding. I am asking you only to look at Him. For who can prevent you from turning the eyes of your soul (just for a moment, if you can do no more) upon this Lord? You are capable of looking at very ugly *and loathsome* things: can you not, then, look at the most beautiful thing imaginable? Your Spouse never takes His eyes off you, daughters. He has borne with thousands of foul and abominable sins which you have committed against Him, yet even they have not been enough to make Him cease looking upon you. Is it such a great matter, then, for you to avert the eyes *of your soul* from outward things and sometimes to look at Him? See, He is only waiting for us to look at Him, as He says to the Bride.[97] If you want Him[98] you will find Him. He longs so much for us to look at Him once more that it will not be for lack of effort on His part if we fail to do so.

A wife, they say, must be like this if she is to have a happy married life with her husband. If he is sad, she must show signs of sadness; if he is merry, even though she may not in fact be so, she must appear merry too. See what slavery you have escaped from, sisters! Yet this, without any pretence, is really how we are treated by the Lord. He becomes subject to us and is pleased to let you be the mistress and to conform to your will. If you are happy, look upon your risen Lord, and the very thought of how He rose from the sepulchre will gladden you. How bright and how beautiful was He then! How majestic![99] How victorious! How joyful! He was like one emerging from a battle in which He had gained a great kingdom, all of which He desires you to have—and with it Himself. Is it such a great thing that you should turn your eyes but once and look upon Him Who has made you such great gifts?

If you are suffering trials, or are sad, look upon Him on His way to the Garden. What sore distress He must have borne in His soul, to describe His own suffering as He did and to complain of it! Or look upon Him bound to the Column, full of pain, His flesh all torn to pieces by His great love for you. How much He suffered, persecuted by some, spat upon by others, denied by His friends, and even deserted by them, with none to take His part, frozen with the cold and left so completely alone that you may well comfort each other! Or look upon Him bending under the weight of the Cross and not even allowed to take breath: He will look upon you with His lovely and compassionate eyes, full of tears, and in comforting your grief will forget His own because you are bearing Him company in order to comfort Him and turning your head to look upon Him.

"O Lord of the world, my true Spouse!" you may say to Him, if seeing Him in such a plight has filled your heart with such tenderness that you not only desire to look upon Him but love to speak to Him, not using forms of prayer, but words issuing from the compassion of your heart, which means so much to Him: "Art Thou so needy, my Lord and my Good, that Thou wilt accept poor companionship like mine? Do I read in Thy face that Thou hast found comfort, even in me? How can it be possible, Lord, that the angels are leaving Thee alone and that Thy Father is not comforting Thee?

"If Thou, Lord, art willing to suffer all this for me, what am I suffering for Thee? What have I to complain of? I am ashamed, Lord, when I see Thee in such a plight, and if in any way I can imitate Thee I will suffer all trials that come to me and count them as a great blessing. Let us go both together, Lord: whither Thou goest, I must go; through whatsoever Thou passest, I must pass." Take up this cross, sisters: never mind if the Jews trample upon you provided you can save Him some of His trials. Take no heed of what they say to you; be deaf to all detraction; stumble and fall with your Spouse, but do not draw back from your cross or give it up. Think often of the weariness of His journey and of how much harder His trials were than those which you have to suffer. However hard you may imagine yours to be, and however much affliction they may cause you, they will be a source of comfort to you, for you will see that they are matters for scorn compared with the trials endured by the Lord.

You will ask me, sisters, how you can possibly do all this, and say that, if you had seen His Majesty with your bodily eyes at the time when He lived in the world, you would have done it willingly and gazed at Him for ever. Do not believe it: anyone who will not make the slight effort necessary for recollection in order to gaze upon this Lord present within her, which she can do without danger and with only the minimum of trouble, would have been far less likely to stand at the foot of the Cross with the Magdalen, who looked death *(as they say)* straight in the face. What the glorious Virgin and this blessed saint must have suffered! What threats, what malicious words, what shocks, what insults! For the people they were dealing with were not exactly polite to them. No, indeed; theirs was the kind of courtesy you might meet in hell, for they were the ministers of the devil himself. Yet, terrible as the sufferings of these women must have been, they would not have noticed them in the presence of pain so much greater.

So do not suppose, sisters, that you would have been prepared to endure such great trials then, if you are not ready for such trifling ones now. Practise enduring these and you may be given others which are greater. *Believe that I am telling the truth when I say that you can do this, for I am speaking from experience.* You will find it very helpful if you can get an image or a picture of this Lord—one that you like—not to wear round your neck and never look at but to use regularly whenever you talk to Him, and He will tell you what to say. If words do not fail you when you talk to people *on earth,* why should they do so when you talk to

God? Do not imagine that they will—I shall certainly not believe that they have done so if you once form the habit. For when you never have intercourse with a person he soon becomes a stranger to you, and you forget how to talk to him; and before long, even if he is a kinsman, you feel as if you do not know him, for both kinship and friendship lose their influence when communication ceases.

It is also a great help to have a good book, written in the vernacular, simply as an aid to recollection. With this aid you will learn to say your vocal prayers well, *I mean, as they ought to be said*—and little by little, persuasively and methodically, you will get your soul used to this, so that it will no longer be afraid of it. Remember that many years have passed since it went away from its Spouse, and it needs very careful handling before it will return home. We sinners are like that: we have accustomed our souls and minds to go after their own pleasures (or pains, it would be more correct to say) until the unfortunate soul no longer knows what it is doing. When that has happened, a good deal of skill is necessary before it can be inspired with enough love to make it stay at home; but unless we can gradually do that we shall accomplish nothing. Once again I assure you that, if you are careful to form habits of the kind I have mentioned, you will derive such great profit from them that I could not describe it even if I wished. Keep at the side of this good Master, then, and be most firmly resolved to learn what He teaches you; His Majesty will then ensure your not failing to be good disciples, and He will never leave you unless you leave Him. Consider the words uttered by those Divine lips: the very first of them will show you at once what love He has for you, and it is no small blessing and joy for the pupil to see that his Master loves Him.

CHAPTER TWENTY-SEVEN

Describes the great love shown us by the Lord in the first words of the Paternoster and the great importance of our making no account of good birth if we truly desire to be the daughters of God.

"Our Father, which art in the Heavens." O my Lord, how Thou dost reveal Thyself as the Father of such a Son, while Thy Son reveals Himself as the Son of such a Father! Blessed be Thou for ever and ever. Ought not so great a favour as this, Lord, to have come at the end of the prayer? Here, at the very beginning, Thou dost fill our hands and grant us so great a favour that it would be a very great blessing if our understanding could be filled with it so that the will would be occupied and we should be unable to say another word. Oh, how appropriate, daughters, would perfect contemplation be here! Oh, how right would the soul be to enter within itself, so as to be the better able to rise above itself, that this holy Son might show it the nature of the place where He says His Father dwells—namely, the Heavens! Let us leave earth, my daughters, for it is not right that a favour like this should be prized so little, and that, after we have realized how great this favour is, we should remain on earth any more.

O Son of God and my Lord! How is it that Thou canst give us so much with Thy first word? It is so wonderful that Thou shouldst descend to such a degree of humility as to join with us when we pray and make Thyself the Brother of creatures so miserable and lowly! How can it be that, in the name of Thy Father, Thou shouldst give us all that there is to be given, by willing Him to have us as His children—and Thy word cannot fail? [It seems that] Thou dost oblige Him to fulfil Thy word, a charge by no means light, since, being our Father, He must bear with us, however great our offences. If we return to Him, He must pardon us, as He pardoned the prodigal son, must comfort us in our trials, and must sustain us, as such a Father is bound to do, for He must needs be better than any earthly father, since nothing good can fail to have its perfection in Him. *He must cherish us; He must sustain us;* and at the last He must make us participants and fellow-heirs with Thee.

Behold, my Lord, with the love that Thou hast for us and with Thy humility, nothing can be an obstacle to Thee. And then, Lord, Thou hast been upon earth and by taking our nature upon Thee hast clothed Thyself with humanity: Thou hast therefore some reason to care for our advantage. But behold, Thy Father is in Heaven, as Thou hast told us, and it is right that Thou shouldst consider His honour. Since Thou hast offered Thyself to be dishonoured by us, leave Thy Father free. Oblige Him not to do so much for people as wicked as I, who will make Him such poor acknowledgment.

O good Jesus! How clearly hast Thou shown that Thou art One with Him and that Thy will is His and His is Thine! How open a confession is this, my Lord! What is this love that Thou hast for us? Thou didst deceive the devil, and conceal from him that Thou art the Son of God, but Thy great desire for our welfare overcomes all obstacles to Thy granting us this greatest of favours. Who but Thou could do this, Lord? I cannot think how the devil failed to understand from that word of Thine Who Thou wert, beyond any doubt. I, at least, my Jesus, see clearly that Thou didst speak as a dearly beloved son both for Thyself and for us, and Thou hast such power that what Thou sayest in Heaven shall be done on earth. Blessed be Thou for ever, my Lord, Who lovest so much to give that no obstacle can stay Thee.

Do you not think, daughters, that this is a good Master, since He begins by granting us this great favour so as to make us love to learn what He teaches us? Do you think it would be right for us, while we are repeating this prayer with our lips, to stop trying to think of what we are saying, lest picturing such love should tear our hearts to pieces? No one who realized His greatness could possibly say it would be. What son is there in the world who would not try to learn who his father was if he had one as good, and of as great majesty and dominion, as ours? Were God not all this, it would not surprise me if we had no desire to be known as His children; for the world is such that, if the father is of lower rank than his son, the son feels no honour in recognizing him as his father. This does not apply here: God forbid that such a thing should ever happen in this house—it would turn the place into hell. Let the sister who is of the highest birth speak of her father least; we must all be equals.

O College of Christ, in which the Lord was pleased that Saint Peter, who was a fisherman, should have more authority than Saint Bartholomew, who was the son of a king! His Majesty knew what a fuss would be made in the world about who was fashioned from the finer clay— which is like discussing whether clay is better for bricks or for walls. Dear Lord, what a trouble we make about it! God deliver you, sisters, from such contentions, even if they be carried on only in jest; I hope that His Majesty will indeed deliver you. If anything like this should be going on among you, apply the remedy immediately, and let the sister concerned fear lest she be a Judas among the Apostles. *Do what you can to get rid of such a bad companion. If you cannot,* give her penances *heavier than for anything else* until she realizes that she has not deserved to be even the basest clay. You have a good Father, given you by the good Jesus: let no other father be known or referred to here. Strive, my daughters, to be such that you deserve to find comfort in Him and to throw yourselves into His arms. You know that, if you are good children, He will never send you away. And who would not do anything rather than lose such a Father?

Oh, thank God, what cause for comfort there is here! Rather than write more about it I will leave it for you to think about; for, however much your thoughts may wander, between such a Son and such a Father there must needs be the Holy Spirit. May He enkindle your will and bind you to Himself with the most fervent love, since even the great advantage you gain will not suffice to do so.

CHAPTER TWENTY-EIGHT

Describes the nature of the Prayer of Recollection and sets down some of the means by which we can make it a habit.

Consider now what your Master says next: "Who art in the Heavens." Do you suppose it matters little what Heaven is and where you must seek your most holy Father? I assure you that for minds which wander it is of great importance not only to have a right belief about this but to try to learn it by experience, for it is one of the best ways of concentrating the mind and effecting recollection in the soul.

You know that God is everywhere; and *this is a great truth, for,* of course, wherever the king is, or so they say, the court is too: that is to say, wherever God is, there is Heaven. No doubt you can believe that, in any place where His Majesty is, there is fulness of glory. Remember how Saint Augustine tells us about his seeking God in many places and eventually finding Him within himself. Do you suppose it is of little importance that a soul which is often distracted should come to understand this truth and to find that, in order to speak to its Eternal Father and to take its delight in Him, it has no need to go to Heaven or to speak in a loud voice? However quietly we speak, He is so near that He will hear us: we need no wings to go in search of Him but have only to find a place where we can be alone and look upon Him present within us. Nor need we feel strange in the presence of so kind a Guest; we must talk to Him very humbly, as we should to our father, ask Him for things as we should ask a father, tell Him our troubles, beg Him to put them right, and yet realize that we are not worthy to be called His children.

Avoid being bashful with God, as some people are, in the belief that they are being humble. It would not be humility on your part if the King were to do you a favour and you refused to accept it; but you would be showing humility by taking it, and being pleased with it, yet realizing how far you are from deserving it. A fine humility it would be if I had the Emperor of Heaven and earth in my house, coming to it to do me a favour and to delight in my company, and I were so humble that I would not answer His questions, nor remain with Him, nor accept what He gave me, but left Him alone. Or if He were to speak to me and beg me to ask for what I wanted, and I were so humble that I preferred to remain poor and even let Him go away, so that He would see I had not sufficient resolution.

Have nothing to do with that kind of humility, daughters, but speak with Him as with a Father, a Brother, a Lord and a Spouse—and, sometimes in one way and sometimes in another, He will teach you what you must do to please Him. Do not be foolish; ask Him to let you speak to Him, and, as He is your Spouse, to treat you as His brides. *Remember how important it is for you to have understood this truth—that the Lord is within us and that we should be there with Him.*

If one prays in this way, the prayer may be only vocal, but the mind will be recollected much sooner; and this is a prayer which brings with it many blessings. It is called recollection because the soul collects together all the faculties and enters within itself to be with its God. Its Divine Master comes more speedily to teach it, and to grant it the Prayer of Quiet, than in any other way. For, hidden there within itself, it can think about the Passion, and picture the Son, and offer Him to the Father, without wearying the mind by going to seek Him on Mount Calvary, or in the Garden, or at the Column.

Those who are able to shut themselves up in this way within this little Heaven of the soul, wherein dwells the Maker of Heaven and earth, and who have formed the habit of looking at nothing and staying in no place which will distract these outward senses, may be sure that they are walking on an excellent road, and will come without fail to drink of the water of the fountain, for they will journey a long way in a short time. They are like one who travels in a ship, and, if he has a little good wind, reaches the end of his voyage in a few days, while those who go by land take *much* longer.

These souls have already, as we may say, put out to sea; though they have not sailed quite out of sight of land, they do what they can to get away from it, in the time at their disposal, by recollecting their senses. If their recollection is genuine, the fact becomes very evident, for it produces certain effects which I do not know how to explain but which anyone will recognize who has experience of them. It is as if the soul were rising from play, for it sees that worldly things are nothing but toys; so in due course it rises above them, like a person entering a strong castle, in order that it may have nothing more to fear from its enemies. It withdraws the senses from all outward things and spurns them so completely that, without its understanding how, its eyes close and it cannot see them and the soul's spiritual sight becomes clear. Those who walk along this path almost invariably close their eyes when they say their prayers; this, for many reasons, is an admirable custom, since it means that they are making an effort not to look at things of the world. The effort has to be made only at the beginning; later it becomes unnecessary: eventually, in fact, it would cost a greater effort to open the eyes during prayer than to close them. The soul seems to gather up its strength and to master itself at the expense of the body, which it leaves weakened and alone: in this way it becomes stronger for the fight against it.

This may not be evident at first, if the recollection is not very profound—for at this stage it is sometimes more so and sometimes less. At first it may cause a good deal of trouble, for the body insists on its rights, not understanding that if it refuses to admit defeat it is, as it were, cutting off its own head. But if we cultivate the habit, make the necessary effort and practise the exercises for several days, the benefits will reveal themselves, and when we begin to pray we shall realize that the bees are coming to the hive and entering it to make the honey, and all without any effort of ours. For it is the Lord's will that, in return for the time which their efforts have cost them, the soul and the will should be given this power over the senses. They will only have to make a sign to show that they wish to enter into recollection and the senses will obey and allow themselves to be recollected. Later they may come out again, but it is a great thing that they should ever have surrendered, for if they come out it is as captives and slaves and they do none of the harm that they might have done before. When the will calls them afresh they respond more quickly, until, after they have entered the soul many times, the Lord is pleased that they should remain there altogether in perfect contemplation.

What has been said should be noted with great care, for, though it seems obscure, it will be understood by anyone desirous of putting it into practice. The sea-voyage, then, can be made; and, as it is very important that we should not travel too slowly, let us just consider how we can get accustomed to these good habits. Souls who do so are more secure from many occasions of sin, and the fire of Divine love is the more readily enkindled in them; for they are so near that fire that, however little the blaze has been fanned with the understanding, any small spark that flies out at them will cause them to burst into flame. When no hindrance comes to it from outside, the soul remains alone with its God and is thoroughly prepared to become enkindled.

And now let us imagine that we have within us a palace of priceless worth, built entirely of gold and precious stones—a palace, in short, fit for so great a Lord. Imagine that it is partly your doing that this palace should be what it is—and this is really true, for there is no building so beautiful as a soul that is pure and full of virtues, and, the greater these virtues are, the more brilliantly do the stones shine. Imagine that within the palace dwells this great King, Who has vouchsafed to become your

Father and Who is seated upon a throne of supreme price—namely, your heart.

At first you will think this irrelevant—I mean the use of this figure to explain my point—but it may prove very useful, especially to persons like yourselves. For, as we women are not learned or *fine-witted,* we need all these things to help us realize that we actually have something within us incomparably more precious than anything we see outside. Do not let us suppose that the interior of the soul is empty; God grant that only women may be so thoughtless as to suppose that. If we took care always to remember what a Guest we have within us, I think it would be impossible for us to abandon ourselves to *vanities and* things of the world, for we should see how worthless they are by comparison with those which we have within us. What does an animal do beyond satisfying his hunger by seizing whatever attracts him when he sees it? There should surely be a great difference between the brute beasts and ourselves, *as we have such a Father.*

Perhaps you will laugh at me and say that this is obvious enough; and you will be right, though it was some time before I came to see it. I knew perfectly well that I had a soul, but I did not understand what that soul merited, or Who dwelt within it, until I closed my eyes to the vanities of this world in order to see it. I think, if I had understood then, as I do now, how this great King *really* dwells within this little palace of my soul, I should not have left Him alone so often, but should have stayed with Him and never have allowed His dwelling-place to get so dirty. How wonderful it is that He Whose greatness could fill a thousand worlds, and very many more, should confine Himself within so small a space, *just as He was pleased to dwell within the womb of His most holy Mother!* Being the Lord, He has, of course, perfect freedom, and, as He loves us, He fashions Himself to our measure.

When a soul sets out upon this path, He does not reveal Himself to it, lest it should feel dismayed at seeing that its littleness can contain such greatness; but gradually He enlarges it to the extent requisite for what He has to set within it. It is for this reason that I say He has perfect freedom, since He has power to make the whole of this palace great.

213

The important point is that we should be absolutely resolved to give it to Him for His own and should empty it so that He may take out and put in just what He likes, as He would with something of His own. His Majesty is right in demanding this; let us not deny it to Him. And, as He refuses to force our will, He takes what we give Him but does not give Himself wholly until *He sees that* we are giving ourselves wholly to Him. This is certain, and, as it is of such importance, I often remind you of it. Nor does He work within the soul as He does when it is wholly His and keeps nothing back. I do not see how He can do so, since He likes everything to be done in order. If we fill the palace with vulgar people and all kinds of junk, how can the Lord and His Court occupy it? When such a crowd is there it would be a great thing if He were to remain for even a short time.

Do you suppose, daughters, that He is alone when He comes to us? Do you not see that His *most holy* Son says: "Who art in the Heavens?" Surely such a King would not be abandoned by His courtiers. They stay with Him and pray to Him on our behalf and for our welfare, for they are full of charity. Do not imagine that Heaven is like this earth, where, if a lord or prelate shows anyone favours, whether for some particular reason or simply because he likes him, people at once become envious, and, though the poor man has done nothing to them, he is maliciously treated, *so that his favours cost him dear.*

CHAPTER TWENTY-NINE

Continues to describe methods for achieving this Prayer of Recollection. Says what little account we should make of being favoured by our superiors.

For the love of God, daughters, avoid making any account of these favours. You should each do your duty; and, if this is not appreciated by your superior, you may be sure that it will be appreciated and rewarded by the Lord. We did not come here to seek rewards in this life, *but only in the life to come.* Let our thoughts always be fixed upon what endures, and not trouble themselves with earthly things which do not endure even for a lifetime. For to-day some other sister will be in your superior's good books; whereas to-morrow, if she sees you exhibiting some additional virtue, it is with you that she will be better pleased—and if she is not it is of little consequence. Never give way to these thoughts, which sometimes begin in a small way but may cost you a great deal of unrest. Check them by remembering that your kingdom is not of this world, and that everything comes quickly to an end, *and that there is nothing in this life that goes on unchangingly.*

But even that is a poor remedy and anything but a perfect one; it is best that this state of things should continue, and that you should be humbled and out of favour, and should wish to be so for the sake of the Lord Who dwells in you. Turn your eyes upon yourself and look at yourself inwardly, as I have said. You will find your Master; He will not fail you: indeed, the less outward comfort you have, the [much] greater the joy He will give you. He is full of compassion and never fails those who are afflicted and out of favour if they trust in Him alone. Thus David tells us that *he never saw the just forsaken,*[100] *and again, that* the Lord is with the afflicted.[101] Either you believe this or you do not: if you do, *as you should,* why do you wear yourselves to death with worry?

O my Lord, if we had a real knowledge of Thee, we should make not the slightest account of anything, since Thou givest so much to those who will set their whole trust on Thee. Believe me, friends, it is a great thing to realize the truth of this so that we may see how deceptive are earthly *things and* favours when they deflect the soul in any way from its course and hinder it from entering within itself.[102] God help me! If only someone could make you realize this! I myself, *Lord,* certainly cannot; I know that [in truth] I owe *Thee* more than anyone else but I cannot realize this myself as well as I should.

Returning to what I was saying, I should like to be able to explain the nature of this holy companionship with our great Companion, the Holiest of the holy, in which there is nothing to hinder the soul and her Spouse from remaining alone together, when the soul desires to enter within herself, to shut the door behind her so as to keep out all that is worldly and to dwell in that Paradise with her God. I say "desires," because you must understand that this is not a supernatural state but depends upon our volition, and that, by God's favour, we can enter it of our own accord: *this condition must be understood of everything that we say in this book can be done,* for without it nothing can be accomplished and we have not the power to think a single good thought. For this is not a silence of the faculties: it is a shutting-up of the faculties within itself by the soul.

There are many ways in which we can gradually acquire this habit, as various books tell us. We must cast aside everything else, they say, in order to approach God inwardly and we must retire within ourselves even during our ordinary occupations. If I can recall the companionship which I have within my soul for as much as a moment, that is of great utility. *But as I am speaking only about the way to recite vocal prayers well, there is no need for me to say as much as this. All I want is that we should know[103] and abide with the Person with Whom we are speaking, and not turn our backs upon Him; for that, it seems to me, is what we are doing when we talk to God and yet think of all kinds of vanity. The whole mischief comes from our not really grasping the fact that He is near us, and imagining Him far away—so far, that we shall have to go to Heaven in order to find Him. How is it, Lord, that we do not look at Thy face, when it is so near us? We do not think people are listening to us when we are speaking to them unless we see them looking at us. And do we close our eyes so as not to see that Thou art looking at us? How can we know if Thou hast heard what we say to Thee?*

The great thing I should like to teach you is that, in order to accustom ourselves gradually to giving our minds confidence, so that we may readily understand what we are saying, and with Whom we are speaking, we must recollect our outward senses, take charge of them ourselves and give them something which will occupy them. It is in this way that we have Heaven within ourselves since the Lord of Heaven is there. If once we accustom ourselves to being glad[104] that there is no need to raise our voices in order to speak to Him, since His Majesty will make us conscious that He is there, we shall be able to say the Paternoster and whatever other prayers we like with great peace of mind, and the Lord Himself will help us not to grow tired. Soon after we have begun to force ourselves to remain near the Lord, He will give us indications by which we may understand that, though we have had to say the Paternoster many times, He heard us the first time. For He loves to save us worry; and, even though we may take a whole hour over saying it once, if we can realize that we are with Him, and what it is we are asking Him, and how willing He is, *like any father,* to grant it to us, and how He loves to be with us, *and comfort us,* He has no wish for us to tire our brains by a great deal of talking.

For love of the Lord, then, sisters, accustom yourselves to saying the Paternoster in this recollected way, and before long you will see how you gain by doing so. It is a method of prayer which establishes habits that prevent the soul from going astray and the faculties from becoming restless. This you will find out in time: I only beg you to test it, even at the cost of a little trouble, which always results when we try to form a new habit. I assure you, however, that before long you will have the great comfort of finding it unnecessary to tire yourselves with seeking this holy Father to Whom you pray, for you will discover Him within you.

May the Lord teach this to those of you who do not know it: for my own part I must confess that, until the Lord taught me this method, I never knew what it was to get satisfaction and comfort out of prayer, and it is because I have always gained such great benefits from this custom of interior recollection[105] that I have written about it at such length. Perhaps you all know this, but some sister may come to you who will not know it, so you must not be vexed at my having spoken about it here.

I conclude by advising anyone who wishes to acquire it (since, as I say, it is in our power to do so) not to grow weary of trying to get used to the method which has been described, for it is equivalent to a gradual gaining of the mastery over herself and is not vain labour. To conquer oneself for one's own good is to make use of the senses in the service of the interior life. If she is speaking she must try to remember that there is One within her to Whom she can speak; if she is listening, let her remember that she can listen to Him Who is nearer to her than anyone else. Briefly, let her realize that, if she likes, she need never withdraw from this good companionship, and let her grieve when she has left her Father alone for so long though her need of Him is so sore.

If she can, let her practise recollection many times daily; if not, let her do so occasionally. As she grows accustomed to it, she will feel its benefits, either sooner or later. Once the Lord has granted it to her, she would not exchange it for any treasure.

Nothing, sisters, can be learned without a little trouble, so do, for the love of God, look upon any care which you take about this as well spent. I know that, with God's help, if you practise it for a year, or perhaps for only six months, you will be successful in attaining it. Think what a short time that is for acquiring so great a benefit, for you will be laying a good foundation, so that, if the Lord desires to raise you up to achieve great things, He will find you ready, because you will be close to Himself. May His Majesty never allow us to withdraw ourselves from His presence. Amen.

CHAPTER THIRTY

Describes the importance of understanding what we ask for in prayer. Treats of these words in the Paternoster: "Sanctificetur nomen tuum, adveniat regnum tuum."[106] *Applies them to the Prayer of Quiet, and begins the explanation of them.*

We must now come to consider the next petition in our good Master's prayer, in which He begins to entreat His holy Father on our behalf, and see what it is that He entreats, as it is well that we should know this.

What person, however careless, who had to address someone of importance, would not spend time in thinking how to approach him so as to please him and not be considered tedious? He would also think what he was going to ask for and what use he would make of it, especially if his petition were for some particular thing, as our good Jesus tells us our petitions must be. This point seems to me *very* important. Couldst Thou not, my Lord, have ended this prayer in a single sentence, by saying: "Give us, Father, whatever is good for us?" For, in addressing One Who knows everything, there would seem to be no need to say any more.

This would have sufficed, O Eternal Wisdom, as between Thee and Thy Father. It was thus that Thou didst address Him in the Garden, telling Him of Thy will and Thy fear, but leaving Thyself in His hands. But Thou knowest us, my Lord, and Thou knowest that we are not as resigned as wert Thou to the will of Thy Father; we needed, therefore, to be taught to ask for particular things so that we should stop *for a moment* to think if what we ask of Thee is good for us, and if it is not, should not ask for it. For, being what we are and having our free will, if we do not receive what we ask for, we shall not accept what the Lord gives us. The gift might be the best one possible—but we never think we are rich unless we actually see money in our hands.

Oh, God help me! What is it that sends our faith to sleep, so that we cannot realize how certain we are, on the one hand, to be punished, and, on the other, to be rewarded? It is for this reason, daughters, that it is good for you to know what you are asking for in the Paternoster, so that, if the Eternal Father gives it you, you shall not cast it back in His face. You must think carefully if what you are about to ask for will be good for you; if it will not, do not ask for it, but ask His Majesty to give you light. For we are blind and often we have such a loathing for life-giving food that we cannot eat it but prefer what will cause us death—and what a death: so terrible and eternal!

Now the good Jesus bids us say these words, in which we pray that this Kingdom may come in us: "Hallowed be Thy Name, Thy Kingdom come in us." Consider now, daughters, how great is our Master's wisdom. I am thinking here of what we are asking in praying for this kingdom, and it is well that we should realize this. His Majesty, knowing of how little we are capable, saw that, unless He provided for us by giving us His Kingdom here on earth, we could neither hallow nor praise nor magnify nor glorify *nor exalt* this holy name of the Eternal Father in a way befitting it. The good Jesus, therefore, places these two petitions next to each other. Let us understand this thing that we are asking for, daughters, and how important it is that we should pray for it without ceasing and do all we can to please Him Who will give it us: it is for that reason that I want to tell you what I know about the matter now. If you do not like the subject, think out some other meditations for yourselves, for our Master will allow us to do this, provided we submit in all things to the teaching of the [Holy Roman] Church, as I do here. *In any case I shall not give you this book to read until persons who understand these matters have seen it: so, if there is anything wrong with it, the reason will be, not wickedness, but my imperfect knowledge.*

To me, then, it seems that, of the many joys to be found in the kingdom of Heaven, the chief is that we shall have no more to do with the things of earth; for in Heaven we shall have an intrinsic tranquillity and glory, a joy in the rejoicings of all, a perpetual peace, and a great interior satisfaction which will come to us when we see that all are hallowing and praising the Lord, and are blessing His name, and that none is offending Him. For all love Him there and the soul's one concern is loving Him, nor can it cease from loving Him because it knows Him. And this is how we should love Him on earth, though we cannot do so with the same perfection nor yet all the time; still, if we knew Him, we should love Him very differently from the way we do now.

It looks as though I were going to say that we must be angels to make this petition and to say our vocal prayers well. This would indeed be our Divine Master's wish, since He bids us make so sublime a petition. You may be quite sure that He never tells us to ask for impossibilities, so it must be possible, with God's help, for a soul living in that state of exile to reach such a point, though not as perfectly as those who have been freed from this prison, for we are making a sea-voyage and are still on the journey. But there are times when we are wearied with travelling and the Lord grants our faculties tranquillity and our soul quiet, and while they are in that state He gives us a clear understanding of the nature of the gifts He bestows upon those whom He brings to His Kingdom. Those to whom, while they are still on earth, He grants what we are asking Him for receive pledges which will give them a great hope of eventually attaining to a perpetual enjoyment of what on earth He only allows them to taste.

If it were not that you would tell me I am treating of contemplation, it would be appropriate, in writing of this petition, to say a little about the beginning of pure contemplation, which those who experience it call the Prayer of Quiet; but, as I have said, I am discussing vocal prayer here, and anyone ignorant of the subject might think that the two had nothing to do with one another, though I know this is *certainly* not true. Forgive my wanting to speak of it, for I know there are many people who practise vocal prayer in the manner already described and are raised by God to the higher kind of contemplation without *having had any hand in this themselves* or *even* knowing how it has happened. *For this reason, daughters, I attach great importance to your saying your vocal prayers well.* I know a nun who could never practise anything but vocal prayer but who kept to this and found she had everything else; yet if she omitted saying her prayers her mind wandered so much that she could not endure it. May we all practise such mental prayer as that. She would say a number of Paternosters, corresponding to the number of times Our Lord shed His blood, and on nothing more than these and a few other prayers she would spend two or three hours. She came to me once in great distress, saying that she did not know how to practise mental prayer, and that she could not contemplate but could only say vocal prayers. *She was quite an old woman and had lived an extremely good and religious life.* I asked her what prayers she said, and *from her reply* I saw that, though keeping to the Paternoster, she was experiencing pure contemplation, and the Lord was raising her to be with Him in union. She spent her life so well, too, that her actions made it clear she was receiving great favours. So I praised the Lord and envied her her vocal prayer. If this story is true—and it is—none of you who have had a bad opinion of contemplatives can suppose that you will be free from the risk of becoming like them if you say your vocal prayers as they should be said and keep a pure conscience. *I shall have to say still more about this. Anyone not wishing to hear it may pass it over.*

CHAPTER THIRTY-ONE

Continues the same subject. Explains what is meant by the Prayer of Quiet. Gives several counsels to those who experience it. This chapter is very noteworthy.

N ow, daughters, I still want to describe this Prayer of Quiet to you, in the way I have heard it talked about, and as the Lord has been pleased to teach it to me, perhaps in order that I might describe it to you. It is in this kind of prayer, as I have said, that the Lord seems to me to begin to show us that He is hearing our petition: He begins to give us His Kingdom on earth so that we may truly praise Him and hallow His name and strive to make others do so likewise.

This is a supernatural state, and, however hard we try, we cannot reach it for ourselves; for it is a state in which the soul enters into peace, or rather in which the Lord gives it peace through His presence, as He did to that just man Simeon.[107] In this state all the faculties are stilled. The soul, in a way which has nothing to do with the outward senses, realizes that it is now very close to its God, and that, if it were but a little closer, it would become one with Him through union. This is not because it sees Him either with its bodily or with its spiritual eyes. The just man Simeon saw no more than the glorious Infant—a poor little Child, Who, to judge from the swaddling-clothes in which He was wrapped and from the small number of the people whom He had *as a retinue* to take Him up to the Temple, might well have been the son of these poor people rather than the Son of his Heavenly Father. But the Child Himself revealed to him Who He was. Just so, though less clearly, does the soul know Who He is. It cannot understand how it knows Him, yet it sees that it is in the Kingdom (or at least is near to the King Who will give it the Kingdom), and it feels such reverence that it dares to ask nothing. It is, as it were, in a swoon, both inwardly and outwardly, so that the outward man (let me call it the "body," and then you will understand me better) does not wish to move, but rests, like one who has almost reached the end of his journey, so that it may the better start again upon its way, with redoubled strength for its task.

The body experiences the greatest delight and the soul is conscious of a deep satisfaction. So glad is it merely to find itself near the fountain that, even before it has begun to drink, it has had its fill. There seems nothing left for it to desire. The faculties are stilled and have no wish to move, for any movement they may make appears to hinder the soul from loving God. They are not completely lost, however, since, two of them being free, they can realize in Whose Presence they are. It is the will that is in captivity now; and, if while in this state it is capable of experiencing any pain, the pain comes when it realizes that it will have to resume its liberty. The mind tries to occupy itself with only one thing, and the memory has no desire to busy itself with more: they both see that this is the one thing needful and that anything else will unsettle them. Persons in this state prefer the body to remain motionless, for otherwise their peace would be destroyed: for this reason they dare not stir. Speaking is a distress to them: they will spend a whole hour on a single repetition of the Paternoster. They are so close to God that they know they can make themselves understood by signs. They are in the palace, near to their King, and they see that He is already beginning to give them His Kingdom on earth. *Sometimes tears come to their eyes, but they weep very*

gently and quite without distress: their whole desire is the hallowing of this name.
They seem not to be in the world, and have no wish to see or hear
anything but their God; nothing distresses them, nor does it seem that
anything can possibly do so. In short, for as long as this state lasts, they
are so overwhelmed and absorbed by the joy and delight which they
experience that they can think of nothing else to wish for, and will gladly
say with Saint Peter: "Lord, let us make here three mansions."[108]

Occasionally, during this Prayer of Quiet, God grants the soul another favour which is hard to understand if one has not had long experience of it. But any of you who have had this will at once recognize it
and it will give you great comfort to know what it is. I believe God
often grants this favour together with the other. When this quiet is felt
in a high degree and lasts for a long time, I do not think that, if the will
were not made fast to something, the peace could be of such long dura-
tion. Sometimes it goes on for a day, or for two days, and we find
ourselves—I mean those who experience this state—full of this joy without understanding the reason. They see clearly that their whole self is
not in what they are doing, but that the most important faculty is absent—namely, the will, which I think is united with its God—and that
the other faculties are left free to busy themselves with His service. For
this they have much more capacity at such a time, though when attending
to worldly affairs they are dull and sometimes stupid.

It is a great favour which the Lord grants to these souls, for it unites
the active life with the contemplative. At such times they serve the Lord
in both these ways at once; the will, while in contemplation, is working
without knowing how it does so; the other two faculties are serving
Him as Martha did. Thus Martha and Mary work together. I know
someone to whom the Lord often granted this favour; she could not
understand it and asked a great contemplative[109] about it, he told her
that what she described was quite possible and had happened to himself.
I think, therefore, that as the soul experiences such satisfaction in this
Prayer of Quiet the will must be almost continuously united with Him
Who alone can give it happiness.

I think it will be well, sisters, if I give some advice here to any of you whom the Lord, out of His goodness alone, has brought to this state, as I know that this has happened to some of you. First of all, when such persons experience this joy, without knowing whence it has come to them, but knowing at least that they could not have achieved it of themselves, they are tempted to imagine that they can prolong it and they may even try not to breathe. This is ridiculous: we can no more control this prayer than we can make the day break, or stop night from falling; it is supernatural and something we cannot acquire. The most we can do to prolong this favour is to realize that we can neither diminish nor add to it, but, being most unworthy and undeserving of it, can only receive it with thanksgiving. And we can best give thanks, not with many words, but by lifting up our eyes, like the publican.[110]

It is well to seek greater solitude so as to make room for the Lord and allow His Majesty to do His own work in us. The most we should do is occasionally, and quite gently, to utter a single word, like a person giving a little puff to a candle, when he sees it has almost gone out, so as to make it burn again; though, if it were fully alight, I suppose the only result of blowing it would be to put it out. I think the puff should be a gentle one because, if we begin to tax our brains by making up long speeches, the will may become active again.

Note carefully, friends, this piece of advice which I want to give you now. You will often find that these other two faculties are of no help to you. It may come about that the soul is enjoying the highest degree of quiet, and that the understanding has soared so far aloft that what is happening to it seems not to be going on in its own house at all; it *really* seems to be a guest in somebody else's house, looking for other lodgings, since its own lodging no longer satisfies it and it cannot remain there for long together. Perhaps this is only my own experience and other people do not find it so. But, speaking for myself, I sometimes long to die because I cannot cure this wandering of the mind. At other times the mind seems to be settled in its own abode and to be remaining there with the will as its companion. When all three faculties work together it is wonderful. The harmony is like that between husband and wife: if they are happy and love each other, both desire the same thing; but if the husband is unhappy in his marriage he soon begins to make the wife restless. Just so, when the will finds itself in this state of quiet, it must take no more notice of the understanding than it would of a madman, for, if it tries to draw the understanding along with it, it is bound to grow preoccupied and restless, with the result that this state of prayer will be all effort and no gain and the soul will lose what God has been giving it without any effort of its own.

Pay great attention to the following comparison, which *the Lord suggested to me when I was in this state of prayer, and which* seems to me very appropriate. The soul is like an infant still at its mother's breast: such is the mother's care for it that she gives it its milk without its having to ask for it so much as by moving its lips. That is what happens here. The will simply loves, and no effort needs to be made by the understanding, for it is the Lord's pleasure that, without exercising its thought, the soul should realize that it is in His company, and should merely drink the milk which His Majesty puts into its mouth and enjoy its sweetness. The Lord desires it to know that it is He Who is granting it that favour and that in its enjoyment of it He too rejoices. But it is not His will that the soul should try to understand how it is enjoying it, or what it is enjoying; it should lose all thought of itself, and He Who is at its side will not fail to see what is best for it. If it begins to strive with its mind so that the mind may be apprised of what is happening and thus induced to share in it,[111] it will be quite unable to do so, and the soul will perforce lose the milk[112] and forgo that Divine sustenance.

This state of prayer is different from that in which the soul is wholly united with God, for in the latter state it does not even swallow its nourishment: the Lord places this within it, and it has no idea how. But in this state it even seems to be His will that the soul should work a little, though so quietly that it is hardly conscious of doing so. What disturbs it is the understanding and this is not the case when there is union of all the three faculties, since He Who created them suspends them: He keeps them occupied with the enjoyment that He has given them, without their knowing, or being able to understand, the reason. *Anyone who has had experience of this kind of prayer will understand quite well what I am saying if, after reading this, she considers it carefully, and thinks out its meaning: otherwise it will be Greek*[113] *to her.*

Well, as I say, the soul is conscious of having reached this state of prayer, which is a quiet, deep *and peaceful* happiness of the will, without being able to decide precisely what it is, although it can clearly see how it differs from the happiness of the world. To have dominion over the whole world, with all its happiness, would not suffice to bring the soul such inward satisfaction as it enjoys now in the depths of its will. For other kinds of happiness in life, it seems to me, touch only the outward part of the will, which we might describe as its rind.

When one of you finds herself in this sublime state of prayer, which, as I have already said, is most markedly supernatural, and the understanding (or, to put it more clearly, the thought) wanders off after the most ridiculous things in the world, she should laugh at it and treat it as the silly thing it is, and remain in her state of quiet. For thoughts will come and go, but the will is mistress and all-powerful, and will recall them without your having to trouble about it. But if you try to drag the understanding back by force, you lose your power over it, which comes from your taking and receiving that Divine sustenance, and neither will nor understanding will gain[114], but both will be losers. There is a saying that, if we try very hard to grasp all, we lose all; and so I think it is here. Experience will show you the truth of this; and I shall not be surprised if those of you who have none think this very obscure and unnecessary. But, as I have said, if you have only a little experience of it you will understand it and be able to profit by it, and you will praise the Lord for being pleased to enable me to explain it.

Let us now conclude by saying that, when the soul is brought to this state of prayer, it would seem that the Eternal Father has already granted its petition that He will give it His Kingdom on earth. O blessed request, in which we ask for so great a good without knowing what we do! Blessed manner of asking! It is for this reason, sisters, that I want us to be careful how we say this prayer, the Paternoster, and all other vocal prayers, *and what we ask for in them.* For *clearly,* when God has shown us this favour, we shall have to forget worldly things, all of which the Lord of the world has come and cast out. I do not mean that everyone who experiences the Prayer of Quiet must perforce be detached from everything in the world; but at least I should like all such persons to know what they lack and to humble themselves *and not to make so great a petition as though they were asking for nothing, and, if the Lord gives them what they ask for, to throw it back in His face.* They must try to become more and more detached from everything, for otherwise they will only remain where they are. If God gives a soul such pledges, it is a sign that He has great things in store for it. It will be its own fault if it does not make great progress. But if He sees that, after He has brought the Kingdom of Heaven into its abode, it returns to earth, not only will He refrain from showing it the secrets of His Kingdom but He will grant it this other favour only for short periods and rarely.

I may be mistaken about this, but I have seen it and know that it happens, and, for my own part, I believe this is why spiritual people are not much more numerous. They do not respond to so great a favour in a practical way: instead of preparing themselves to receive this favour again, they take back from the Lord's hands the will which He considered His own and centre it upon base things. So He seeks out others who love Him in order to grant them His greater gifts, although He will not take away all that He has given from those who live in purity of conscience. But there are persons—and I have been one of them—to whom the Lord gives tenderness of devotion and holy inspirations and light on everything. He bestows this Kingdom on them and brings them to this Prayer of Quiet, and yet they deafen their ears to His voice. For they are so fond of talking and of repeating a large number of vocal prayers in a great hurry, as though they were anxious to finish their task of repeating them daily, that when the Lord, as I say, puts His Kingdom into their very hands, *by giving them this Prayer of Quiet and this inward peace,* they do not accept it, but think that they will do better to go on reciting their prayers, which only distract them from their purpose.

Do not be like that, sisters, but be watchful when the Lord grants you this favour. Think what a great treasure you may be losing and realize that you are doing much more by occasionally repeating a single petition of the Paternoster than by repeating the whole of it many times in a hurry *and not thinking what you are saying.* He to Whom you are praying is very near to you and will not fail to hear you; and you may be sure that you are truly praising Him and hallowing His name, since you are glorifying the Lord as a member of His household and praising Him with increasing affection and desire so that it seems you can never forsake His service. *So I advise you to be very cautious about this, for it is of the greatest importance.*

Chapter Thirty-Two

Expounds these words of the Paternoster: "Fiat voluntas tua sicut in coelo et in terra."[115] Describes how much is accomplished by those who repeat these words with full resolution and how well the Lord rewards them for it.

Now that our good Master has asked on our behalf, and has taught us ourselves to ask, for a thing so precious that it includes all we can desire on earth, and has granted us the great favour of making us His brethren, let us see what He desires us to give to His Father, and what He offers Him on our behalf, and what He asks of us, for it is right that we should render Him some service in return for such great favours. O good Jesus! Since Thou givest so little (little, that is to say, on our behalf) how canst Thou ask [so much] for us? What we give is in itself nothing at all by comparison with all that has been given us and with the greatness of Our Lord. But in truth, my Lord, Thou dost not leave us with nothing to give and we give all that we can—I mean if we give in the spirit of these words: "Thy will be done; as in Heaven, so on earth."

Thou didst well, O our good Master, to make this last petition, so that we may be able to accomplish what Thou dost promise in our name. For truly, Lord, hadst Thou not done this, I do not think it would have been possible *for us to accomplish it*. But, since Thy Father does what Thou askest Him in granting us His Kingdom on earth, I know that we can truly fulfil Thy word by giving what Thou dost promise in our name. For since my earth has now become Heaven, it will be possible for Thy will to be done in me. Otherwise, on an earth so wretched as mine, and so barren of fruit, I know not, Lord, how it could be possible. It is a great thing that Thou dost offer.

When I think of this, it amuses me that there should be people who dare not ask the Lord for trials, thinking that His sending them to them depends upon their asking for them! I am not referring to those who omit to ask for them out of humility because they think themselves to be incapable of bearing them, though for my own part I believe that He who gives them love enough to ask for such a stern method of proving it will give them love enough to endure it. I should like to ask those who are afraid to pray for trials lest they should at once be given them what they mean when they beg the Lord to fulfil His will in them. Do they say this because everyone else says it and not because they want it to be done? That would not be right, sisters. Remember that the good Jesus is our Ambassador here, and that His desire has been to mediate between us and His Father at no small cost to Himself: it would not be right for us to refuse to give what He *promises and* offers on our behalf or to say nothing about it. Let me put it in another way. Consider, daughters, that, whether we wish it or no, God's will must be done, and must be done both in Heaven and on earth. Believe me, then, do as I suggest and make a virtue of necessity.

O my Lord, what a great comfort it is to me that Thou didst not entrust the fulfilment of Thy will to one so wretched as I! Blessed be Thou for ever and let all things praise Thee. May Thy name be for ever glorified. I should indeed have had to be good, Lord, if the fulfilment or non-fulfilment of Thy will [in Heaven and on earth] were in my hands. But as it is, though my will is not yet free from self-interest, I give it to Thee freely. For I have proved, by long experience, how much

I gain by leaving it freely in Thy hands. O friends, what a great gain is this—and how much we lose through not fulfilling our promises to the Lord in the Paternoster, and giving Him what we offer Him!

Before I tell you in what this gain consists, I will explain to you how much you are offering, lest later you should exclaim that you had been deceived and had not understood what you were saying. Do not behave like some religious among us, who do nothing but promise, and then excuse ourselves for not fulfilling our promises by saying that we had not understood what we were promising. That may well be true, *for it is easy to say things and hard to put them into practice, and anyone who thought that there was no more in the one than in the other certainly did not understand.* It seems very easy to say that we will surrender our will to someone, until we try it and realize that it is the hardest thing we can do if we carry it out as we should. Our superiors do not always treat us strictly when they see we are weak; and sometimes they treat both weak and strong in the same way. That is not so with the Lord; He knows what each of us can bear, and, when He sees that one of us is strong, He does not hesitate to fulfil His will in him.

So I want you to realize with Whom (as they say) you are dealing and what the good Jesus offers on your behalf to the Father, and what you are giving Him when you pray that His will may be done in you: it is nothing else than this that you are praying for. Do not fear that He will give you riches or pleasures or *great* honours or any such earthly things; His love for you is not so poor as that. And He sets a very high value on what you give Him and desires to recompense you for it since He gives you His Kingdom while you are still alive. Would you like to see how He treats those who make this prayer from their hearts? Ask His glorious Son, Who made it thus in the Garden. Think with what resolution and fullness of desire He prayed; and consider if the will of God was not perfectly fulfilled in Him through the trials, sufferings, insults and persecutions which He gave Him, until at last His life ended with death on a Cross.

So you see, daughters, what God gave to His best Beloved, and from that you can understand what His will is. These, then, are His gifts in this world. He gives them in proportion to the love which He bears us.

He gives more to those whom He loves most, and less to those He loves least; and He gives in accordance with the courage which He sees that each of us has and the love we bear to His Majesty. When He sees a soul who loves Him greatly, He knows that soul can suffer much for Him, whereas one who loves Him little will suffer little. For my own part, I believe that love is the measure of our ability to bear crosses, whether great or small. So if you have this love, sisters, try not to let the prayers you make to so great a Lord be words of mere politeness but brace yourselves to suffer what His Majesty desires. For if you give Him your will in any other way, you are just showing Him a jewel, making as if to give it to Him and begging Him to take it, and then, when He puts out His hand to do so, taking it back and holding on to it tightly.

Such mockery is no fit treatment for One who endured so much for us. If for no other reason than this, it would not be right to mock Him so often—and it is by no means seldom that we say these words to Him in the Paternoster. Let us give Him once and for all the jewel which we have so often undertaken to give Him. For the truth is that He gives it to us first so that we may give it back to Him. *Ah, my God! How well Jesus knows us and how much He thinks of our good! He did not say we must surrender our wills to the Lord until we had been well paid for this small service. It will be realized from this how much the Lord intends us to gain by rendering it to Him: even in this life He begins to reward us for this, as I shall presently explain.* Worldly people will do a great deal if they sincerely resolve to fulfil the will of God. But you, daughters, must both say and act, and give Him both words and deeds, as I really think we religious do. Yet sometimes not only do we undertake to give God the jewel but we even put it into His hand and then take it back again. We are so generous all of a sudden, and then we become so mean, that it would have been better if we had stopped to think before giving.

The aim of all my advice to you in this book is that we should surrender ourselves wholly to the Creator, place our will in His hands and detach ourselves from the creatures. As you will already have understood how important this is, I will say no more about it, but I will tell you why our good Master puts these words here. He knows how much we shall gain by rendering this service to His Eternal Father. We are preparing ourselves for the time, which will come very soon, when we shall find ourselves at the end of our journey and shall be drinking of living water from the fountain I have described. Unless we make a total surrender of our will to the Lord, *and put ourselves in His hands* so that He may do in all things what is best for us in accordance with His will, He will never allow us to drink of it. This is the perfect contemplation of which you asked me to write to you.

In this matter, as I have already said, we can do nothing of ourselves, either by working hard or by making plans, nor is it needful that we should. For everything else hinders and prevents us from saying [with real resolution], "Fiat voluntas tua": that is, may the Lord fulfil His will in me, in every way and manner which Thou, my Lord, desirest. If Thou wilt do this by means of trials, give me strength and let them come. If by means of persecutions and sickness and dishonour and need, here I am, my Father, I will not turn my face away from Thee nor have I the right to turn my back upon them. For Thy Son gave Thee this will of mine in the name of us all and it is not right that I for my part should fail. Do Thou grant me the grace of bestowing on me Thy Kingdom so that I may do Thy will, since He has asked this of me. Dispose of me as of that which is Thine own, in accordance with Thy will.

Oh, my sisters, what power this gift has! If it be made with due resolution, it cannot fail to draw the Almighty to become one with our lowliness and to transform us into Himself and to effect a union between the Creator and the creature. Ask yourselves if that will not be a rich reward for you, and if you have not a good Master. For, knowing how the good will of His Father is to be gained, He teaches us how and by what means we must serve Him.

The more *resolute we are in soul and the more* we show Him by our actions that the words we use to Him are not words of mere politeness, the more and more does Our Lord draw us to Himself and raise us above all *petty* earthly things, and above ourselves, in order to prepare us to receive great favours *from Him,* for His rewards for our service will not end with this life. So much does He value this service of ours that we do not know for what more we can ask, while His Majesty never wearies of giving. Not content with having made this soul one with Himself, through uniting it to Himself, He begins to cherish it, to reveal secrets to it, to rejoice in its understanding of what it has gained and in the knowledge which it has of all He has yet to give it. He causes it gradually to lose its exterior senses so that nothing may occupy it. This we call rapture. He begins to make such a friend of the soul that not only does He restore its will to it but He gives it His own also. For, now that He is making a friend of it, He is glad to allow it to rule with Him, as we say, turn and turn about. So He does what the soul asks of Him, just as the soul does what He commands, only in a much better way, since He is all-powerful and can do whatever He desires, and His desire never comes to an end.

But the poor soul, despite its desires, is *often* unable to do all it would like, nor can it do anything at all unless it is given the power.[116] And so it grows richer and richer; and the more it serves, the greater becomes its debt; and often, growing weary of finding itself subjected to all the inconveniences and impediments and bonds which it has to endure while it is in the prison of this body, it would gladly pay something of what it owes, for it is quite worn out. But even if we do all that is in us, how can we repay God, since, as I say, we have nothing to give save what we have first received? We can only learn to know ourselves and do what we can—namely, surrender our will and fulfil God's will in us. Anything else must be a hindrance to the soul which the Lord has brought to this state. It causes it, not profit, but harm, for nothing but humility is of any use here, and this is not acquired by the understanding but by a clear perception of the truth, which comprehends in one moment what could not be attained over a long period by the labour of the imagination—namely, that we are nothing and that God is infinitely great.

I will give you one piece of advice: do not suppose that you can reach this state by your own effort or diligence; that would be too much to expect. On the contrary, you would turn what devotion you had quite cold. You must practise simplicity and humility, for those are the virtues which achieve everything. You must say: "Fiat voluntas tua."

CHAPTER THIRTY-THREE

Treats of our great need that the Lord should give us what we ask in these words of the Paternoster: "Panem nostrum quotidianum da nobis hodie."[117]

The good Jesus understands, as I have said, how difficult a thing He is offering on our behalf, for He knows our weakness, and how often we show that we do not understand what the will of the Lord is, since we are weak while He is so merciful. He knows that some means must be found by which we shall not omit to give what He has given on our behalf, for if we did that it would be anything but good for us, since everything we gain comes from what we give. Yet He knows that it will be difficult for us to carry this out; for if anyone were to tell some wealthy, pampered person that it is God's will for him to moderate his eating so that others, who are dying of hunger, shall have at least bread to eat, he will discover a thousand reasons for not understanding this but interpreting it in his own way. If one tells a person who speaks ill of others that it is God's will that he should love his neighbour as himself,[118] he will lose patience and no amount of reasoning will convince him. If one tells a religious who is accustomed to liberty and indulgence that he must be careful to set a good example and to remember that when he makes this petition it is his duty to keep what he has sworn and promised, and that not in word alone; that it is the will of God that he should fulfil his vows and see that he gives no occasion for scandal by acting contrarily to them, even though he may not actually break them; that he has taken the vow of poverty and must keep it without evasions, because that is the Lord's will—it would be impossible, in spite of all this, that some religious should not still want their own way. What would be the case, then, if the Lord had not done most of what was necessary by means of the remedy He has given us? There would have been very few who could have fulfilled this petition, which the Lord made to the Father on our behalf: "Fiat voluntas tua." Seeing our need, therefore, the good Jesus has sought the admirable means whereby He has shown us the extreme love which He has for us, and in His own name and in that of His brethren He has made this petition: "Give us, Lord, this day our daily bread."

For the love of God, sisters, let us realize the meaning of our good Master's petition, for our very life depends on our not disregarding it. Set very little store by what you have given, since there is so much that you will receive. It seems to me, in the absence of a better opinion, that the good Jesus knew what He had given for us and how important it was for us to give this to God, and yet how difficult it would be for us to do so, as has been said, because of our natural inclination to base things and our want of love and courage. He saw that, before we could be aroused, we needed His aid, not once but every day, and it must have been for this reason that He resolved to remain with us. As this was so weighty and important a matter, He wished it to come from the hand of the Eternal Father. Though both Father and Son are one and the same, and He knew that whatever He did on earth God would do in Heaven, and would consider it good, since His will and the Father's will were one, yet the humility of the good Jesus was such that He wanted, as it were, to ask leave of His Father, for He knew that He was His beloved Son and that He was well pleased with Him. He knew quite well that in this petition He was asking for more than He had asked for in the others, but He already knew what death He was to suffer and what dishonours and affronts He would have to bear.

What father could there be, Lord, who, after giving us his son, and such a Son, would allow Him to remain among us day by day to suffer as He had done already? None, Lord, in truth, but Thine: well dost Thou know of Whom Thou art asking this. God help me! What a great love is that of the Son and what a great love is that of the Father! I am not so much amazed at the good Jesus, because, as He had already said "Fiat voluntas tua," He was bound, being Who He is, to put what He had said into practice. Yes, for He is not like us; knowing that He was carrying out His words by loving us as He loves Himself, He went about seeking how He could carry out this commandment more perfectly, even at His own cost. But how, Eternal Father, couldst Thou consent to this? How canst Thou see Thy Son every day in such wicked hands? Since first Thou didst permit it and consent to it, Thou seest how He has been treated. How can Thy Mercy, day by day and every day,[119] see Him affronted? And how many affronts are being offered to-day to this Most Holy Sacrament? How often must the Father see Him in the hands of His enemies? What desecrations these heretics commit!

O Eternal Lord! How canst Thou grant such a petition? How canst Thou consent to it? Consider not His love, which, for the sake of fulfilling Thy will and of helping us, would allow Him to submit day by day to being cut to pieces. It is for Thee to see to this, my Lord, since Thy Son allows no obstacle to stand in His way. Why must all the blessings that we receive be at His cost? How is it that He is silent in face of all, and cannot speak for Himself, but only for us? Is there none who will speak for this most loving Lamb? *Give me permission to speak for Him, Lord, since Thou hast been pleased to leave Him in our power, and let me beseech Thee on His behalf, since He gave Thee such full obedience and surrendered Himself to us with such great love.*

I have been reflecting how in this petition alone the same words are repeated: first of all the Lord speaks of "our daily bread" and asks Thee to give it, and then He says: "Give it us to-day, Lord."[120] He lays the matter before His Father in this way: the Father gave us His Son once and for all to die for us, and thus He is our own; yet He does not want the gift to be taken from us until the end of the world but would have it left to be a help to us every day. Let this melt your hearts, my daughters, and make you love your Spouse, for there is no slave who would willingly call himself by that name, yet the good Jesus seems to think it an honour.

O Eternal Father, how great is the merit of this humility! With what a treasure are we purchasing Thy Son! How to sell Him we already know, for He was sold for thirty pieces of silver; but, if we would purchase Him, no price is sufficient. Being made one with us through the portion of our nature which is His, and being Lord of His own will, He reminds His Father that, as our nature is His, He is able to give it to us, and thus He says "our bread." He makes no difference between Himself and us, though we make one between ourselves and Him through not giving ourselves daily for His Majesty's sake.

CHAPTER THIRTY-FOUR

We have now reached the conclusion that the good Jesus, being ours,
asks His Father to let us have Him daily—which appears to
mean "for ever." *While writing this I have been wondering
why, after saying "our 'daily' bread," the Lord repeated the idea in the
words "Give us this day, Lord." I will tell you my own foolish idea: if it
really is foolish, well and good—in any case, it is quite bad enough that I should
interfere in such a matter at all. Still, as we are trying to understand what we are
praying for, let us think carefully what this means, so that we may pray rightly,
and thank Him Who is taking such care about teaching us.* This bread, then, is
ours daily, it seems to me, because we have Him here on earth, *since He
has remained with us here and we receive Him;* and, if we profit by His
company, we shall also have Him in Heaven, for the only reason He
remains with us is to help and encourage and sustain us so that we shall
do that will, which, as we have said, is to be fulfilled in us.

In using the words "this day" He seems to me to be *thinking of a day
of the length of this life.* And a day indeed it is! As for the unfortunate souls

who *will* bring damnation upon themselves and will not have fruition of Him in the world to come, *they are His own creatures, and He did everything to help them on, and was with them, to strengthen them, throughout the "to-day" of this life, so* it is not His fault if they are vanquished. They will have no excuse to make nor will they be able to complain of the Father for taking this bread from them at the time when they most needed it. Therefore the Son prays the Father that, since this life lasts no more than a day, He will allow Him to spend it in our service.[121] As His Majesty has already given His Son to us, by sending Him, of His will alone, into the world, so now, of that same will, He is pleased not to abandon us, but to remain here with us for the greater glory of His friends and the discomfiture of His enemies. He prays for nothing more than this "to-day" since He has given us this most holy Bread. He has given it to us for ever, as I have said, as the sustenance and manna of humanity. We can have it whenever we please and we shall not die of hunger save through our own fault, for, in whatever way the soul desires to partake of food, it will find joy and comfort in the Most Holy Sacrament. There is no need or trial or persecution that cannot be easily borne if we begin to *partake and* taste of those which He Himself bore, *and to make them the subject of our meditations.*

With regard to other bread[122]—*the bread of bodily necessaries and sustenance— I neither like to think that the Lord is always being reminded of it nor would I have you remember it yourselves. Keep on the level of the highest contemplation, for anyone who dwells there no more remembers that he is in the world than if he had already left it—still less does he think about food. Would the Lord ever have insisted upon our asking for food, or taught us to do so by His own example? Not in my opinion. He teaches us to fix our desires upon heavenly things and to pray that we may begin to enjoy these things while here on earth: would He, then, have us trouble about so petty a matter as praying for food? As if He did not know that, once we begin to worry about the needs of the body, we shall forget the needs of the soul! Besides, are we such moderately minded people that we shall be satisfied with just a little and pray only for a little? No: the more food we are given, the less we shall get of the water from Heaven. Let those of you, daughters, who want more of the necessaries of life pray for this.*

Join with the Lord, then, daughters, in begging the Father to let you have your Spouse to-day, so that, *as long as you live,* you may never find yourself in this world without Him. Let it suffice to temper your great joy that He should remain disguised beneath these accidents of bread and wine, which is a real torture to those who have nothing else to love and no other consolation. Entreat Him not to fail you but to prepare you to receive Him worthily.

As for that other bread, have no anxiety about it if you have truly resigned yourselves to God's will. I mean that at these hours of prayer you are dealing with more important matters and there is time enough for you to labour and earn your daily bread. Try never at any time to let your thoughts dwell on this; work with your body, for it is good for you to try to support yourselves, but let your soul be at rest. Leave anxiety about this to your Spouse, as has been said at length already, and He will always bear it for you. *Do not fear that He will fail you if you do not fail to do what you have promised and to resign yourselves to God's will. I assure you, daughters, that, if I myself were to fail in this, because of my wickedness, as I have often done in the past, I would not beg Him to give me that bread, or anything else to eat. Let Him leave me to die of hunger. Of what use is life to me if it leads me daily nearer to eternal death?*

If, then, you are really surrendering yourselves to God, as you say, cease to be anxious for yourselves, for He bears your anxiety, and will bear it always. It is as though a servant had gone into service and were anxious to please his master in everything. The master is bound to give him food for so long as he remains in his house, and in his service, unless he is so poor that he has food neither for his servant nor for himself. Here, however, the comparison breaks down, for God is, and will always be, rich and powerful. It would not be right for the servant to go to his master *every day* and ask him for food when he knew that his master would see that it was given him and so he would be sure to receive it. *To do this would be a waste of words.* His master would quite properly tell him that he should look after his own business of serving and pleasing him, for, if he worried himself unnecessarily, he would not do his work as well as he should. So, sisters, those who will may worry about asking for earthly

245

bread; let our own task be to beg the Eternal Father that we may merit our heavenly bread, so that, although our bodily eyes cannot feast themselves on the sight of Him since He is thus hidden from us, He may reveal Himself to the eyes of the soul and may make Himself known to us as another kind of food, full of delight and joy, which sustains our life.

Do you suppose that this most holy food is not *ample* sustenance even for the body and a potent medicine for bodily ills? I am sure that it is. I know a person who was subject to serious illnesses and often suffered great pain; and this pain was taken away from her in a flash[123] and she became quite well again. This often occurs, I believe; and cures are recorded from quite definite illnesses which could not be counterfeited. As the wondrous effects produced by this most holy bread in those who worthily receive it are very well known, I will not describe all the things that could be related about this person I mentioned, though I have been enabled to learn about them and I know that they are not fabrications. The Lord had given this person such a lively faith that, when she heard people say they wished they had lived when Christ walked on this earth, she would smile to herself, for she knew that we have Him as truly with us in the Most Holy Sacrament as people had Him then, and wonder what more they could possibly want.

I know, too, that for many years this person, though by no means perfect, always tried to strengthen her faith, when she communicated, by thinking that it was exactly as if she saw the Lord entering her house, with her own bodily eyes, for she believed in very truth that this Lord was entering her poor abode, and she ceased, as far as she could, to think of outward things, and went into her abode with Him. She tried to recollect her senses so that they might all become aware of this great blessing, or rather, so that they should not hinder the soul from becoming conscious of it. She imagined herself at His feet and wept with the Magdalen exactly as if she had seen Him with her bodily eyes in the Pharisee's house. Even if she felt no devotion, faith told her that it was good for her to be there.

For, unless we want to be foolish and to close our minds to facts, we cannot suppose that this is the work of the imagination, as it is when we think of the Lord on the Cross, or of other incidents of the Passion, and picture within ourselves how these things happened. This is something which is happening now; it is absolutely true; and we have no need to go and seek Him somewhere a long way off. For we know that, until the accidents of bread have been consumed by our natural heat, the good Jesus is with us and we should [not lose so good an opportunity but should] come to Him. If, while He went about in the world, the sick were healed merely by touching His clothes, how can we doubt that He will work miracles when He is within us, if we have faith, or that He will give us what we ask of Him since He is in our house? His Majesty is not wont to offer us too little payment for His lodging if we treat Him well.

If you grieve at not seeing Him with the eyes of the body, remember that that would not be good for us, for it is one thing to see Him glorified and quite another to see Him as He was when He lived in the world. So weak is our nature that nobody could endure the sight—in fact, there would be no one left to endure it, for no one would wish to remain in the world any longer. Once having seen this Eternal Truth, people would realize that all the things we prize here are mockery and falsehood. And if such great Majesty could be seen, how could a miserable sinner like myself, after having so greatly offended Him, remain so near to Him? Beneath those accidents of bread, we can approach Him; for, if the King disguises Himself, it would seem that we need not mind coming to Him without so much circumspection and ceremony: by disguising Himself, He has, as it were, obliged Himself to submit to this. Who, otherwise, would dare to approach Him so unworthily, with so many imperfections and with such lukewarm zeal?

Oh, we know not what we ask! How much better does His Wisdom know what we need! He reveals Himself to those who He knows will profit by His presence; though unseen by bodily eyes, He has many ways of revealing Himself to the soul through deep inward emotions and by various other means. Delight to remain with Him; do not lose such an excellent time for talking with Him as the hour after Communion. *Remember that this is a very profitable hour for the soul; if you spend it in the company of the good Jesus, you are doing Him a great service. Be very careful, then, daughters, not to lose it.* If you are compelled by obedience to do something else, try to leave your soul with the Lord. *For He is your Master, and, though it be in a way you may not understand, He will not fail to teach you.* But if you take your thoughts elsewhere, and pay no *more* attention to Him *than if you had not received Him,* and care nothing for His being within you, how can He make Himself known to you? *You must complain, not of Him, but of yourself.* This, then, is a good time for our Master to teach us and for us to listen to Him. *I do not tell you to say no prayers at all, for if I did you would take hold of my words and say I was talking about contemplation, which you need practise only if the Lord brings you to it. No: you should say the Paternoster, realize that you are verily and indeed in the company of Him Who taught it you* and kiss His feet in gratitude to Him for having desired to teach you and beg Him *to show you how to pray and* never to leave you.

You may be in the habit of praying while looking at a picture of Christ, but *at a time like this* it seems foolish to me to turn away from *the living image*—the Person Himself—to look at His picture. Would it not be foolish if we had a portrait of someone whom we dearly loved and, when the person himself came to see us, we refused to talk with him and carried on our entire conversation with the portrait? Do you know when I find the use of a picture an excellent thing, and take great pleasure in it? When the person is absent and we are made to feel his loss by our great aridity, it is then that we find it a great comfort to look at the picture of Him Whom we have such reason to love. *This is a great inspiration,* and *makes us* wish that, in whichever direction we turn our eyes, we could see the picture. What can we look upon that is better or more attractive to the sight than upon Him Who so dearly loves us and contains within Himself all good things? Unhappy are those heretics, who through their own fault have lost this comfort, as well as others.

When you have received the Lord, and are in His very presence, try to shut the bodily eyes and to open the eyes of the soul and to look into your own hearts. I tell you, and tell you again, for I should like to repeat it often, that if you practise this habit *of staying with Him, not just once or twice, but* whenever you communicate, and strive to keep your conscience clear so that you can often rejoice in this your Good, He will not, as I have said, come so much disguised as to be unable to make His presence known to you in many ways, according to the desire which you have of seeing Him. So great, indeed, may be your longing for Him that He will reveal Himself to you wholly.

But if we pay no heed to Him save when we have received Him, and go away from Him in search of other and baser things, what can He do? Will He have to drag us by force to look at Him *and be with Him* because He desires to reveal Himself to us? No; for when He revealed Himself to all men plainly, and told them clearly who He was, they did not treat Him at all well—very few of them, indeed, even believed Him. So He grants us an exceeding great favour when He is pleased to show us that it is He Who is in the Most Holy Sacrament. But He will not reveal Himself openly and communicate His glories and bestow His treasures save on those who He knows greatly desire Him, for these are His true friends. I assure you that anyone who is not a true friend and does not come to receive Him as such, after doing all in his power to prepare for Him, must never importune Him to reveal Himself to him. Hardly is the hour over which such a person has spent in fulfilling the Church's commandment than he goes home and tries to drive Christ out of the house. What with all his other business and occupations and worldly hindrances, he seems to be making all possible haste to prevent the Lord from taking possession of the house which is His own.

CHAPTER THIRTY-FIVE

Describes the recollection which should be practised after Communion. Concludes this subject with an exclamatory prayer to the Eternal Father.

I have written at length about this, although, when writing of the Prayer of Recollection, I spoke of the great importance of our entering into solitude with God. When you hear Mass without communicating, daughters, you may communicate spiritually, which is extremely profitable, and afterwards you may practise inward recollection in exactly the same way, for this impresses upon us a deep love of the Lord. If we prepare to receive Him, He never fails to give, and He gives in many ways that we cannot understand. It is as if we were to approach a fire: it might be a very large one, but, if we remained a long way from it and covered our hands, we should get little warmth from it, although we should be warmer than if we were in a place where there was no fire at all. But when we try to approach the Lord there is this difference: if the soul is properly disposed, and comes with the intention of driving out the cold, and stays for some time where it is, it will retain its warmth for several hours, *and if any little spark flies out, it will set it on fire.*

It is of such importance, daughters, for us to prepare ourselves in this way that you must not be surprised if I often repeat this counsel. If at first you do not get on with this practice (which may happen, for the devil will try to oppress and distress your heart, knowing what great harm he can do in this way), the devil will make you think that you can find more devotion in other things and less in this. But [trust me and] do not give up this method, for the Lord will use it to prove your love for Him. Remember that there are few souls who stay with Him and follow Him in His trials; let us endure something for Him and His Majesty will repay us. Remember, too, that there are actually people who not only have no wish to be with Him but who insult Him and *with great irreverence drive Him away from their homes.* We must endure something, therefore, to show Him that we have the desire to see Him. *In many places He is neglected and ill-treated, but* He suffers everything, and will continue to do so, if He finds but one single soul which will receive Him and love to have Him as its Guest.[124] Let this soul be yours, then, for, if there were none, the Eternal Father would rightly refuse to allow Him to remain with us. Yet the Lord is so good a Friend to those who are His friends, and so good a Master to those who are His servants, that, when He knows it to be the will of His Beloved Son, He will not hinder Him in so excellent a work, in which His Son so fully reveals the love which He has for His Father, *as this wonderful way which He seeks of showing how much He loves us and of helping us to bear our trials.*

Since, then, Holy Father, Who art in the Heavens, Thou dost will and accept this (and it is clear that Thou couldst not deny us a thing which is so good for us) there must be someone, as I said at the beginning, who will speak for Thy Son, for He has never defended Himself. Let this be the task for us, daughters, though, having regard to what we are, it is presumptuous of us to undertake it. Let us rely, however, on Our Lord's command to us to pray to Him, and, in fulfilment of our obedience to Him, let us beseech His Majesty, in the name of the good Jesus, that, as He has left nothing undone that He could do for us in granting sinners so great a favour, He may be pleased of His mercy to prevent Him from being so ill-treated. Since His Holy Son has given us this excellent way in which we can offer Him up frequently as a sacrifice, let us make use of this precious gift so that it may stay the advance of such terrible evil and irreverence as in many places is paid to this Most Holy Sacrament. For these Lutherans *seem to want to drive Him out of the world again: they* destroy churches, cause the loss of many priests and abolish the sacraments.[125] *And there is something of this even among Christians, who sometimes go to church meaning to offend Him rather than to worship Him.*

Why is this, my Lord and my God? Do Thou bring the world to an end or give us a remedy for such grievous wrongs, which even our wicked hearts cannot endure. I beseech Thee, Eternal Father, endure it no longer: quench this fire, Lord, for Thou canst do so if Thou wilt. Remember that Thy Son is still in the world; may these dreadful things be stopped out of respect for Him, horrible and abominable and foul as they are. With His beauty and purity He does not deserve to be in a house where such things happen. Do this, Lord, not for our sake, for we do not deserve it, but for the sake of Thy Son. We dare not entreat Thee that He should no longer stay with us, *for Thou hast granted His prayer to Thee to leave Him with us for to-day—that is, until the end of the world.* If He were to go, what would become of us? *It would be the end of everything.* If anything can placate Thee it is to have on earth such a pledge as this. Since some remedy must be found for this, then, my Lord, I beg Thy Majesty to apply it. *For if Thou wilt, Thou art able.*

O my God, if only I could indeed importune Thee! If only I had served Thee well so that I might be able to beg of Thee this great favour as a reward for my services, for Thou leavest no service unrewarded! But I have not served Thee, Lord; indeed, it may perhaps be for my sins, and because I have so greatly offended Thee, that so many evils come. What, then, can I do, my Creator, but present to Thee this most holy Bread, which, though Thou gavest it to us, I return to Thee, beseeching Thee, by the merits of Thy Son, to grant me this favour, which on so many counts He has merited? Do Thou, Lord, calm this sea, and no longer allow this ship, which is Thy Church, to endure so great a tempest. Save us, my Lord, for we perish.[126]

CHAPTER THIRTY-SIX

Treats of these words in the Paternoster: "Dimitte nobis debita nostra."[127]

O ur good Master sees that, if we have this heavenly food, everything is easy for us, except when we are ourselves to blame, and that we are well able to fulfil our undertaking to the Father that His will shall be done in us. So He now asks Him to forgive us our debts, as we ourselves forgive others. Thus, continuing the prayer which He is teaching us, He says these words: "And forgive us, Lord, our debts, even as we forgive them to our debtors."

Notice, sisters, that He does not say: "as we shall forgive." We are to understand that anyone who asks for so great a gift as that just mentioned, and has already yielded his own will to the will of God, must have done this already. And so He says: "as we forgive our debtors." Anyone, then, who sincerely repeats this petition, "Fiat voluntas tua," must, at least in intention, have done this already. You see now why the saints rejoiced in insults and persecutions: it was because these gave them something to present to the Lord when they prayed to Him. What can a poor creature like myself do, who has had so little to forgive others and has so much to be forgiven herself? This, sisters, is something which we should consider carefully; it is such a serious and important matter that God should pardon us our sins, which have merited eternal fire, that we must pardon all trifling things which have been done to us *and which are not wrongs at all, or anything else. For how is it possible, either in word or in deed, to wrong one who, like myself, has deserved to be plagued by devils for ever? Is it not only right that I should be plagued*[128] *in this world too?* As I have so few, Lord, even of these trifling things, to offer Thee, Thy pardoning of me must be a free gift: there is abundant scope here for Thy mercy. *Thy Son must pardon me, for no one has done me any injustice, and so there has been nothing that I can pardon for Thy sake. But take my desire to do so, Lord, for I believe I would forgive any wrong if Thou wouldst forgive me and I might unconditionally do Thy will. True, if the occasion were to arise, and I were condemned without cause, I do not know what I should do. But at this moment I see that I am so guilty in Thy sight that everything I might have to suffer would fall short of my deserts, though anyone not knowing, as Thou knowest, what I am, would think I was being wronged.* Blessed be Thou, Who endurest one that is so poor: when Thy *most holy* Son makes this petition in the name of all mankind, I cannot be included, being such as I am and having nothing to give.

And supposing, my Lord, that there are others who are like myself but have not realized that this is so? If there are any such, I beg them, in Thy name, to remember this truth, and to pay no heed to little things about which they think they are being slighted, for, if they insist on these nice points of honour, they become like children building houses of straw. Oh, God help me, sisters! If we only knew what honour really is and what is meant by losing it! I am not speaking now about ourselves, for it would indeed be a bad business if we did not understand this; I am speaking of myself as I was when I prided myself on my honour without knowing what honour meant; I just followed the example of others. Oh, how easily I used to feel slighted! I am ashamed to think of it now; and I was not one of those who worried most about such things either. But I never grasped the essence of the matter, because I neither thought nor troubled about true honour, which it is good for us to have because it profits the soul. How truly has someone said: "Honour and profit cannot go together." I do not know if this was what that person was thinking of when he said it; but it is literally true, for the soul's profit and what the world calls honour can never be reconciled. Really, the topsy-turviness of the world is terrible. Blessed be the Lord for taking us out of it! *May His Majesty grant that this house shall always be as far from it as it is now! God preserve us from religious houses where they worry about points of honour! Such places never do much honour to God.*

God help us, how absurd it is for religious to connect their honour with things so trifling that they amaze me! You know nothing about this, sisters, but I will tell you about it so that you may be wary. You see, sisters, the devil has not forgotten us. He has invented honours of his own for religious houses and has made laws by which we go up and down in rank, as people do in the world. Learned men have to observe this with regard to their studies (a matter of which I know nothing): anyone, for example, who has got as far as reading theology must not descend and read philosophy—that is their kind of honour, according to which you must always be going up and never going down. Even if someone were commanded by obedience to take a step down, he would *in his own mind* consider himself slighted; and then someone would take his part [and say] it was an insult; next, the devil would discover reasons for this—and he seems to be an authority even in God's own law. Why, among ourselves, anyone who has been a prioress is thereby incapacitated from holding any lower office *for the rest of her life.* We must defer to the senior among us, and we are not allowed to forget it either: sometimes it would appear to be a positive merit for us to do this, because it is a rule of the Order.

The thing is enough to make one laugh—or, it would be more proper to say, to make one weep. After all, the Order does not command us not to be humble: it commands us to do everything in due form. And in matters which concern my own esteem I ought not to be so formal as to insist that this detail of our Rule shall be kept as strictly as the rest, which we may in fact be observing very imperfectly. We must not put all our effort into observing just this one detail: let my interests be looked after by others—I will forget about myself altogether. The fact is, although we shall never rise as far as Heaven in this way, we are attracted by the thought of rising higher, and we dislike climbing down. O, Lord, Lord, art Thou our Example and our Master? Yes, indeed. And wherein did Thy honour consist, O Lord, Who hast honoured us?[129] Didst Thou perchance lose it when Thou wert humbled even to death? No, Lord, rather didst Thou gain it for all.

For the love of God, sisters! We have lost our way; we have taken the wrong path from the very beginning. God grant that no soul be lost through its attention to these wretched niceties about honour, when it has no idea wherein honour consists. We shall get to the point of thinking that we have done something wonderful because we have forgiven a person for some trifling thing, which was neither a slight nor an insult nor anything else. Then we shall ask the Lord to forgive us as people who have done something important, just because we have forgiven someone. Grant us, my God, to understand how little we understand ourselves and how empty our hands are when we come to Thee that Thou, of Thy mercy, mayest forgive us. For in truth, Lord, since all things have an end and punishment is eternal, I can see nothing meritorious which I may present to Thee that Thou mayest grant us so great a favour. Do it, then, for the sake of Him Who asks it of Thee, *and Who may well do so, for He is always being wronged and offended.*

How greatly the Lord must esteem this mutual love of ours one for another! *For, having given Him our wills, we have given Him complete rights over us, and we cannot do that without love. See, then, sisters, how important it is for us to love one another and to be at peace.* The good Jesus might have put everything else before our love for one another, and said: "Forgive us, Lord, because we are doing a great deal of penance, or because we are praying often, and fasting, and because we have left all for Thy sake and love Thee greatly." But He has never said: "Because we would lose our lives for Thy sake"; or any of these [numerous] other things which He might have said. He simply says: "Because we forgive." Perhaps *the reason He said this rather than anything else* was because He knew that our fondness for this dreadful honour made mutual love the hardest virtue for us to attain, though it is the virtue dearest to His Father. *Because of its very difficulty* He put it where He did, and *after having asked for so many great gifts for us,* He offers it on our behalf to God.

Note particularly, sisters, that He says: "As we forgive." As I have said, He takes this for granted. And observe especially with regard to it that unless, after experiencing the favours granted by God in the prayer that I have called perfect contemplation, a person is very resolute, and makes a point, if the occasion arises, of forgiving, not [only] these mere nothings which people call wrongs, but any wrong, however grave, you need not think much of that person's prayer.[130] For wrongs have no effect upon a soul whom God draws to Himself in such sublime prayer as this, nor does it care if it is highly esteemed or no. That is not quite correct: it does care, for honour distresses much more than dishonour and it prefers trials to a great deal of rest and ease. For anyone to whom the Lord has really given His Kingdom no longer wants a kingdom in this world, knowing that he is going the right way to reign in a much more exalted manner, and having already discovered by experience what great benefits the soul gains and what progress it makes when it suffers for God's sake. For only very rarely does His Majesty grant it such great consolations, and then only to those who have willingly borne many trials for His sake. For contemplatives, as I have said elsewhere in this book, have to bear heavy trials, and therefore the Lord seeks out for Himself souls of great experience.

Understand, then, sisters, that as these persons have already learned to rate everything at its proper valuation, they pay little attention to things which pass away. A great wrong, or a great trial, may cause them some momentary distress, but they will hardly have felt it when reason will intervene, and will seem to raise its standard aloft, and drive away their distress by giving them the joy of seeing how God has entrusted them with the opportunity of gaining, in a single day, more lasting favours and graces in His Majesty's sight than they could gain in ten years by means of trials which they sought on their own account. This, as I understand (and I have talked about it with many contemplatives), is quite usual, and I know for a fact that it happens. Just as other people prize gold and jewels, so these persons prize and desire trials, for they know quite well that trials will make them rich.

Such persons would never on any account esteem themselves: they want their sins to be known and like to speak about them to people who they see have any esteem for them. The same is true of their descent, which they know quite well will be of no advantage to them in the kingdom which has no end. If being of good birth were any satisfaction to them, it would be because this would enable them to serve God better. If they are not well born, it distresses them when people think them better than they are, and it causes them no distress to disabuse them, but only pleasure. The reason for this is that those to whom God grants the favour of possessing such humility and great love for Him forget themselves when there is a possibility of rendering Him greater services, and simply cannot believe that others are troubled by things which they themselves do not consider as wrongs at all.

These last effects which I have mentioned are produced in persons who have reached a high degree of perfection and to whom the Lord commonly grants the favour of uniting them to Himself by perfect contemplation. But the first of these effects—namely, the determination to suffer wrongs even though such suffering brings distress—is very quickly seen in anyone to whom the Lord has granted this grace of prayer as far as the stage of union. If these effects are not produced in a soul and it is not strengthened by prayer, you may take it that this was not Divine favour but indulgence and illusion coming from the devil, *which he makes us think to be good,* so that we may attach more importance to our honour.

It may be that, when the Lord first grants these favours, the soul will not immediately attain this fortitude. But, if He continues to grant them, He will soon give it fortitude—certainly, at least, as regards forgiveness, if not in the other virtues as well. I cannot believe that a soul which has approached so nearly to Mercy Itself, and has learned to know itself and the greatness of God's pardon, will not immediately and readily forgive, and be mollified and remain on good terms with a person who has done it wrong. For such a soul remembers the consolation and grace which He has shown it, in which it has recognized the signs of great love, and it is glad that the occasion presents itself for showing Him some love in return.

I repeat that I know many persons to whom Our Lord has granted the grace of raising them to supernatural experiences and of giving them this prayer, or contemplation, which has been described; and although I may notice other faults and imperfections in them, I have never seen such a person who had this particular fault, nor do I believe such a person exists, if the favours he has received are of God. If any one of you receives high favours, let her look within herself and see if they are producing these effects, and, if they are not, let her be very fearful, and believe that these consolations are not of God, Who, as I have said, when He visits the soul, always enriches it. That is certain; for, although the grace and the consolations may pass quickly, it can be recognized in due course through the benefits which it bestows on the soul. And, as the good Jesus knows this well, He gives a definite assurance to His Holy Father that we are forgiving our debtors.

CHAPTER THIRTY-SEVEN

Describes the excellence of this prayer called the Paternoster, and the many ways in which we shall find consolation in it.

The sublimity of the perfection of this evangelical prayer is something for which we should give great praise to the Lord. So well composed by the good Master was it, daughters, that each of us may use it in her own way. I am astounded when I consider that in its few words are enshrined all contemplation and perfection, so that if we study it no other book seems necessary. For thus far in the Paternoster the Lord has taught us the whole method of prayer and of high contemplation, from the very beginnings of mental prayer, to Quiet and Union. With so true a foundation to build upon, I could write a great book on prayer if only I knew how to express myself. As you have seen, Our Lord is beginning here to explain to us the effects which it produces, when the favours come from Him.

I have wondered why His Majesty did not expound such obscure and sublime subjects in greater detail so that we might all have understood them. It has occurred to me that, as this prayer was meant to be a general one for the use of all, so that everyone could interpret it as he thought right, ask for what he wanted and find comfort in doing so, He left the matter in doubt;[131] and thus contemplatives, who no longer desire earthly things, and persons greatly devoted to God, can ask for the heavenly favours which, through the great goodness of God, may be given to us on earth. Those who still live on earth, and must conform to the customs of their state, may also ask for the bread which they need for their own maintenance and for that of their households, as is perfectly just and right, and they may also ask for other things according as they need them.

(Blessed be His name for ever and ever. Amen. For His sake I entreat the Eternal Father to forgive my debts and grievous sins: though no one has wronged me, and I have therefore no one to forgive,[132] I have myself need for forgiveness every day. May He give me grace so that every day I may have some petition to lay before Him.)

The good Jesus, then, has taught us a sublime method of prayer, and begged that, in this our life of exile, we may be like the angels, if we endeavour, with our whole might, to make our actions conform to our words—in short, to be like the children of such a Father, and the brethren of such a Brother. His Majesty knows that if, as I say, our actions and our words are one, the Lord will unfailingly fulfil our petitions, give us His kingdom and help us by means of supernatural gifts, such as the Prayer of Quiet, perfect contemplation and all the other favours which the Lord bestows on our trifling efforts—and everything is trifling which we can achieve and gain by ourselves alone.

It must be realized, however, that these two things—surrendering our will to God and forgiving others—apply to all. True, some practise them more and some less, as has been said: those who are perfect will surrender their wills like the perfect souls they are and will forgive others with the perfection that has been described. For our own part, sisters, we will do what we can, and the Lord will accept it all. It is as if He were to make a kind of agreement on our behalf with His Eternal Father, and to say: "Do this, Lord, and My brethren shall do that." It is certain that He for His own part will not fail us. Oh, how well He pays us and how limitless are His rewards!

We may say this prayer only once, and yet in such a way that He will know that there is no duplicity about us and that we shall do what we say; and so He will leave us rich. We must never be insincere with Him, for He loves us, in all our dealings with Him, to be honest, and to treat Him frankly and openly, never saying one thing and meaning another; and then He will always give us more than we ask for. Our good Master knows that those who attain real perfection in their petitions will reach this high degree through the favours which the Father will grant them, and is aware that those who are already perfect, or who are on the way to perfection, do not and cannot fear, for they say they have trampled the world beneath their feet, and the Lord of the world is pleased with them. They will derive the greatest hope of His Majesty's pleasure from the effects which He produces in their souls; absorbed in these joys, they wish they were unable to remember that there is any other world at all, and that they have enemies.

O Eternal Wisdom! O good Teacher! What a wonderful thing it is, daughters, to have a wise and prudent Master who foresees our perils! This is the greatest blessing that the spiritual soul *still on earth* can desire, because it brings complete security. No words could ever exaggerate the importance of this. The Lord, then, saw it was necessary to awaken such souls and to remind them that they have enemies, and how much greater danger they are in if they are unprepared, and, since if they fall it will be from a greater height, how much more help they need from the Eternal Father. So, lest they should fail to realize their danger and suffer deception, He offers these petitions so necessary to us all while we live in this exile: "And lead us not, Lord, into temptation, but deliver us from evil."

CHAPTER THIRTY-EIGHT

Treats of the great need which we have to beseech the Eternal Father to grant us what we ask in these words: "Et ne nos inducas in tentationem, sed libera nos a malo."[133] *Explains certain temptations. This chapter is noteworthy.*

There are great things here for us to meditate upon, sisters, and to learn to understand as we pray. Remember I consider it quite certain that those who attain perfection do not ask the Lord to deliver them from trials, temptations, persecutions and conflicts—and that is another sure and striking sign that these favours and this contemplation which His Majesty gives them are coming from the Spirit of the Lord and are not illusions. For, as I said a little way back, perfect souls *are in no way repelled by trials, but rather* desire them and pray for them and love them. They are like soldiers: the more wars there are, the better they are pleased, because they hope to emerge from them with the greater riches.[134] If there are no wars, they serve for their pay, but they know they will not get very far on that.

Believe me, sisters, the soldiers of Christ—namely, those who experience contemplation and practise prayer—are always ready for the hour of conflict. They are never very much afraid of their open enemies, for they know who they are and are sure that their strength can never prevail against the strength which they themselves have been given by the Lord: they will always be victorious and gain great riches, so they will never turn their backs on the battle. Those whom they fear, and fear rightly, and from whom they always beg the Lord to deliver them, are enemies who are treacherous, devils who transform themselves and come and visit them in the disguise of angels of light. The soul fails to recognize them until they have done it a great deal of harm; they suck our life-blood and put an end to our virtues and we go on yielding to temptation without knowing it. From these enemies let us pray the Lord often, in the Paternoster, to deliver us: may He not allow us to run into temptations which deceive us; may their poison be detected; and may light and truth not be hidden from us. How rightly does our good Master teach us to pray for this and pray for it in our name!

Consider, daughters, in how many ways these enemies do us harm. Do not suppose that the sole danger lies in their making us believe that the consolations and the favours which they can counterfeit to us come from God. This, I think, in a way, is the least harmful thing they can do; it may even help some whom this sensible devotion entices to spend more time in prayer and thus to make greater progress. Being ignorant that these consolations come from the devil, and knowing themselves to be unworthy of such favours, they will never cease to give thanks to God and will feel the greater obligation to serve Him; further, they will strive to prepare themselves for more favours which the Lord may grant them, since they believe them to come from His hand.

Always strive after humility, sisters, and try to realize that you are not worthy of these graces, and do not seek them. It is because many souls do this, I feel sure, that the devil loses them: he thinks that he has caused their ruin, but out of the evil which he has been trying to do the Lord brings good. For His Majesty regards our intention, which is to please Him and serve Him and keep near to Him in prayer, and the Lord is faithful. We shall do well to be cautious, and not to let our humility break down or to become in any way vainglorious. Entreat the Lord to deliver you from this, daughters, and you need then have no fear that His Majesty will allow you to be comforted much by anyone but Himself.

Where the devil can do great harm without our realizing it is in making us believe that we possess virtues which we do not: that is pestilential. For, when consolations and favours come to us, we feel that we are doing nothing but receive, and have the greater obligation to serve; but when we suffer from this other delusion we think that we are giving and serving, and that the Lord will be obliged to reward us; and this, little by little, does us a great deal of harm. On the one hand, our humility is weakened, while, on the other, we neglect to cultivate that virtue, believing we have already acquired it. *We think we are walking safely, when, without realizing it, we stumble, and fall into a pit from which we cannot escape. Though we may not consciously have committed any mortal sin which would have sent us infallibly to hell, we have sprained our ankles and cannot continue on that road which I began to speak about and which I have not forgotten. You can imagine how much progress will be made by anyone who is at the bottom of a huge pit: it will be the end of him altogether and he will be lucky if he escapes falling right down to hell: at best, he will never get on with his journey. This being so, he will be unable to help either himself or others. It will be a bad thing for others, too, for, once the pit has been dug, a great many passers-by may fall into it. Only if the person who has fallen in gets out of it and fills it up with earth will further harm to himself and others be prevented. But I warn you that this temptation is full of peril. I know a great deal about it from experience, so I can describe it to you, though not as well as I should like.* What can we do about it, sisters? To me the best thing seems to be what our Master teaches us: to pray, and to beseech the Eternal Father not to allow us to fall into temptation.

There is something else, too, which I want to tell you. If we think the Lord has given us a certain grace, we must understand that it is a blessing which we have received but which He may take away from us again, as indeed, in the great providence of God, often happens. Have you never observed this yourselves, sisters? I certainly have: sometimes I think I am extremely detached, and, in fact, when it comes to the test, I am; yet at other times I find I have such attachment to things which the day before I should perhaps have scoffed at that I hardly know myself. At some other time I seem to have so much courage that I should not quail at anything I was asked to do in order to serve God, and, when I am tested, I find that I really can do these things. And then on the next day I discover that I should not have the courage to kill an ant for God's sake if I were to meet with any opposition about it. Sometimes it seems not to matter in the least if people complain or speak ill of me, and, when the test comes, I still feel like this—indeed, I even get pleasure from it. And then there come days when a single word distresses me and I long to leave the world altogether, for everything in it seems to weary me. And I am not the only person to be like this, for I have noticed the same thing in many people better than myself, so I know it can happen.

That being so, who can say that he possesses any virtue, or that he is rich, if at the time when he most needs this virtue he finds himself devoid of it? No, sisters: let us rather think of ourselves as lacking it and not run into debt without having the means of repayment. Our treasure must come from elsewhere and we never know when God will leave us in this prison of our misery without giving us any. If others, thinking we are good, bestow favours and honours upon us, both they and we shall look foolish when, as I say, it becomes clear that our virtues are only lent us. The truth is that, if we serve the Lord with humility, He will sooner or later succour us in our needs. But, if we are not strong in this virtue, the Lord will leave us to ourselves, as they say, at every step. This is a great favour on His part, for it helps us to realize fully that we have nothing which has not been given us.

And now you must take note of this other piece of advice. The devil makes us believe that we have some virtue—patience, let us say—because we have determination and make continual resolutions to suffer a great deal for God's sake. We really and truly believe that we would suffer all this, and the devil encourages us in the belief, and so we are very pleased. I advise you to place no reliance on these virtues: we ought not to think that we know anything about them beyond their names, or to imagine that the Lord has given them to us, until we come to the test. For it may be that at the first annoying word which people say to you your patience will fall to the ground. Whenever you have frequently to suffer, praise God for beginning to teach you this virtue, and force yourself to suffer patiently, for this is a sign that He wants you to repay Him for the virtue which He is giving you, and you must think of it only as a deposit, as has already been said.

The devil has yet another temptation, which is to make us appear very poor in spirit: we are in the habit of saying that we want nothing and care nothing about anything: but as soon as the chance comes of our being given something, even though we do not in the least need it, all our poverty of spirit disappears. Accustoming ourselves to saying this goes far towards making us think it true. It is very important always to be on the watch and to realize that this is a temptation, both in the things I have referred to and in many others. For when the Lord really gives one of these solid virtues, it seems to bring all the rest in its train: that is a very well-known fact. But I advise you once more, even if you think you possess it, to suspect that you may be mistaken; for the person who is truly humble is always doubtful about his own virtues; very often they seem more genuine and of greater worth when he sees them in his neighbours.

The devil makes you think you are poor, and he has some reason for doing so, because you have made (with the lips, of course) a vow of poverty, as have some other people who practise prayer. I say "with the lips" because, if before making the vow we really meant in our hearts what we were going to say, the devil could not possibly lead us into that temptation—not even in twenty years, or in our entire lifetime—for we should see that we were deceiving the whole world, and ourselves into the bargain. Well, we make our vow of poverty, and then one of us, believing herself all the time to be keeping it, says: "I do not want anything, but I am having this because I cannot do without it: after all, if I am to serve God, I must live, and He wants us to keep these bodies of ours alive." So the devil, in his angelic disguise, suggests to her that there are a thousand different things which she needs and that they are all good for her. And all the time he is persuading her to believe that she is still being true to her vow and possesses the virtue of poverty and that what she has done is no more than her duty.

And now let us take a test case, for we can only get to the truth of this by keeping a continual watch on ourselves: then, if there is any cause for anxiety on our part, we shall at once recognize the symptoms. Here is someone who has a larger income than he needs—I mean, needs for the necessaries of life—and, though he could do with a single manservant, he keeps three. Yet, when he is sued in the courts in connection with a part of his property, or some poor peasant omits to pay him his dues, he gets as upset and excited about it as if his life were at stake. He says he must look after his property or he will lose it, and considers that that justifies him. I do not suggest that he ought to neglect his property: whether or no things go well with him, he should look after it. But a person whose profession of poverty is a genuine one makes so little account of these things that, although for various reasons he attends to his own interests, he never worries about them, because he never supposes he will lose everything he has; and, even if he should do so, he would consider it of no great moment, for the matter is one of secondary importance to him and not his principal concern. His thoughts rise high above it and he has to make an effort to occupy himself with it at all.

Now monks and nuns are demonstrably poor—they must be so, for they possess nothing: sometimes because there is nothing for them to possess. But if a religious of the type just mentioned is given anything, it is most unlikely that he will think it superfluous. He always likes to have something laid by; if he can get a habit of good cloth, he will not ask for one of coarse material. He likes to have some trifle, if only books, which he can pawn or sell, for if he falls ill he will need extra comforts. Sinner that I am! Is this the vow of poverty that you took? Stop worrying about yourself and leave God to provide for you, come what may. If you are going about trying to provide for your own future, it would be less trouble for you to have a fixed income. This may not involve any sin, but it is as well that we should learn to recognize our imperfections, so that we can see how far we are from possessing the virtue of poverty, which we must beg and obtain from God. If we think we already possess it, we shall grow careless, and, what is worse, we shall be deceiving ourselves.

The same thing happens with regard to humility.[135] *We think that we have no desire for honour and that we care nothing about anything; but as soon as our honour comes to be slighted in some detail our feelings and actions at once show that we are not humble at all. If an opportunity occurs for us to gain more honour, we do not reject it; even those who are poor, and to whom I have just referred, are anxious to have as much profit as possible—God grant we may not go so far as actually to seek it! We always have phrases on our lips about wanting nothing, and caring nothing about anything, and we honestly think them to be true, and get so used to repeating them that we come to believe them more and more firmly. But when, as I say, we keep on the watch, we realize that this is a temptation, as regards both the virtue I have spoken of and all the rest; for when we really have one of these solid virtues, it brings all the rest in its train: that is a very well-known fact.*

CHAPTER THIRTY-NINE

Continues the same subject and gives counsels concerning different kinds of temptation. Suggests two remedies by which we may be freed from temptations.[136]

Beware also, daughters, of certain kinds of humility which the devil inculcates in us and which make us very uneasy about the gravity of our *past* sins. There are many ways in which he is accustomed to depress us so that in time we withdraw from Communion and give up our private prayer, because the devil suggests to us that we are not worthy to engage in it. When we come to the Most Holy Sacrament, we spend the time during which we ought to be receiving grace in wondering whether we are properly prepared or no. The thing gets to such a pass that a soul can be made to believe that, through being what it is, it has been forsaken by God, and thus it almost doubts His mercy. Everything such a person does appears to her to be dangerous, and all the service she renders, however good it may be, seems to her fruitless. She loses confidence and sits with her hands in her lap because she thinks she can do nothing well and that what is good in others is wrong in herself.

Pay great attention, daughters, to this point which I shall now make, because sometimes thinking yourselves so wicked may be humility and virtue and at other times a very great temptation. I have had experience of this, so I know it is true. Humility, however deep it be, neither disquiets nor troubles nor disturbs the soul; it is accompanied by peace, joy and tranquillity. Although, on realizing how wicked we are, we can see clearly that we deserve to be in hell, and are distressed by our sinfulness, and rightly think that everyone should hate us, yet, if our humility is true, this distress is accompanied by an interior peace and joy of which we should not like to be deprived. Far from disturbing or depressing the soul, it enlarges it and makes it fit to serve God better. The other kind of distress only disturbs and upsets the mind and troubles the soul, so grievous is it. I think the devil is anxious for us to believe that we are humble, and, if he can, to lead us to distrust God.

When you find yourselves in this state, cease thinking, so far as you can, of your own wretchedness, and think of the mercy of God and of His love and His sufferings for us. If your state of mind is the result of temptation, you will be unable to do even this, for it will not allow you to quiet your thoughts or to fix them on anything but will only weary you the more: it will be a great thing if you can recognize it as a temptation. This is what happens when we perform excessive penances in order to make ourselves believe that, because of what we are doing, we are more penitent than others. If we conceal our penances from our confessor or superior, or if we are told to give them up and do not obey, that is a clear case of temptation. Always try to obey, however much it may hurt you to do so, for that is the greatest possible perfection.

There is another very dangerous kind of temptation: a feeling of security caused by the belief that we shall never again return to our past faults and to the pleasures of the world. "I know all about these things now," we say, "and I realize that they all come to an end and I get more pleasure from the things of God." If this temptation comes to beginners it is very serious; for, having this sense of security, they think nothing of running once more into occasions of sin. They soon come up against these—and then God preserve them from falling back farther than before!

The devil, seeing that here are souls which may do him harm and be of great help to others, does all in his power to prevent them from rising again. However many consolations and pledges of love the Lord may give you, therefore, you must never be so sure of yourselves that you cease to be afraid of falling back again, and you must keep yourselves from occasions of sin.

Do all you can to discuss these graces and favours with someone who can give you light and have no secrets from him. However sublime your contemplation may be, take great care both to begin and to end every period of prayer with self-examination. If these favours come from God, you will do this more frequently, without either taking or needing any advice from me, for such favours bring humility with them and always leave us with more light by which we may see our own unworthiness. I will say no more here, for you will find many books which give this kind of advice. I have said all this because I have had experience of the matter and have sometimes found myself in difficulties of this nature. Nothing that can be said about it, however, will give us complete security.

What, then, Eternal Father, can we do but flee to Thee and beg Thee not to allow these enemies of ours to lead us into temptations? If attacks are made upon us publicly, we shall easily surmount them, with Thy help. But how can we be ready for these treacherous assaults,[137] my God? We need constantly to pray for Thy help. Show us, Lord, some way of recognizing them and guarding against them. Thou knowest that there are not many who walk along this road, and if so many fears are to beset them, there will be far fewer.

What a strange thing it is! You might suppose that the devil never tempted those who do not walk along the road of prayer! People get a greater shock when deception overtakes a single one of the many persons who are striving to be perfect than when a hundred thousand others are deceived and fall into open sin, whom there is no need to look at in order to see if they are good or evil, for Satan can be seen at their side a thousand leagues away. But as a matter of fact people are right about this, for very few who say the Paternoster in the way that has been described are deceived by the devil, so that, if the deception of one of them causes surprise, that is because it is a new and an unusual thing. For human nature is such that we scarcely notice what we see frequently but are astounded at what we see seldom or hardly at all. And the devils themselves encourage this astonishment, for if a single soul attains perfection it robs them of many others.

It is so strange, I repeat, that I am not surprised if people are amazed at it; for, unless they are altogether at fault, they are much safer on this road than on any other, just as people who watch a bull-fight from the grand-stand are safer than the men who expose themselves to a thrust from the bull's horns. This comparison, which I heard somewhere, seems to me very exact. Do not be afraid to walk on these roads, sisters, for there are many of them in the life of prayer— and some people get most help by using one of them and others by using another, as I have said. This road is a safe one and you will the more readily escape from temptation if you are near the Lord than if you are far away from Him. Beseech and entreat this of Him, as you do so many times each day in the Paternoster.

CHAPTER FORTY

Describes how, by striving always to walk in the love and fear of God, we shall travel safely amid all these temptations.

S how us, then, O our good Master, some way in which we may live through this most dangerous warfare without frequent surprise. The best way that we can do this, daughters, is to use the love and fear given us by His Majesty. For love will make us quicken our steps, while fear will make us look where we are setting our feet so that we shall not fall on a road where there are so many obstacles. Along that road all living creatures must pass, and if we have these two things we shall certainly not be deceived.

You will ask me how you can tell if you *really* have these two very, very great virtues.[138] You are right to ask, for we can never be quite definite and certain about it; if we were sure that we possessed love, we should be sure that we were in a state of grace. But you know, sisters, there are some indications which are in no way secret but so evident that even a blind man, as people say, could see them. You may not wish to heed them, but they cry so loud for notice that they make quite an uproar, for there are not many who possess them to the point of perfection and thus they are the more readily noticed. Love and fear of God! These are two strong castles whence we can wage war on the world and on the devils.

Those who really love God love all good, seek all good, help forward all good, praise all good, and invariably join forces with good men and help and defend them. They love only truth and things worthy of love. Do you think it possible that anyone who really and truly loves God can love vanities, riches, worldly pleasures or honours? Can he engage in strife or feel envy? No; for his only desire is to please the Beloved. Such persons die with longing for Him to love them and so they will give their lives to learn how they may please Him better. Will they hide their love? No: if their love for God is genuine love they cannot. Why, think of Saint Paul or the Magdalen. One of these—Saint Paul—found in three days that he was sick with love. The Magdalen discovered this on the very first day. And how certain of it they were! For there are degrees of love for God, which shows itself in proportion to its strength. If there is little of it, it shows itself but little; if there is much, it shows itself a great deal. But it always shows itself, whether little or much, provided it is real love for God.

But to come to what we are chiefly treating of now—the deceptions and illusions practised against contemplatives by the devil—such souls have no little love; for had they not a great deal they would not be contemplatives, and so their love shows itself plainly and in many ways. Being a great fire, it cannot fail to give out a very bright light. If they have not much love, they should proceed with many misgivings and realize that they have great cause for fear; and they should try to find out what is wrong with them, say their prayers, walk in humility and beseech the Lord not to lead them into temptation, into which, I fear, they will certainly fall unless they bear this sign. But if they walk humbly and strive to discover the truth and do as their confessor bids them and tell him the plain truth, then *the Lord is faithful, and,* as has been said, by using the very means with which he had thought to give them death, the devil will give them life, with however many fantasies and illusions he tries to deceive them. *If they submit to the teaching of the Church, they need not fear; whatever fantasies and illusions the devil may invent, he will at once betray his presence.*

But if you feel this love for God which I have spoken of, and the fear which I shall now describe, you may go on your way with happiness and tranquillity. In order to disturb the soul and keep it from enjoying these great blessings, the devil will suggest to it a thousand false fears and will persuade other people to do the same; for if he cannot win souls he will at least try to make them lose something, and among the losers will be those who might have gained greatly had they believed that such great favours, bestowed upon so miserable a creature, come from God, and that it is possible for them to be thus bestowed, for sometimes we seem to forget His past mercies.

Do you suppose that it is of little use to the devil to suggest these fears? No, it is most useful to him, for there are two *well-known* ways in which he can make use of this means to harm us, *to say nothing of others.* First, he can make those who listen to him fearful of engaging in prayer, because they think that they will be deceived. Secondly, he can dissuade many from approaching God who, as I have said, see that He is so good that He will hold intimate converse with sinners. Many such souls think that He will treat them in the same way, and they are right: I myself know certain persons inspired in this way who began the habit of prayer and in a short time became truly devout and received great favours from the Lord.

Therefore, sisters, when you see someone to whom the Lord is granting these favours, praise Him fervently, yet do not imagine that she is safe, but aid her with more prayer, for no one can be safe in this life amid the engulfing dangers of this stormy sea. Wherever this love is, then, you will not fail to recognize it; I do not know how it could be concealed. For they say that it is impossible for us to hide our love even for creatures, and that, the more we try to conceal it, the more clearly is it revealed. And yet this is so worthless that it hardly deserves the name of love, for it is founded upon nothing at all: *it is loathsome, indeed, to make this comparison.* How, then, could a love *like God's* be concealed— so strong, so righteous, continually increasing, never seeing cause for ceasing to manifest itself, and resting upon the firm foundation of the love which is its reward? As to the reality of this reward there can be no doubt, for it is manifest in Our Lord's great sorrows, His trials, the shedding of His blood and even the loss of His life. Certainly, then, there is no doubt as to this love. *It is indeed love, and deserves that name, of which worldly vanities have robbed it.* God help me! How different must the one love be from the other to those who have experience of both!

May His Majesty be pleased to grant us to *experience* this before He takes us from this life, for it will be a great thing at the hour of death, *when we are going we know not whither,* to realize that we shall be judged by One Whom we have loved above all things, *and with a passion that makes us entirely forget ourselves.* Once our debts have been paid we shall be able to walk in safety. We shall not be going into a foreign land, but into our own country, for it belongs to Him Whom we have loved so truly and Who Himself loves us. *For this love of His, besides its other properties, is better than all earthly affection in that, if we love Him, we are quite sure that He loves us too.* Remember, my daughters, the greatness of the gain which comes from this love, and of our loss if we do not possess it, for in that case we shall be delivered into the hands of the tempter, hands so cruel and so hostile to all that is good, and so friendly to all that is evil.

What will become of the poor soul when it falls into these hands after emerging from all the pains and trials of death? How little rest it will have! How it will be torn as it goes down to hell! What swarms and varieties of serpents it will meet! How dreadful is that place! How miserable that lodging! Why, a pampered person (and most of those who go to hell are that) can hardly bear to spend a single night in a bad inn: what, then, will be the feelings of that wretched soul when it is condemned to such an inn as this and has to spend eternity there?[139] Let us not try to pamper ourselves, daughters. We are quite well off here: there is only a single night for us to spend in this bad inn. Let us praise God and strive to do penance in this life. How sweet will be the death of those who have done penance for all their sins and have not to go to purgatory! It may be that they will begin to enjoy glory even in this world, and will know no fear, but only peace.

Even if we do not attain to this, sisters, let us beseech God that, if in due course we must suffer these pains, it may be with a hope of emerging from them. Then we shall suffer them willingly and lose neither the friendship nor the grace of God. May He grant us these in this life so that we may not unwittingly fall into temptation.

CHAPTER FORTY-ONE

Speaks of the fear of God and of how we must keep ourselves from venial sins.

How I have enlarged on this subject! Yet I have not said as much about it as I should like; for it is a delightful thing to talk about this love *of God*. What, then, must it be to possess it? May the Lord, for His own sake, give it me! *May I not depart from this life till there is nothing in it that I desire, till I have forgotten what it is to love anything but Thee and till I deny the name of love to any other kind of affection— for all love is false but love of Thee, and, unless the foundations of a building are true, the building itself will not endure. I do not know why it surprises us to hear people say: "So-and-so has made me a poor return for something." "Someone else does not like me." I laugh to myself when I hear that. What other sort of return do you expect him to make you? And why do you expect anyone to like you? These things will show you what the world is; your love itself becomes your punishment, and the reason why you are so upset about it is that your will strongly resents your involving it in such childish pastimes.*

Let us now come to the fear of God—*though I am sorry not to be able to say a little about this worldly love, which, for my sins, I know well and should like to acquaint you with, so that you may free yourself from it for ever. But I am straying from my subject and shall have to pass on.*

This fear of God is another thing with which those who possess it and those who have to do with them are very familiar. But I should like you to realize that at first it is not very deep, save in a few people, to whom, as I have said, the Lord grants such great favours as to make them rich in virtues *and to raise them, in a very short time, to great heights of prayer.* It is not recognizable, therefore, at first, in everyone. As it increases, it grows stronger each day, and then, of course, it can be recognized, for those who possess it forsake sin, and occasions of sin, and bad company, and other signs of it are visible in them. When at last the soul attains to contemplation, of which we are chiefly treating at the moment, its fear of God is plainly revealed, and its love is not dissembled even outwardly. However narrowly we watch such persons, we shall not find them growing careless; for, close as our watch on them may be, the Lord so preserves them that they would not knowingly commit one venial sin even to further their own interests, and, as for mortal sin, they fear it like fire. These are the illusions, sisters, which I should like you always to fear; let us always beseech God that temptation may not be strong enough for us to offend Him but that He may send it to us in proportion to the strength which He gives us to conquer it. *If we keep a pure conscience, we can suffer little or no harm.* That is the important point; and that is the fear which I hope will never be taken from us, for it is that fear which will stand us in good stead.

Oh, what a great thing it is not to have offended the Lord, so that the servants and slaves of hell[140] may be kept under control! In the end, whether willingly or no, we shall all serve Him—they by compulsion and we with our whole heart. So that, if we please Him, they will be kept at bay and will do nothing that can harm us, however much they lead us into temptation and lay secret snares for us.

Keep this in mind, for it is very important advice, so do not neglect it until you find you have such a fixed determination not to offend the Lord that you would rather lose a thousand lives *and be persecuted by the whole world,* than commit one mortal sin, and until you are most careful not to commit venial sins. I am referring now to sins committed knowingly: as far as those of the other kind are concerned, who can fail to commit them frequently? But it is one thing to commit a sin knowingly and after long deliberation, and quite another to do it so suddenly that the knowledge of its being a venial sin and its commission are one and the same thing, and we hardly realize what we have done, *although we do to some extent realize it.* From any sin, however small, committed with full knowledge, may God deliver us, especially since we are sinning against so great a Sovereign and realizing that He is watching us! That seems to me to be a sin committed of malice aforethought; it is as though one were to say: "Lord, although this displeases Thee, I shall do it. I know that Thou seest it and I know that Thou wouldst not have me do it; but, though I understand this, I would rather follow my own whim and desire than Thy will." If we commit a sin in this way, however slight, it seems to me that our offence is not small but very, very great.

For the love of God, sisters, *never be careless about this—and, glory be to the Lord, you are not so at present.* If you would gain this fear of God, *remember the importance of habit and of starting to realize what a serious thing it is to offend Him. Do your utmost to learn this and to turn it over in your minds;* for our life, and much more than our life, depends upon this virtue being firmly planted in our souls. Until you are conscious within your soul of possessing it, you need always to exercise very great care and to avoid all occasions of sin and any kind of company which will not help you to get nearer to God. Be most careful, in all that you do, to bend your will to it; see that all you say tends to edification; flee from all places where there is conversation which is not pleasing to God. Much care is needed if this fear *of God* is to be thoroughly impressed upon the soul; though, if one has true love, it is quickly acquired. Even when the soul has that firm inward determination which I have described, not to offend God for the sake of any creature, *or from fear of a thousand deaths,* it may subsequently fall from time to time, for we are weak and cannot trust ourselves, and, the more determined we are, the less self-confidence we should have, for confidence must come from God. But, when we find ourselves in this state, we need not feel constrained or depressed, for the

Lord will help us and the habits we have formed will be of assistance to us so that we shall not offend Him; we shall be able to walk in holy freedom, and associate with anyone, as seems right to us, even with dissolute people. *These will do you no harm, if you hate sin.* Before we had this true fear of God worldly people would have been poisonous to us and would have helped to ruin our souls; but now they will often help us to love God more and to praise Him for having delivered us from what we see to be a notorious danger. And whereas we for our part may previously have helped to foster their weaknesses, we shall now be help-ing to repress them, because they will restrain themselves in our pres-ence, and this is a compliment which they will pay us without our desiring it.

I often praise the Lord (though I also wonder why it should be so) that merely by his presence, and without saying a word, a servant of God should frequently prevent people from speaking against Him. It may be as it is in worldly intercourse: a person is always spoken of with respect, even in his absence, before those who are known to be his friends, lest they should be offended. Since this servant of God is in a state of grace, this grace must cause him to be respected, however lowly his station, for people will not distress him in a matter about which they know him to feel so strongly as giving offence to God. I really do not know the reason for this but I do know that it very commonly happens. Do not be too strict with yourselves, then, for, if your spirit begins to quail, it will do great harm to what is good in you and may sometimes lead to scrupulosity, which is a hindrance to progress both in yourselves and in others. Even if things are not as bad as this, a person, however good in herself, will not lead many souls to God if they see that she is so strict and timorous. Human nature is such that these characteristics will frighten and oppress it and lead people to avoid the road you are taking, even if they are quite clear it is the best one.

Another source of harm is this: we may judge others unfavourably, though they may be holier than ourselves, because they do not walk as we do, but, in order to profit their neighbours, talk freely and without restraint. You think such people are imperfect; and if they are good and yet at the same time of a lively disposition, you think them dissolute. This is especially true of those of us who are unlearned and are not sure what we can speak about without committing sin. It is a very dangerous state of mind, leading to great uneasiness and to continual temptation, because it is unfair to our neighbour. It is very wrong to think that everyone who does not follow in your own timorous footsteps has something the matter with her. Another danger is that, when it is your duty to speak, and right that you should speak, you may not dare to do so lest you say too much and may perhaps speak well of things that you ought to hate.

Try, then, sisters, to be as pleasant as you can, without offending God, and to get on as well as you can with those you have to deal with, so that they may like talking to you and want to follow your way of life and conversation, and not be frightened and put off by virtue. This is very important for nuns: the holier they are, the more sociable they should be with their sisters. Although you may be very sorry if all your sisters' conversation is not just as you would like it to be, never keep aloof from them if you wish to help them and to have their love. We must try hard to be pleasant, and to humour the people we deal with and make them like us, especially our sisters.

So try, my daughters, to bear in mind that God does not pay great attention to all the trifling matters which occupy you, and do not allow these things to make your spirit quail and your courage fade, for if you do that you may lose many blessings. As I have said, let your intention be upright and your will determined not to offend God. But do not let your soul dwell in seclusion, or, instead of acquiring holiness, you will develop many imperfections, which the devil will implant in you in other ways, in which case, as I have said, you will not do the good that you might, either to yourselves or to others.

You see that, with these two things—love and fear of God—we can travel along this road in peace and quietness, *and not think at every step that we can see some pitfall, and that we shall never reach our goal.*[141] *Yet we cannot be sure of reaching it, so* fear will always lead the way, and then we shall not grow careless, for, as long as we live, we must never feel completely safe or we shall be in great danger. And that was our Teacher's meaning when at the end of this prayer He said these words to His Father, knowing how necessary they were: *"But deliver us from evil. Amen."*

CHAPTER FORTY-TWO

Treats of these last words of the Paternoster: "Sed libera nos a malo. Amen." "But deliver us from evil. Amen."

I think the good Jesus was right to ask this for Himself, for we know how weary of this life He was when at the Supper He said to His Apostles: "With desire I have desired to sup with you"[142]—and that was the last supper of His life. From this it can be seen how weary He must have been of living; yet nowadays people are not weary even at a hundred years old, but always want to live longer. It is true, however, that we do not live so difficult a life or suffer such trials or such poverty as His Majesty had to bear. What was His whole life but a continuous death, with the picture of the cruel death that He was to suffer always before His eyes? And this was the least important thing, with so many offenses being committed against His Father and such a multitude of souls being lost. If to any human being full of charity this is a great torment, what must it have been to the boundless and measureless charity of the Lord? And how right He was to beseech the Father to deliver Him from so many evils and trials and to give Him rest for ever in His Kingdom, of which He was the true heir.

By the word "Amen," as it comes at the end of every prayer, I understand that the Lord is begging that we may be delivered from all evil for ever. *It is useless, sisters, for us to think that, for so long as we live, we can be free from numerous temptations and imperfections and even sins; for it is said that whosoever thinks himself to be without sin deceives himself, and that is true. But if we try to banish bodily ills and trials—and who is without very many and various trials of such kinds?—is it not right that we should ask to be delivered from sin?*

Still, let us realize that what we are asking here—this deliverance from all evil—seems an impossibility, whether we are thinking of bodily ills, as I have said, or of imperfections and faults in God's service. I am referring, not to the saints, who, as Saint Paul said, can do all things in Christ[143] *but to sinners like myself. When I find myself trammelled by weakness, lukewarmness, lack of mortification and many other things, I realize that I must beg for help from the Lord.*

You, daughters, must ask as you think best. Personally, I shall find no redress in this life, so I ask the Lord to deliver me from all evil "for ever." What good thing shall we find in this life, sisters, in which we are deprived of our great Good and are absent from Him? Deliver me, Lord, from this shadow of death; deliver me from all these trials; deliver me from all these pains; deliver me from all these changes, from all the formalities with which we are forced to comply for as long as we live, from all the many, many, many things which weary and depress me, and the enumeration of all of which would weary the reader if I were to repeat them. This life is unendurable. The source of my own depression must be my own wicked life and the realization that even now I am not living as I should, so great are my obligations.

I beseech the Lord, then, to deliver me from all evil for ever, since I cannot pay what I owe, and may perhaps run farther into debt each day. And the hardest thing to bear, Lord, is that I cannot know with any certainty if I love Thee and if my desires are acceptable in Thy sight. O my God and Lord, deliver me from all evil and be pleased to lead me to that place where all good things are to be found. What can be looked for on earth by those to whom Thou hast given some knowledge of what the world is and those who have a living faith in what the Eternal

Father has laid up for them *because His Son asks it of Him and teaches us to ask Him for it too?*

When contemplatives ask for this with fervent desire and full determination it is a *very* clear sign that *their contemplation is genuine and that* the favours which they receive in prayer are from God. Let those who have these favours,[144] then, prize them highly. But if I myself make this request it is not for that reason (I mean, it must not be taken as being for that reason); it is because I am wearied by so many trials and because my life has been so wicked that I am afraid of living any longer. It is not surprising if those who share in the favours of God should wish to pass to a life where they no longer enjoy mere sips at them: *being already partakers in some knowledge of His greatness, they would fain see it in its entirety. They have no desire to remain* where there are so many hindrances to the enjoyment of so many blessings; nor that they should desire to be where the Sun of justice never sets. Henceforward all the things they see on earth seem dim to them and I wonder that they can live *for even an hour.* No one can be content to do so who has begun to enjoy such things, and has been given the Kingdom of God on earth, and must live to do, not his own will, but the will of the King.

Oh, far other must be that life in which we no longer desire death! How differently shall we then incline our wills towards the will of God! His will is for us to desire truth, whereas we desire falsehood; His will is for us to desire the eternal, whereas we prefer that which passes away; His will is for us to desire great and sublime things, whereas we desire the base things of earth; He would have us desire only what is certain, whereas here on earth we love what is doubtful. What a mockery it all is, my daughters, unless we beseech God to deliver us from these perils for ever and to keep us from all evil! And although our desire for this may not be perfect, let us strive to make the petition. What does it cost us to ask it, since we ask it of One Who is so powerful? *It would be insulting a great emperor to ask him for a farthing.* Since we have already given Him our will, let us leave the giving to His will, so that we may be the more surely heard; and may His name be for ever hallowed in the Heavens and on the earth and may His will be ever done in me. Amen.

You see now, friends, what is meant by perfection in vocal prayer, in which we consider and know to Whom the prayer is being made, Who is making it and what is its object. When you are told that it is not good for you to practise any but vocal prayer, do not be discouraged, but read this with great care and beg God to explain to you anything about prayer which you cannot understand. For no one can deprive you of vocal prayer or make you say the Paternoster hurriedly, without understanding it. If anyone tries to do so, or advises you to give up your prayer, take no notice of him. You may be sure he is a false prophet; and in these days, remember, you must not believe everyone, for, though you may be told now that you have nothing to fear, you do not know what is in store for you. I had intended, as well as saying this, to talk to you a little about how you should say the Ave Maria, but I have written at such length that that will have to be left over. If you have learned how to say the Paternoster well, you will know enough to enable you to say all the other vocal prayers you may have to recite.

Now let us go back and finish the journey which I have been describing, for the Lord seems to have been saving me labour by teaching both you and me the Way which I began to outline to you and by showing me how much we ask for when we repeat this evangelical prayer. May He be for ever blessed, for it had certainly never entered my mind that there were such great secrets in it. You have now seen that it comprises the whole spiritual road, right from the beginning, until God absorbs the soul and gives it to drink abundantly of the fountain of living water which I told you was at the end of the road. It seems, sisters, that the Lord's will has been to teach us what great consolation is comprised in it, and this is a great advantage to those who cannot read. If they understood this prayer, they could derive a great deal of sound instruction from it and would find it a real comfort. *Our books may be taken from us, but this is a book which no one can take away, and it comes from the lips of the Truth Himself, Who cannot err.*

As we repeat the Paternoster so many times daily, then, as I have said, let us delight in it and strive to learn from so excellent a Master the humility with which He prays, and all the other things that have been described. May His Majesty forgive me for having dared to speak of such high matters. Well does His Majesty know that *I should not have ventured to do so, and that* my understanding would not have been capable of it, had He not taught me what I have said. Give thanks to Him for this, sisters, for He must have done it because of the humility with which you asked me to write it for you in your desire to be instructed by one so unworthy.

Well, sisters, Our Lord seems not to want me to write any more, for, although I had intended to go on, I can think of nothing to say. The Lord has shown you the road and has taught me what I wrote in the book which, as I say, I have already written.[145] *This tells you how to conduct yourselves on reaching this fount of living water and what the soul experiences when there, and how God satiates it and takes away its thirst for earthly things, and makes it grow in things pertaining to God's service. This will be very helpful to those who have reached the fount, and will give them a great deal of light.*

Before you see this book I shall give it to my confessor, Father Presentado Domingo Báñez *of the Order of Saint Dominic.* If he thinks you will benefit by it, and gives it you to read, and if you find it of any comfort, I, too, shall be comforted. *If he gives you this book, he will give you the other*[146] *as well.* Should it be found unsuitable for anyone to read, you must take the will for the deed, as I have obeyed your command by writing it.[147] I consider myself well repaid for my labour in writing, though it has certainly been no labour to me to think about what I have been going to say, *as the Lord has taught me the secrets of this evangelical prayer, which has been a great comfort to me.* Blessed and praised be the Lord, from Whom comes all the good that we speak and think and do. Amen.

NOTES

1. Cf. Vol. I, pp. 2–5, above
2. See also the reference, in the "General Argument" of the Valladolid redaction, to her being Prioress of St. Joseph's when the book was written. Presumably the original draft is meant.
3. E.g., at places where a chapter ends in E. but not in V.
4. One special case of this class is the suppression in V. of one out of two or three almost but not quite synonymous adjectives referring to the same noun.
5. With few exceptions, the footnotes to *The Way of Perfection* are the translators. Square brackets are therefore not used to distinguish them from those of P. Silverio, as elsewhere. Ordinary brackets, in the footnote translations, are placed round words inserted to complete the sense.
6. This title, in St. Teresa's hand, appears on the first page of the Valladolid autograph (V.) which, as we have said in the Introduction, is the basis of the text here used. The Escorial autograph (E.) has the words "Treatise of the Way of Perfection" in an unknown hand, followed by the Prologue, in St. Teresa's. The Toledo copy (T.) begins with the Protestation.
7. These lines, also in St. Teresa's hand, follow the title in the Valladolid autograph. P. Báñez added, in his own writing, the words: "I have seen this book and my opinion of it is written at the end and signed with my name." Cf. ch. 42, below.
8. This Protestation, taken from T., was dictated by St. Teresa for the edition of *The Way of Perfection* published at Évora in 1583 by D. Teutonio de Braganza.
9. The words "Fray Domingo Bañes" are crossed out, probably by P. Báñez himself. T. has: "from the Father Master Fray Domingo Báñez, Professor at Salamanca." Báñez was appointed to a Chair at Salamanca University in 1577.
10. The pronoun *(quien)* in the Spanish is singular, but in the sixteenth century it could have plural force and the context would favour this. A manuscript note in V., however (not by P. Báñez, as the Paris Carmelites—*Oeuvres,* V, 30—suggest), evidently takes the reference to be to St. Gregory, for it says: "And he wrote something on Job, and the *Morals,* importuned by servants of God, and trusting in their prayers, as he himself says."

11. French Protestantism which had been repressed during the reigns of Francis I and Henry II, increased after the latter's death in 1559, and was still doing so at the time of the foundation of St. Joseph's.

12. *Lit.:* "and bad."

13. Allá se lo hayan. "And serve them right!" would, in most contexts, be a more exact rendering of this colloquial phrase, but there is no suspicion of Schadenfreude here.

14. An apparent reference to St. Mark xiii, 31.

15. In the Spanish the subject is in the singular: P. Báñez inserted "the house," but crossed this out later.

16. St. Teresa liked to have hermitages in the grounds of her convents to give the nuns opportunity for solitude.

17. *Lit.:* "making this corner." The reference is to St. Joseph's, Ávila.

18. The italicized lines which follow, and are in the nature of a digression, do not appear in V., and in E. they have been crossed out.

19. Here follow two erased lines which are illegible but for the words "Thou didst honour the world." The exact sense of the following words ("We can . . . in secret") is affected by these illegible lines and must be considered uncertain.

20. *Lit.:* "of those." P. Báñez wrote in the margin "of the mansions" using the word which is thus translated in the titles of the seven main divisions of the Interior Castle. T. has: "of the houses."

21. *Lit.,* "poor little one."

22. *Lit.:* "are seldom ordered in such a way as."

23. "Other" is not in the Spanish. "When they are only between," is the reading of T., which also omits: "and become a pest."

24. Here begins the passage reproduced in the Appendix to Chapter 4, below.

25. Honra.

26. *Lit.:* "I beg her who is in the position of a senior *(mayor).*" *Mayor* was the title given to the superior at the Incarnation, Ávila, and many other convents in Spain, at that time.

27. *Lit.:* "There remains, as people say, no patience"; but, as the phrase "as people say" (which E. omits) suggests that this was a popular phrase, I have translated rather more freely and picturesquely. T. has (after "ache too"): "and it upsets us, and so on."

28. *Ternura. Lit.:* "tenderness."

29. *Lit.:* "My life!" "My soul!" "My good!"

30. *Lit.:* de darnos todas a Él todo: "giving ourselves wholly to Him wholly."

31. The thirteenth was St. Teresa.

32. De sus tierras. The phrase will also bear the interpretation: "from their own countries."

33. The sense of this passage, especially without the phrase from E. which V. omits, is not very clear. T. remodels thus: "You know there is no worse thief for the perfection of the soul than the love of ourselves, for unless etc."

34. Here, in the margin, is written: "Humility and mortification, very great virtues."

35. *Lit.:* "to contrive not to die." But the reading of E. ("to think that we came to the convent for no other reason than to serve our bodies and look after them") suggests that this is what is meant.

36. *Lit.:* "which can be suffered on foot."

37. *Lit.:* "to look at (or to) what is needful"—the phrase is ambiguous and might mean: "to worry about their own needs." The word translated "people" is feminine.

38. *Lit.:* "awakens."

39. *Lit.:* "Do you know why, apart from other things?"

40. *Lit.:* "did them to Him."

41. *Lit.:* "to this college of Christ."

42. I.e., St. Joseph's, Ávila.

43. An untranslatable play upon words: corto y no muy cortado—as though "sharpened" could be used in the sense of "refined."

44. Proverbs xxiv, 16.
45. The first four paragraphs of this chapter originally formed part of V., but, after writing them, St. Teresa tore them out of the manuscript, as though, on consideration, she had decided not to leave on record her knowledge of such a worldly game as chess. The allegory, however, is so expressive and beautiful that it has rightly become famous, and from the time of Fray Luis de León all the editions have included it. The text here followed is that of E.
46. Chess was very much in vogue in the Spain of St. Teresa's day and it was only in 1561 that its great exponent Ruy López de Segura had published his celebrated treatise, in Spanish, entitled "Book of the liberal invention and art of the game of chess."
47. *Lit.:* "the great virtues." In V. St. Teresa originally began this sentence thus: "In the last chapter I said that the King of glory, etc.," and ended it: "to gain the virtues which I there described as great." Later she altered it to read as above.
48. *Lit.:* "out of his hands," but the meaning, made more explicit in V., is evident. On the doctrinal question involved in this paragraph, see Introduction, above. P. Silverio (III, 75–6), has a more extensive note on the subject than can be given here and cites a number of Spanish authorities, from P. Juan de Jesús María (Theologia Mystica, Chap. III) to P. Seisdedos Sanz (Principios fundamentales de la mística, Madrid, 1913, II, 61–77.)
49. *Lit.:* "and tenderness."
50. *Lit.:* "low," contrasting with "high" at the end of the sentence.
51. Acts x, 34.
52. St. Luke xiv, 10.
53. *Lit.:* "These others."
54. *Lit.:* "would give them nothing," but the reference seems to be to payment.
55. *Lit.:* "very, very certain"—a typically Teresan repetition.
56. *Lit.:* "who is such."
57. *Lit.:* "so many days."
58. *Lit.:* "It will have to go as it comes out."
59. St Teresa is probably referring to the treatises of Luis de Granada and St. Peter of Alcántara (S.S.M, 1, 40–52, II, 106–20). Cf. Constitutions (Vol. III, p. 236, below).
60. *Lit.:* "of his doing something on (the horse) which is not graceful."
61. St. John iv, 13.
62. *Lit.:* "But this one—no, no."
63. The author probably refers to herself: Cf. Life, Chapter XX, and Relations, passim.
64. *Lit.:* "drowned."
65. *Lit.:* "We eat it without measure."
66. *Lit.:* "to cut the thread."
67. Presumably a reminiscence of Romans vii, 24 or Philippians i, 23.
68. This, too, is generally taken as referring to St. Teresa herself.
69. Cassian: Conferences, II. v.
70. E. ends the chapter here. This final paragraph appears to be based upon St. John vii, 37.
71. There is a reference here to St. John xiv, 2.
72. St. John vii, 37.
73. *Lit.:* "these are they who are, etc."
74. Cuenta de perdones: a bead larger in size than the remainder in the rosary and carrying special indulgences for the souls in purgatory.
75. *Lit.:* "of beginning so great a good."
76. *Lit.:* "save in God"—i.e., save as those whose life is centred in God: not necessarily, I think, only of God.
77. "Do not be surprised, daughters, for this is the royal road (camino real) to Heaven." A more idiomatic translation of camino real would be "king's highway."
78. *Lit.:* "determined determination": this doubling of words is not uncommon in St. Teresa.
79. *Lit.:* "are such ingenious geniuses."

80. V.: alguna consideración: the use of the singular form in a plural sense, with the shade of meaning which might be conveyed by "some occasional thoughts," is common in Spanish. E. uses one of St. Teresa's characteristic diminutives (see Vol. 1, p. xxi) alguna consideracioncita—"some (occasional) trifling thoughts."
81. This is generally taken as referring to St. Teresa's visit to Doña Luisa de la Cerda in 1562.
82. *Lit.:* "to call her 'Honour.'" The point of this delightfully unaffected reminiscence, omitted in V. and inserted here rather for its attractiveness than for its artistic appropriateness, is that "Your Honour" (Vuestra Merced: now abbreviated to Vd. and used as the third personal pronoun of ordinary polite address) was an expression merely of respect and not of rank: the Saint often uses it, for example, in addressing her confessors. It was as though a peer of the realm were to say "Just call me 'Sir.'"
83. For "fears" the original has "things"; but that seems to be the meaning.
84. *Lit.:* "a thing."
85. *Lit.:* "a Beauty . . . itself," as though referring to obras: "works."
86. *Lit.:* "Yes, approach God, and, in approaching, try."
87. The words "think about our Spouse" appear in no manuscript but were added by Luis de León.
88. Este cuidadito: lit., "this little attentiveness"—another characteristic diminuitive.
89. *Lit.:* "a nothing at all" (una nonada).
90. No es nada delicado mi Dios. "Fastidious" might be nearer to the characteristically bold adjective of the original.
91. St. Luke xi, 9.
92. *Lit.:* "the good."
93. The word rendered "discuss," both here and below, is a strong one, entrometerse, to intermeddle.
94. More literally: "consider," "reflect."
95. *Lit.:* "and that His greatness is addressing her."
96. algarabía. *Lit.:* "Arabic" and hence "gibberish," "jargon."
97. A vague reminiscence of some phrase from Canticles: perhaps ii, 14, 16, v, 2, or vi, 12.
98. Or "love Him." The verb in the Spanish can have either meaning.
99. *Lit.:* "With what majesty!"
100. Psalm xxxvi (A.V., xxxvii, 25).
101. Psalm xxxiii 20-1 (A.V., xxxiv, 19–20).
102. *Lit.* "when they deflect the soul in any way from going within itself."
103. *Lit.:* "see."
104. *Lit.:* "once we begin to be glad."
105. *Lit.:* "of recollection within me."
106. "Hallowed be Thy name. Thy kingdom come."
107. The allusion is, of course, to St. Luke ii, 25 ("just and devout"), 29.
108. Moradas. The "three tabernacles" of St. Matthew xvii, 4.
109. In the margin of T. the author adds, in her own hand, that this contemplative was St. Francis Borgia, Duke of Gandía. No doubt, then, the other person referred to was St. Teresa herself. The addition reads: "who was a religious of the Company of Jesus, who had been Duke of Gandía," and to this are added some words, also in St. Teresa's hand, but partially scored out and partially cut by the binder, which seem to be: "who knew it well by experience."
110. St. Luke xviii, 13. St. Teresa apparently forgot that the publican "would not so much as lift his eyes towards heaven."
111. *Lit.:* "and drawn along with it"; the same phrase is found at the end of the preceding paragraph.
112. *Lit.* "let the milk fall out of its mouth."
113. Algarabía. Cf. n. 96 above.
114. *Lit.:* "neither the one nor the other will gain."

NOTES

115. "Thy will be done: as in Heaven, so on earth."
116. *Lit.* "given it."
117. "Give us this day our daily bread."
118. *Lit.:* "should want as much for himself as for his neighbour, and for his neighbour as for himself." The italicized phrase is found in E. only.
119. *Lit.:* "each day, each day."
120. This, as will be observed from the title to this chapter, is the order of the words in the Latin.
121. *Lit.:* "in service"—en servidumbre, a strong word, better rendered, perhaps, "servitude," and not far removed from "slavery."
122. The whole of this paragraph is lightly crossed out in the manuscript.
123. *Lit.:* "as if by (someone's) hand." St. Teresa is thought here to be referring to herself.
124. *Lit.:* "and have him within itself with love."
125. The sense of the verb here rendered "cause the loss of" is vague. Literally the phrase reads: "so many priests are lost."
126. St. Matthew viii, 25.
127. "Forgive us our debts."
128. *Lit.:* "ill-treated." The same verb is used in the following sentence.
129. *Lit.:* "our Honourer"—Honrador nuestro: a rather unusual phrase which T. changes into the quite conventional honrado Maestro—"honoured Master."
130. St. Teresa left this sentence uncompleted. Luis de León added: "You need not . . . prayer" in his edition, since when it has always been included. It figures as an anonymous correction in T.
131. *Lit.:* "He left it thus confused." Here follows in E., in place of the rest of this paragraph, a passage which interrupts the trend of the thought, and therefore, in the text above, is printed in italics and in brackets at the end of this paragraph.
132. The words "though . . . forgive" are crossed out in the manuscript, as is the following sentence "May He . . . before Him."
133. "And lead us not into temptation, but deliver us from evil."
134. *Lit.:* "gains," as also in the next paragraph. E. has: "because they have hopes of becoming rich." The reference in both manuscripts is, of course, to the spoils and booty of war.
135. It will be noticed that this paragraph is similar to the last paragraph in the text of V. (p. 254, above). The differences, however, are so wide that each of the two is given as it stands.
136. A marginal addition made, in the autograph, to the title by another hand reads: "This chapter is very noteworthy, both for those tempted by false kinds of humility and for confessors." This is found in T. and in most of the editions.
137. *Lit.:* "these treasons."
138. *Lit.:* "these two virtues, so great, so great."
139. *Lit.:* "to an inn for ever, ever, for eternity." The repetition of "ever" (siempre) reminds one of the famous reminiscence of St. Teresa's childhood, to be found in her Life, Chap. I.
140. *Lit.:* "the infernal slaves."
141. Or "for [if we do this] we shall never reach our goal."
142. St. Luke xxii, 15.
143. Philippians iv, 13.
144. *Lit.:* "Let those who are so."
145. The Life.
146. The Life. I do not know what reason St. Teresa had to suppose this, but the Spanish of E. ("también os dará el otro") is quite definite.
147. *Lit.:* "you will take my will, as I have obeyed your command with the work" [i.e. in deed].